Archives of the Airwaves Volume 4

Archives of the Airwaves Volume 4

Roger C. Paulson

BearManor Media
2006

Archives of the Airwaves, Volume 4
© 2006 by Roger C. Paulson
All rights reserved.

For information, address:
BearManor Media
P. O. Box 750
Boalsburg, PA 16827

bearmanormedia.com

Cover design by John Teehan

Typesetting and layout by John Teehan

Published in the USA by BearManor Media

ISBN—1-59393-048-8

– M –

MA AND PA

Humorous dialog, using Cape Cod (Massachusetts) as its setting, was the format for the radio episodes of Ma and Pa.

The series began as a thirty minute weekly summer show in 1936 sustained by the CBS network. It returned to the CBS lineup on January 5, 1937. The fifteen minute serial was initially heard on Tuesday, Thursday, and Saturday under the sponsorship of The Atlantic Refining Company's White Flash Gasoline. However, after a few weeks, the schedule was changed to Monday through Friday.

Margaret Dee played Ma and Parker Fennelly played Pa, also heard in the cast were Harry Humphreys and Ruth Russell. Del Sharbut was the announcer.

The final broadcast of Ma and Ma aired on June 25, 1937.

MA PERKINS

Ma Perkins (aka Oxydol's Own Ma Perkins) was one of a half dozen or so of the best remembered and longest running daytime serial dramas on radio.

Ma Perkins was a strong, but kindly, widow who managed a lumberyard and reared her three children as a single parent in the mythical town of Rushville Center.

The serial was initially a local presentation heard over Cincinnati's station WLW beginning on August 14, 1933. By December 4th, Procter and Gamble's Oxydol Soap Powder began sponsorship; they preceeded to move Ma to the Chicago studios of WLS, and expand the listening audience by way of the NBC Red network. In 1942 the CBS network bought the series; but until 1948, Ma and her brood continued to be heard over the NBC network in addition to the CBS airing at different times of the day. After that, CBS claimed exclusive rights to broacast the series.

The role of Ma Perkins, the small town matriarch, was played from the beginning by Virginia Payne, despite the fact she was only twenty-three years old when the show went on the air in 1933. Virginia also did double duty when portraying another character in the story named Gladys Pendleton. Ma's daughter Fay Perkins Henderson was played by Rita Ascot, Cheer Brentson (who was also heard as Greta, the maid and Catherine Shaughnessey), Margaret Draper, Laurette Fillbrandt (who was also heard for a time as Ma's other daughter Evey), Marjorie Hannan, and Joan Tompkins. Ma's other daughter Evey Perkins Fitz was played by Kay Campbell (who was also heard as Doris Fairchild), Laurette Fillbrandt (who was also heard for a time as Ma's other daughter Fay), and Dora Johnson.

Ma's son John, who was killed during World War II and buried "somewhere in Germany," was played by Gil Faust. This wartime twist in the storyline evoked anger and concern from radio listeners who felt it was poor for home front morale. Other principal members of the cast included Charles Egleston and Edwin Wolfe as Shuffle Shober, Ma's partner in the lumberyard business; Murray Forbes (who also played Hunkins) as Willie Fitz, Evey's husband and lumberyard manager; Bobby Ellis, Cecil Roy, and Arthur Young as Junior Fitz. To mention a few of the more familiar radio voices that contributed to the endless parade of actors who appeared with Ma; there was Rye Billsbury, Herb Butterfield, Fran Carlon, Maurice Copeland, Constance Crowder, Nancy Douglass, Patricia Dunlap, Wilms Herbert, John Larkin, Forrest Lewis, Marilou Neumayer, Nanette Sargent, Les Tremayne, Beryl Vaughn, and Beverly Younger.

The theme music was a variation of My Old Kentucky Home by Larry Larson. The musical director was Clark "Doc" Whipple, Irma Glen and Elwyn were the orgainsts, and Julie Conway was heard as the "Oxydol Sparkle". The announcers were Jack Brinkley, Bob Brown, Dan Donaldson, Charles Lyon, Marvin Miller, Bob Pfeiffer, Charlie Warren (a "house name" used by both Dan Donaldson and Marvin Miller due to name conflict), and Dick Wells.

Ma Perkins ended her lengthy tenure on the airwaves of twenty-seven years on November 25, 1960.

ALAN MAC ATEER

Journeyman actor Alan MacAteer was heard in the supporting cast of several radio series. He played Daniel on Lora Lawton and Pop (the stage doorman) on Mary Noble, Backstage Wife. Other radio credits included: Stella Dallas, Great Plays, David Harum, Mr. District Attorney, Radio Guild, Renfrew of the Mounted, Wings Over America, and Don Winslow of the Navy.

MacAteer appeared in a few stage productions and was seen on television as a regular on The Kraft Music Hall Presents and Dave King Show.

JACK MAC BRYDE

A native of Troy, New York; actor Jack MacBryde began playing youthful roles on the stage with a local stock company, later graduating to the vaudeville circuit and performing in dozens of productions on the legitimate stage.

In 1928 MacBryde made his radio debut on The Eveready Hour, and thereafter followed a busy work schedule on the airwaves.

He played Doc on Against the Storm, Joseph Dyke on Amanda of Honeymoon Hill, Dad Fulton on The Atlantic Family, the doctor and Fred, the mailman on Aunt Jenny, The Old Ranger on Death Valley Days, Dan Cassidy on Eno Crime Clues, Peewee on Peewee and Windy, and Luke Baxter on Young Widder Brown. He was also in the cast of Amateur Gentleman, Arabesque, Big Ben Dream Dramas, By Kathleen Norris, The Campus; Central City, Cimarron Tavern, Dixie's Circus, Evening in Paris, The Gibson Family, Gold Rush, Johnny Hart in Hollywood, Hasten the Day, The Helen Hayes Theatre, Sherlock Holmes, Mandrake the Magician, My True Story, Second Husband, Set Sail, Strange As It Seems, The Texaco Star Theatre, Twenty Thousand Years in Sing Sing, The Rudy Vallee Show, and Leonidas Witherall.

Jack MacBryde's radio credits seem to end with the 1947 season and no further evidence exists he performed after that in any medium; however, there was no confirmation of his retirement or death.

FRANKLYN MAC CORMACK (Franklin H. McCormick)

Announcer and actor Franklyn MacCormack was born in Waterloo, Iowa on March 8, 1908. He was educated at The University of Iowa, after which he followed in his father's footsteps as a stage actor; but in 1930 the lure of the airwaves changed the course of his career. Radio was responsible for shifting his talent from acting to announcing, however, his experience as an actor remained evident in his dramatic approach to announcing; this would ultimately lead him to preside over several programs of poetry recitation and an occasional acting role.

MacCormack was briefly employed by station WIL in St. Louis, but his radio "home" for many years was Chicago's WBBM and WGN.

As a network announcer, his booming voice still reverberates in the memory of many who recall his convincing plea to a juvenile audience to "Eat Wheaties, breakfast of champions" on the Jack Armstrong adventure serial. His other network acting and announcing credits included: A Bouquet for You, Caroline's Golden Store, Easy Aces, Hymns of all Churches, Joan and Kermit, The Junior Nurse Corps, Mary Marlin, Myrt and Marge, Olsen and Johnson, That's Life With Fred Brady, and Woman in White. MacCormack's emotive poetry readings were incorporated into a mid-1930s program with Wayne King's orchestra. Two decades later they again teamed up to bring music and poetry to the airwaves by way of a syndicated show distributed by Ziv Radio Productions. He also combined poetry and intimate conversation with music on such radio series as The Book of Memories, Love Letters, Poetic Melodies, and The Torch Hour.

Franklyn MacCormack was on the air with his all-night radio show airing over WGN in Chicago on June 12, 1971 when he suffered a heart attack; he died a few hours later. He was sixty-three years old.

JEANETTE MAC DONALD

Soprano Jeanette MacDonald was born on June 18, 1907 in Philadelphia, Pennsylvania. As a small child her interest in singing and dancing began to bloom, and by the age of fourteen she made her New York stage debut in the chorus line of musical productions. MacDonald would go on to become a star of stage, screen (often teamed with baritone Nelson Eddy), opera, and recorded on the RCA Victor label. During the 1930s she was frequently heard on radio, and was later seen occasionally on television.

She was introduced to scanners of the kilocycles in 1936 on The Rudy Vallee Show and on October 3, 1937 joined the cast of the Vicks Open House program. Although regular association with radio shows was limited to the Vick's Open House and Hollywood Hotel, she continued to spread her vocal talents around the airwaves as a guest on numerous programs such as Film Stars on Parade, The Lux Radio Theatre and (Maxwell House) Show Boat.

On television she was seen on The Lux Video Theatre and The Screen Director's Playhouse.

In later years her activity lessened and only ocassionally performed.

Jeanette MacDonald suffered from a heart condition several years before her death. She was admitted to the hospital to undergo heart surgery; but died of a heart attack at the age of fifty-seven on January 14, 1965 before the surgery could be performed. She had been the wife of actor Gene Raymond since 1937.

MARGARET MAC DONALD

Radio personality Margaret MacDonald ran the gamut from actress to news commentator during her 1940s tenure on the airwaves.

She was heard in the title role on the daytime serial drama Kate Hopkins, Angel of Mercy; played Holly on Martha Webster (Life Begins); extolled the virtues of Ivory Snow Soap Powder with announcer Ed Herlihy on Brave Tomorrow; portrayed Dorothy Regeant on Chandu the Magician, and using the name Betty Moore she was The Benjamin Moore Paint Company's spokesperson. In July of 1945 she replaced Bernardine Flynn as the commentator on a weekday news program aimed at a female audience. The fifteen minute series titled Radio Newspaper aired over the CBS network, sponsored by Procter and Gamble's Crisco. The critics noted the program's newsworthiness was diluted to the point of being little more that chitchat; presumably, as a result, Radio Newspaper was cancelled by year's end.

BERNARR MACFADDEN

Publisher, physical culturist, and broadcaster Bernarr Macfadden was born on August 16, 1868 near Mill Springs, Missouri. The colorful, if not downright eccentric, Macfadden began farm work at the age of eleven and spent his early life earning money at odd jobs. In 1924 he entered the field of publishing when he founded The New York Evening Graphic and subsequently his Macfadden Publishing Company. That company circulated such magazines as Liberty, Physical Culture, True Confessions, True Detective Mysteries, True Romance, and True Story.

On radio his publications sponsored several series based on material taken from the pages of his magazines, some even bore the same title as the publication, such as True Story Hour.

Macfadden himself took to the airwaves as early as 1925 with his "sitting-up" exercises broadcast over New York's WOR.

He also appeared on The Physical Culture Magazine Hour and sponsored his own Bernarr Macfadden Hour carried by several east coast stations from August 26th to November 17th of 1936.

In 1941 he sold his interest in the publishing business and acquired a Military Academy and The Physical Culture Hotel.

While in his eighties, he still played tennis, flew his own plane, and made parachute jumps! To the very end he was a advocate of strenuous exercise and fasting. Bernarr Macfadden died on October 12, 1955 at the age of eighty-seven. Death was caused by an attack of jaundice brought on by a three day fast.

EVELYN MAC GREGOR

Songstress Evelyn MacGregor entertained during the 1930s and 1940s on stage, screen, and radio. She toured the vaudeville circuit with The Co-Eds and The Metropolitan Singers, was seen in several film shorts produced by Fox and Pathe, sang with The New York Grand Opera Company, and was heard on radio.

On the latter medium her credits included: The American Album of Familiar Music, The American Melody Hour, The Chesterfield Program, Forty-Five Minutes in Hollywood, Metropolitan Auditions (as a contestant), Monday Merry-Go-Round, and Waltz Time.

Evelyn MacGregor's career faded with the coming of the 1950s.

JOCK MAC GREGOR (Sherman A. MacGregor)

Radio actor and director Jock MacGregor was born in 1896.

As a director he "called the shots" for such radio shows as Bright Horizon; Brownstone Theatre; Cisco Kid; Roger Kilgore, Public Defender; The Mysterious Traveler; Raffles; and The Strange Dr. Weird. He also served as director, producer, and writer for Nick Carter, Master Detective.

Described as having "a distinctive heavy baritone voice that's different," MacGregor enjoyed a busy schedule before the microphone. He was heard on The Aldrich Family; City Desk; Gangbusters; Home of the Brave; John's Other Wife; Lorenzo Jones; Light of the World; Manhattan at Midnight; Martha Webster (Life Begins); The Parker Family; We, the Abbotts; When a Girl Marries; Young Dr. Malone; and hosted For Your Approval.

Jock MacGregor died on February 14, 1984 at the age of eighty-seven.

EDWARD MAC HUGH

Radio gospel singer Edward MacHugh was born on May 26, 1893 in Dundee, Scotland. MacHugh, his mother, and sisters arrived in Canada in 1912;

he later returned to London to study opera at The Royal College of Music. He came to the United States in 1921 where he performed on stage before making his radio debut in 1926 as a singer in Boston, Massachusetts over stations WBZ and WEEI.

In 1933 MacHugh inaugurated his weekday hymn sing over the NBC Blue network as The Gospel Singer. These programs were later broadcast over NBC's Red network and the CBS network.

MacHugh retired from radio in 1945 to spend more time on his Connecticut poultry farm; in 1951 he became an American citizen, and in 1956 he and his wife Jean moved to Florida.

Edward MacHugh died of liver cancer on February 3, 1957 at the age of sixty-three.

CHARLES E. MACK (Charles Emmett Sellers)

Comedian and actor Charles E. Mack was born in White Cloud, Kansas on November 22, 1887. The vaudevillian met his partner George Moran (also see) on the circuit while playing in Over the Top. The pair then formed the blackface act of Moran and Mack (aka Two Black Crows) that went on to perform on stage, radio, in motion pictures, and on the Columbia record label.

In 1928 they were first heard on radio; subsequent airwave credits included: The Eveready Hour, The Majestic Theatre Hour, and guest appearances. The act split up when Mack and his old partner John Swor made a movie; however, Moran and Mack were reunited in 1933.

Charles E. Mack was killed in an automobile accident on January 11, 1934; he was forty-six years old. Also injured in the Arizona crash was his wife, daughter, partner Moran, and producer Mack Sennett.

FLOYD MACK (Floyd MacLaughlin)

Recording business owner Floyd Mack was heard on radio as "The Voice of the Telephone Hour" for many years. From 1940 to 1958 he hosted The Bell System's program of classical and near classical music. Later he continued his musical commentary on the video version of The Telephone Hour from 1959 to 1968.

After retirement, Mack was involved with a senior citizen transportation service.

Floyd Mack died on January 3, 1983 after a long illness; he was seventy years old.

GILBERT MACK

Actor and dialectician Gilbert Mack was born in New York City on November 3, 1912. Mack first performed on the vaudeville stage in 1930 and appeared with such groups as The Collegians, Gobs of Joy, and The Songster Boys; later he was seen in several film shorts and performed in theatrical stock. However, due to Mack's short stature (five foot, four), radio offered him the opportunity for more work. He made his airwaves debut in 1937 and went on to amass an impressive list of supporting roles.

He was heard in the cast of Abbott and Costello; Author, Author; Behind the Mike; Bobby Benson; Big Sister; Chick Carter, Boy Detective; Cloak and Dagger; Cresta Blanca Carnival; Bulldog Drummond; Everyman's Theatre; The Flying Hutchinsons; Gangbusters; Good Neighbors; Grand Central Station; Green Valley, U.S.A.; Harvest of Stars; Inner Sanctum Mysteries; Lights Out; Manhattan at Midnight; Mr. and Mrs. North; Mr. Mercury; My Son and I; Myrt and Marge; The Mysterious Traveler; (Molle) Mystery Theatre; Arch Oboler's Plays; Ellery Queen; Radio Reader's Digest; Screen Guild Theatre; Kate Smith's Bandwagon; Superman; Terry and the Pirates; The Thin Man; Thunder Over Paradise; Dick Tracy; True Detective Mysteries; Two Thousand Plus; We, the People; and many local shows aired over New York City's station WHN.

Mack's exposure on television was limited to a single series, a children's puppet show titled Johnny Jupiter.

HELEN MACK (Helen McDougall)

Actress and director Helen Mack was born in Rock Island, Illinois on November 13, 1913.

She began performing on stage and in motion pictures as a child and continued that career into adulthood, appearing in her last picture in 1946.

On radio her acting talents were used sparingly, taking over the part of Marge on the Myrt and Marge serial when actress Donna Damerel died unexpectedly and as Corliss Archer's mother on the initial brief series of Meet Corliss Archer episodes; however, she was involved with several radio series as the director. She directed such shows as The Amazing Mrs. Danbury. Beulah, A Date With Judy, Richard Diamond, Me and Janie, Meet Corliss Archer, The Saint, and Anne Scotland.

In later years she became semi-retired, but still co-authored a play in 1960 using her married name Helen McAvity.

Helen Mack died of cancer on August 13, 1986 at the age of seventy-three. She was the widow of the late NBC executive Thomas McAvity who died in 1974.

NILA MACK (Nila Mac)

The name of Nila Mack was synonymous with the children's show Let's Pretend, having created and directed the series for twenty two seasons. She was born in Arkansas City, Kansas on October 24, 1891. After completing her education, Nila began her career with a transient theatrical company and toured the vaudeville circuit. During this time she met fellow performer Roy Briant; they were married on March 20, 1913. In 1927 she was widowed at the age of thirty-five and returned to the theatre as an actress and writer for a couple of years before turning her talents to radio. She was in the cast of The Nit Wit

Hour, Radio Guild productions, and other obscure shows before returning to her home town as program director of station WEEB.

During the summer of 1930 Nila Mack found her true niche in radio as a director, starting with the Helen and Mary series, which later evolved into the aforementioned Let's Pretend. She was also involved behind the scenes of The March of Games, Sunday Morning at Aunt Susan's, and was in overall charge of children's programming for the CBS network.

Nila Mack died of a heart attack on January 20, 1953 at the age of sixty-two.

TED MACK (William Edward Maguiness)

Emcee and musician Ted Mack was born in Greeley, Colorado on February 12, 1904. Young Mack learned to play the clarinet and saxophone; later he played with such bands as Benny Goodman, Glenn Miller, Red Nichols, Ben Pollock, and Jack Teagarden. He briefly fronted his own band, but music was not to be his principal forte.

In 1935 he signed on with Major Edward Bowes as a talent scout for the Major's Original Amateur Hour broadcasts. Subsequently he became Bowes' assistant, and eventually took over the reins after the Major's death. In 1948 Mack took his amateurs to television, and soon after revived the radio version of the show. Despite The New York Times' critic Jack Gould's description of Ted Mack's emcee duties as "lackluster and boring," the radio show endured until 1952 and the television sessions until 1970.

In addition, The Ted Mack Family Hour (a video revival of the old Major Bowes' Capitol Family Radio Hour), provided variety entertainment for television audiences in 1951, and in 1955 a similar daily show aired under the title of Ted Mack's Matinee.

Ted Mack died on July 12, 1976 while undergoing treatment for cancer; he was seventy-two years old. He and his wife, Ellen Overholt, had celebrated their fiftieth anniversary the previous March.

GISELE MAC KENZIE (Marie Gisele LaFleche)

Singer and actress Gisele MacKenzie was born in Winnipeg, Manitoba, Canada on January 20, 1927. She gave her first recital on the violin at the age of twelve, later she studied music at The Royal Conservatory in Toronto.

During the 1940s Gisele became a popular radio performer on Canadian radio. In the early 1950s she appeared on several radio shows in the United States, including Bob Crosby's Club Fifteen and The Mario Lanza Show. She also toured the nightclub circuit, recorded on the Capitol label, and became a well-known television personality. On the latter medium she was the star of her own Gisele MacKenzie Show, sang on the video version of Your Hit Parade, played Sid Caesar's wife on The Sid Caesar Show, was a regular on The Woolworth Hour, and was a frequent guest on other shows as both a singer and dramatic actress.

In later years her career was mostly confined to stock company productions.

DON MAC LAUGHLIN

Actor Don MacLaughlin was born on November 24, 1908 in Webster, Iowa. MacLaughlin began acting while attending The University of Arizona, appeared in several Broadway productions, and made his radio debut in 1934.

Of his long list of radio roles, best remembered was his portrayal of David Harding on the Counterspy series. He also shared the title roles with John Lund on Chaplain Jim and Johnny Thomas on Tennessee Jed, he was one of four to play Dr. Jim Brent on Road of Life, he and Vic Perrin were both heard in the principal role of Tex Thorne on The Zane Grey Theatre, was cast as Dwight Swanson on The Romance of Helen Trent, and played Kit Collins on We Love and Learn. Other radio credits included: Aunt Jenny, Buck Private, Dangerous Road, Death Valley Days, Ethel and Albert, The Falcon, Gangbusters, Kate Hopkins, John's Other Wife, Lincoln Highway, Magazine Theatre, Manhattan at Midnight, Mary Marlin, Myrt and Marge, Mystery Man, The O'Neills, Superman, Thunder Over Paradise, The Witch's Tale, and A Woman's Life.

On television MacLaughlin was a fixture on the daytime serial drama As the World Turns in the role of Chris Hughes from 1956 until he faded from the story line in the early 1980s. Before that, he continued his radio portrayal of Dr. Jim Brent on the video version of Road of Life.

Don MacLaughlin died on May 28, 1986 at the age of seventy-nine.

FRED MAC MURRAY

Actor Fred MacMurray was born on August 30, 1908 in Kankakee, Illinois. While attending Carroll College in Wisconsin, MacMurray whet his appetite as a performer by playing the saxophone and singing. This later developed into an association with the bands of Gus Arnheim and George Olsen before turning his attention to acting. He began that phase of his career on the stage, which led to his long and successful tenure on the motion picture screen.

Although recognized mostly for film and television work, he was no stranger to radio listening audiences. MacMurray was one of several to host Hollywood Hotel, co-starred with fellow film star Irene Dunne on Bright Star, presided over a transcribed nostalgic series titled Remember, and made seventeen appearances on The Lux Radio Theatre. He was also heard on such series as Four Star Playhouse, The Magic Key of RCA, and Suspense.

On television Fred MacMurray was the mainstay of the long running comedy series My Three Sons and was frequently seen as a guest on other programs, most notably Bob Hope's show.

Fred MacMurray died of pneumonia on November 5, 1991. He was eighty-three years old.

JOHN MAC PHERSON
See: The Mystery Chef

HAVEN MAC QUARRIE (Frank Haven MacQuarrie)
Emcee and performer Haven MacQuarrie was born in Boston, Massachusetts on April 10, 1894. Young MacQuarrie began his career on the vaudeville stage at the age of fifteen. Later he used those early stage experiences on radio. He served as emcee of such shows as Do You Want to be an Actor?, Noah Webster Says, and Your Marriage Club. He also presided over Haven MacQuarrie Presents, a series of weekly half hour dramas sustained by the NBC Red network during the 1937-38 season. In addition to radio, he continued to entertain on the vaudeville circuit with his brother Earl.

Haven MacQuarrie died of a heart attack on August 4, 1953 at the age of fifty-nine.

GORDON MAC RAE
Singer and actor Gordon MacRae was born on March 12, 1921 in East Orange, New Jersey. Gordon began performing as a child, later he was a page boy at NBC's New York Studios, had a small part in the 1941 Broadway production of Junior Miss, and sang with Horace Heidt's band during 1942-43. His career was then interrupted by World War II military duty; however, the post war era saw him catapulted into stardom. He rose to the top on stage, screen, radio, records, television, and the nightclub circuit.

On radio he hosted his own show, sang the male lead roles on The Railroad Hour, was a regular on The Teentimers Club and The Texaco Star Theatre, and appeared as a frequent guest on shows such as The Voice of Firestone and Yours For a Song.

On television MacRae hosted ther Colgate Comedy Hour, The Lux Video Theatre, and was the star of his own Gordon MacRae Show.

He married actress Sheila Stevens in 1941, and until their divorce in 1967, they often performed together. Their daughter Meredith also became an actress. MacRae married his second wife, Elizabeth Lambert Schrafft, later during the same year of his divorce from Sheila.

Gordon MacRae died on January 24, 1986 at the age of sixty-four. His death was attributed to cancer, complicated by pneumonia.

THE GORDON MAC RAE (SHOW)(SKYLINE ROOF)
Baritone vocalist Gordon MacRae starred on his own sustaining radio show aired over the CBS network during the 1945-46 season (aka Gordon MacRae's Skyline Roof). The series made its debut on December 5, 1945 as a fifteen minute weekday program of music and song. Joining Gordon was singer Sheila Stevens (MacRae's first wife), the orchestra of Archie Bleyer, and announcers Harry Clark and Dan Seymour.

During the summer of 1947 The Gordon MacRae Show filled-in for the vacationing Baby Snooks Show. It was heard over the CBS network sponsored by General Foods' Jello. Also appearing with Gordon was vocalist Marian Bell, Johnny Guarneri's band, and announcer Dan Seymour.

MacRae and announcer Seymour returned to the airwaves with another fifteen minute program of songs in 1950. It was sponsored by The Gulf Oil Company's Gulfspray and Trak.

JOHN MAC VANE

Newsman and author John MacVane was born in Portland, Maine on April 29, 1912. He received his education at Williams College and Oxford University. As a newspaperman he was associated with The Brooklyn Eagle, The New York Sun, and The London Daily Express before becoming a foreign correspondent for The International News Service.

After the outbreak of World War II, and the possibility of a German invasion of England, MacVane was enlisted by the NBC network to report live from London. He later continued his radio coverage of the war from North Africa, and followed the Allied Armies in Europe from the D-Day invasion to Germany's final capitulation.

Following the war, he served as United Nations Correspondent for NBC, and later for ABC. During the 1945-46 season he also broadcast a weekly fifteen minute news report for NBC.

MacVane retired in 1977, but upon his return to his home state of Maine in 1982, he was seen locally on television station WMTW in Poland Springs with a weekly news commentary.

As a writer he authored books on his wartime experiences, UN pamphlets, and a National Educational Television series on Alaska.

John MacVane died of a heart attack on January 28, 1984 at the age of seventy-one.

JERRY MACY

Radio actor Jerry Macy was heard in supporting roles over the airwaves during the 1930s and 40s. He played Mr. Berkeley on Leave it to Mike, Uncle Matthew on McGarry and His Mouse, Ed Norton on The Right to Happiness, Chico on Terry and Ted, Harvey on Trouble House, and Judge Kruger on Valiant Lady. He also appeared on Carnival With Bernie West, The Mighty Show, and The (Molle) Mystery Theatre.

There is no evidence Jerry Macy performed in any other medium than radio.

THE MAD MASTERS

The Mad Masters was a situation comedy which lived up to its title by going far afield to garner a giggle. The off-beat series was first heard on the west coast in 1946 over the ABC network. During the summer of 1947 it originated from the NBC studios in San Francisco and served as the warm weather replacement for Truth or Consequences.

Talent on the show could hardly be classified as household names to coast-to-coast radio listeners. The husband and wife team of Monty and Natalie Masters were the principal players on the sophomoric comedy, aided by supporting actors Helen Kleeb and Henry Leff. Music was provided by Tony Freeman's orchestra with vocals by Paul Waltre.

THE MAD RUSSIAN
See: Bert Gordon

MADAME COURAGEOUS
Madame Courageous was a short-lived daytime serial drama with the all too familiar story line of a divorced mother raising her children alone.

The initial episode aired on September 26, 1938 over the NBC Blue network, sponsored by The Glidden Company's Durkee food products.

Betty Caine played the lead role of Sarah Brayden. Others in the cast were Kathryn Card as Mary Brady, Willard Farnum as Dick Brayden, Barbara Fuller as Peggy Brayden, Donald Krantz as Paul Brayden, Harold Peary as Tom Brayden, and Joan Winters as Cleo Brayden. The announcer was Lynn Brandt.

The quarter hour drama was broadcast on Monday, Wednesday, and Friday over only twenty of the network's affiliate stations.

Madame Courageous left the air on December 23, 1938 after a brief thirteen week run.

MADAME SYLVIA OF HOLLYWOOD
Foreign born (1891) beauty expert Sylvia Wilhelmson was better known to her radio listeners as Madame Sylvia of Hollywood. Her radio series took to the air in the early 1930s over the NBC Red network. However, due in part to lingual limitations with English, the madame had difficulty "getting a word in edge-wise" on her own program and depended on guests to carry the show. By 1934 her improved command of the language, coupled with the help of permanent emcee Percy Hemus, allowed Sylvia to impart her beauty tips and conduct interviews with the Hollywood stars.

The Ralston Purina Company's Ry-Krisp first sponsored Madame Sylvia on a weekly late evening series in 1933, but the following year she was moved to the more appropriate schedule of a twice weekly afternoon program. With the new time schedule came a new gimmick from the sponsor. Three dresses worn on the screen by actress Fay Wray were given away to the listeners sending in the best letters on behalf of their product.

The end came for Madame Sylvia's tenure on the airwaves in 1935.

JOHNNY MADERO, PIER 23
Johnny Madero, Pier 23 was one of a quartet of Jack Webb radio adventures. The tough guy sagas revolved around a San Francisco waterfront charac-

ter named Johnny Madero who rented boats and hired out as a part time private trouble-shooter.

To the theme of I Cover the Waterfront, Madero's first radio encounter with murder and mayhem aired on the West Coast in 1946. On April 24, 1947 the sustaining series made its coast-to-coast debut over the Mutual network.

Jack Webb starred in the title role, William Conrad was heard as the ever meddling cop Warcheck, and Gale Gordon played Father Leahy. Others in the cast were Joan Banks, Francis X. Bushman, John Garfield, and Jean Rogers. Harry Zimmerman was the musical director and Tony LaFrano announced.

The last of Johnny's capers was heard on September 4, 1947 after a run of about five months.

MAGAZINE OF THE AIR
See: Heinz Magazine of the Air

MAGAZINE THEATRE
The Mutual network sustained a series of "true-to-life" stories of adventure, romance, and intrigue during the 1951-52 season. The weekly half hour dramas premiered on February 16, 1951 under the title of Magazine Theatre.

The initial offering starred Don MacLaughlin in I Smuggle for Uncle Sam.

MAGGIE AND JIGGS
See: Bringing Up Father

MAGGI'S PRIVATE WIRE
See: Maggi McNellis

THE MAGIC CARPET PROGRAM
The concept of radio being a magic carpet to transport its listeners on an etherial trip was the basis for the title of several network and local series. Among them was The Anglo-Persians and their Magic Carpet, a popular program of music which began in the pre-network era. The show was on the air from 1924 to 1930 with Lou Katzman conducting the orchestra.

The American Tobacco Company's Lucky Strike Cigarettes was the sponsor for the next Magic Carpet; starting in 1931, it was heard over the NBC Red network. The orchestras of Charlie Agnew, Gus Arnheim, Ben Bernie, Jimmie Grier, Lou Katzman, Vincent Lopez, George Olsen, and Anson Weeks performed from various locations around the country. The radio audience was once again whisked by the mythical magic carpet across the miles and deposited at these ballrooms and nightspots. The host for these fantasy rug rides was Walter O'Keefe, later replaced by Howard Claney. Newscaster Walter Winchell brought the riders up to date with a five minute news capsule aired in midflight. This series of tours concluded with the broadcast of February 18, 1933.

Shortly thereafter, Lucky Strike's Magic Carpet changed its format to a comedy/variety show (aka The Lucky Strike Hour). Funnyman Jack Pearl, in his role as Baron Munchausen, and his sidekick Cliff Hall took over the program. Joining Pearl and Hall was the orchestra of Al Goodman, The DeMarco Sisters, The Leaders Trio, tenor Robert Simmons, and ex-host Howard Claney returned as the announcer. Pearl and company abandoned the show before the close of 1933 for a new Jack Pearl Show and The Magic Carpet was permanently grounded.

MAGIC DETECTIVE
See: Blackstone, Magic Detective

MAGIC ISLAND
The transcribed quarter hour of serialized juvenile fantasy called Magic Island was syndicated and distributed by Lou R. Winston Radio Transcriptions of Hollywood.

Some sources indicated the series was first heard during the 1930s, but The Radio Showbook of 1945 lists 130 episodes also available to local stations that year.

The story line revolved around the adventures of a shipwrecked girl named Joan Gregory and her friend Jerry Hall.

Their magic South Seas island had the ability to appear and disappear at a scientist's command.

THE MAGIC KEY OF RCA
The Magic Key of RCA was a show of magnanimous proportions that brought a wide range of entertainment into living rooms across the nation. The Radio Corporation of America sponsored the hour long Sunday afternoon extravaganza over the NBC Blue network beginning on September 29, 1935.

In addition to showcasing music and drama from around the world, the program hopscotched to various remote pickups where roving reporters John B. Kennedy and Linton Wells would report on some event of interest.

Milton J. Cross and Ben Grauer were the mainstays of the announcing corps; they were aided by Bob Brown, Hal Gibney, Alois Havrilla, Ed Herlihy, Tom Manning, Tex O'Rourke, and John Wald. They all served to introduce an endless list of top performers of that era. Although Frank Black conducted the orchestra on every Magic Key program, legions of other musical aggregations were heard on a guest basis.

During the summer of 1939 The Magic Key of RCA abandoned its traditional Sunday afternoon schedule in favor of a Monday evening hour. Nat Shilkret's orchestra, a parade of guest stars, and announcer LeRoy were heard on this warm weather series. With the coming of the fall season, the death knell sounded for The Magic Key program. It left he air after the broadcast of September 18, 1939.

THE MAGIC OF SPEECH

Vida Ravenscroft Sutton, "an outstanding authority on correct speech," conducted a radio series titled The Magic of Speech.

The program was first broadcast in 1929 over the NBC Red network.

Initially Sutton was heard for fifteen minutes weekly, but the following year her series was expanded to a half hour. In 1936 the program was moved to NBC's Blue network; however, it proved to be the beginning of the end. In 1937, after eight years of teaching people to talk, The Magic of Speech series fell silent.

THE MAGIC VOICE

A romantic drama called The Magic Voice was broadcast twice weekly over the CBS network during the 1932-33 season under the sponsorship of Ex-Lax.

The fifteen minute episodes starred Nick Dawson and Elsie Hitz, who also teamed on similiar shows. Lyle Van was the announcer. The Magic Voice made a return engagement over three stations of the NBC Blue network in 1936. The brief Monday through Friday reprieve lasted only from March 30th to August 28th.

THE MAGNIFICENT MONTIGUE

"Old actors never die, they just go into radio" was the catch phrase used to describe the series titled The Magnificent Montigue. The story line centered on a former Shakespearian actor Edwin Montigue and his actress wife Lily Boheme. Montague, on the downside of his career, was forced to take the role of Uncle Goodheart on a mythical afternoon radio show. Much of the plot revolved around Montigue hiding his present occupation from his Shakespearian actor peers.

The distinguished actor Monty Woolley was cast in the title role, Anne Seymour was heard as is wife, and Pert Kelton played their smart-alecky maid named Agnes. Don Pardo was the announcer and Jack Ward the organist.

The weekly half hour visits with the Montigues were aired over the NBC network during the 1950-51 season for a variety of sponsors.

WALLY MAHER (Walter A. Mayer)

Actor Wally Maher was born on August 4, 1908 in Cincinnati, Ohio. His subsequent show business career encompassed the mediums of stage, screen, and radio; however, he is best remembered for his work on the airwaves.

Maher first appeared on radio in 1929 on Cincinnati's station WLW. He later played Lance Dudley on Brenthouse, Sergeant Matt Grebb on The Line-Up, Ezra on Main Street Sketches, Dan Murray on One Man's Family, Wilbur Hutch on The Tommy Riggs and Betty Lou Show (Quaker Party), the title role on the network version of Michael Shayne, and was one of several to play Archie Goodwin on Nero Wolfe. Maher was also in the cast of Gene Autry's Melody Ranch, The Eddie Bracken Show, Candid Lady, The Chase and Sanborn Program, Circus Days, Good News of 1939-40, Hedda Hopper's Hollywood, I Love a Mystery, Lights Out, The Lux Radio Theatre, Major Hoople, Maisie, Meet Me at Parky's, The Merry Life of Mary Christmas, Irene Rich Dramas, The Sad Sack, and Suspense.

Wally Maher's career was cut short when he died at the age of forty-three on December 21, 1951.

REV. DR. WALTER A. MAIER

Rev. Dr. Walter A. Maier was born in Boston, Massachusetts on October 4, 1893. He studied for the ministry at Concordia Collegiate Institute, Concordia Seminary, Boston University, and Harvand University.

During his life as a Lutheran preacher he taught at Concordia Seminary, authored several books, edited The Walther League Messenger (a Lutheran young people's publication), served on the board of directors of Valparaiso University, and presided over the weekly broadcasts of The Lutheran Hour.

Rev. Dr. Maier was stricken with a coronary thrombosis on December 29, 1949; he died as a result on January 11, 1950 at the age of fifty-six.

MAIN STREET MEMORIES

During 1949 radio personality and author Joe Franklin hosted a transcribed program of nostalgia on Main Street Memories.

Franklin regaled his listening audience with show business yarns, recordings of past stars performances, and interviewed well-known guests.

MAIN STREET MUSIC HALL

Main Street Music Hall was a Saturday afternoon program of music and song sustained over the CBS network during 1949.

Regulars on the series included: vocalists Russ Emery, Nancy Evans, and Earl Wrightson. The orchestra was under the direction of Alfredo Antonini.

MAIN STREET SKECTHES

Light drama set in the mythical town of Titusville was the format for Main Street Sketches. The series got its start over New York's station WOR in 1927 and was later broadcast over the Mutual network.

Don Carney, of Uncle Don fame, wrote the scripts and played the lead role of Luke Higgins. Others included in the cast were Florence Halop as Fanny, Wally Maher as Ezra, Dora Merande as Ivalutta, Peggy Paige as Nancy, Edith Spencer as Sarah, Robert Strauss as Horace, and Walter Tetley as Wilbur.

In 1931 the show became a transcribed feature, and in the fall of 1933 aired under the new title of A New Deal for Main Street (presumably to associate itself to President Roosevelt's "New Deal" administration).

The Main Street dramas were heard on-and-off from its inception in 1927, through 1934.

MAISIE

The adventures of Maisie first appeared on the motion picture screen in 1939, and in 1945 she made her debut in a series adapted for radio. Maisie typified the image of the 1940s bumbling blonde bombshell from Brooklyn, a New York working girl surrounded by an assemblage of characters from a Damon Runyon type saga.

The weekly half hour situation comedy premiered over the CBS network on July 5, 1945, sponsored by Eversharp writing instruments. The show was initially intended to be a summer replacement for Milton Berle, but remained on the network's schedule until the 1947 spring purge of programs. Maisie then moved to the Mutual network for the 1947-48 season.

A revised Maisie format was transcribed and syndicated by New York's station WMGM beginning in November 24, 1949. Although the program originated in New York, the locale for the story line was then shifted to Hollywood.

Actress Ann Sothern recreated her film role as Maisie, John Brown played her boss Mr. Dorsey, and Wally Maher her boy friend Mike. Others in the extensive cast included: Elvia Allman, Bea Benaderet, Hans Conried, Norman Field, Jerry Hausner, Sammie Hill, Florence Lake, Peter Leeds, Sheldon Leonard, Patrick McGeehan, Howard McNear, Paul McVey, Marvin Miller, Frank Nelson, Lurene Tuttle, Donald Woods, and Ben Wright. Music was under the direction of Al Sack and Harry Zimmerman. The announcers were Jack McCoy and Ken Niles.

ARTHUR MAITLAND

Actor Arthur Maitland began his career on the stage in 1894. He later appeared in Broadway productions; founded The Maitland Playhouse in San Francisco; directed The Little Theatre in Louisana, Tennessee, and Georgia, was heard on radio, and was a television pioneer during the late 1930s.

To radio audiences Maitland's voice is remembered for his portrayals on several series. He played school principal Mr. Weatherbee on Archie Andrews, Doc Allen on Aunt Jenny, Zeke Swinney on David Harum, and Silas Drake on Your Family and Mine. He was also heard in the cast of Stella Dallas and Ma Perkins.

Arthur Maitland retired in 1957; he died on May 23, 1959 at the age of eighty-five.

MAJESTIC HOME PROGRAM

See: Ida Bailey Allen

MAJESTIC (THEATRE HOUR) (CURIOSITY SHOP)

A variety series broadcast during the late 1920s and early 1930s, Majestic's Theatre Hour offered radio listeners to the CBS network the best entertainers of that era.

The Grigsby-Grunow Company, manufacturers of Majestic Radios, sponsored the show that bore the product's name.

Among those serving as emcee was Bradford Browne, Wendell Hall, and Lee Seymour. Augmenting the parade of guest stars were such regulars as Eddie Leonard, Moran and Mack with their Two Black Crows act, singers Redferne Hollinshead, Muriel LaFrance, and Lee Morse, and the orchestra of Arnold Johnson.

The Majestic Theatre Hour left the air in the fall of 1930 and was briefly replaced by a half hour version aired under the title The Majestic Curiosity Shop. However, by the start of 1931 new programming filled the CBS network's Sunday night schedule at nine o'clock.

In 1932 a quarter hour Majestic Theatre returned with a new format equally divided between music, song, and commercials for Majestic vacuum tubes. Heard on the show was tenor Arthur Kraft, Hum and Strum, a singing duo identified only as Gene and Charlie, and the Majestic orchestra.

MAJESTIC'S MASTER OF MYSTERY

After several years of sponsoring musical variety programs, The Grigsby-Grunow Company's Majestic radios and vacuum tubes underwrote serialized mystery dramas during 1933-34.

Called Majestic's Master of Mystery, the fifteen minute transcribed episodes were syndicated for broadcast by local stations. The unnamed storyteller, referred to as the Master of Mystery, narrated the mysterious tales.

It is interesting to note an offer from the sponsor to send the listener a "good luck swastika" (an emblem shortly thereafter adopted by Nazi Germany) in return for the end flaps from a Majestic vacuum tube box.

MAJOR BOWES

See: Edward Bowes Capitol Family Hour
The Original Amateur Hour
Shower of Stars

MAJOR HOOPLE

Based on the character in Gene Ahern's comic strip Our Boarding House, the radio comedy series Major Hoople made its debut on June 22, 1942 over the NBC Blue network's airwaves.

Major Amos Hoople and his wife Martha were the owners of a boarding house. Hoople, a pompous braggart, continually aggravated his boarders with prevaricated stories of his wartime heroism.

Major Hoople was played by Arthur Q. Bryan, his wife Martha by Patsy Moran, star boarder and chief cynic Tiffany Twiggs by Mel Blanc, and nephew Alvin by Conrad Binyon and Franklin Bresee. Others included in the cast were John Battle, Evelyn Chevillet, Wally Maher, Ed Max, and Fred McKay. The music was provided by the orchestras of Lou Bring and Walter Greene.

The weekly half hour of sustaining humor was described by Variety in the September 9, 1942 issue as "unfunny, vulgar, and infantile." The Major departed the airwaves later the same month.

MAJOR NORTH, ARMY INTELLIGENCE

Stories of the Army Intelligence's (known as G-2) battle against international espionage was the basis for the radio series called Major North, Army Intelligence. The title was to have been The Man from G-2, but the Army objected to the inference that the dramas were of an official nature.

Based on the writings of Van Wyck Mason, the weekly half hour sustaining programs starred Staats Cotsworth as Major Hugh North and Joan Alexander as his assistant and love interest. Music was conducted by Bernie Green.

The show was heard over the ABC network from April 12, 1945 to February 2, 1946.

MAKE BELIEVE BALLROOM

West Coast announcer Al Jarvis introduced the era of the disc jockey in 1932 with a radio show of recorded music titled The World's Largest Make Believe Ballroom.

In 1935, during lulls in the radio coverage of the murder trial of accused Lindberg kidnapper Bruno Richard Hauptmann, announcer Martin Block borrowed the Jarvis concept. This "fill" music developed into a twenty year tenure on the air for Block's Make Believe Ballroom. His unique format of fifteen minute segments devoted to a single band or vocalist was a hit with his avid listeners.

Although broadcast only in the New York City area over station WNEW, Block and his etherial ballroom were known nationwide.

The last dance on the Make Believe Ballroom aired in 1954.

MAKE BELIEVE TOWN

Film actress Virginia Bruce hosted and narrated a Monday through Friday afternoon drama series called Make Beleive Town (Hollywood). Each complete thirty minute saga depicted a fictional behind the scenes story of movie making in Hollywood, including everything from production problems to temperamental talent.

Make Beleive Town premiered on August 1, 1949 as a sustaining presentation of the CBS network. A varied cast provided the drama, Johnny Jacobs announced, and Ivan Ditmars was at the organ.

The short-lived series left the air after only a few weeks.

MAKE MINE MUSIC

An obscure weekly musical half hour title Make Mine Music aired over the CBS network in 1948.

The show was co-hosted by Billy Leach and Connie Russell.
The orchestra was under the direction of Caesar Petrillo.

MAKE UP YOUR MIND

Make Up Your Mind was a panel quiz show broadcast over the CBS network sponsored by Continental Baking Company's Wonder Bread and Hostess Cakes. It first aired on August 17, 1953, with Jack Sterling serving as emcee. The fifteen minute question and answer sessions occupied a daytime Monday through Friday spot in the network's schedule until the spring of 1956.

MAKING THE MOVIES

Zany funnyman Raymond Knight (of Cuckoo Hour fame) was joined by Katherine Renwick on a weekly "rolllicking half hour of fun" titled Making the Movies. The show premiered over NBC's Blue network flagship station WJZ on March 30, 1932 under the sponsorship of The Kelly-Springfield Tire Company.

The spoof filled program poked fun at comedy films, newsreels, and serials. Making the Movies endured only until June of 1932.

MIKE MALLOY

The crime cases of private investigator Mike Malloy were broadcast over the ABC network during the 1953-54 season.

The sustaining fifteen minute serialized episodes were aired Monday through Friday beginning on October 5, 1953. The prime time series starred Steve Brodie in the title role and featured a varied supporting cast.

Mike Malloy left the air in the spring of 1954.

MATTY MALNECK

Bandleading violinist and composer Matty Malneck was born in Newark, New Jersey on December 9, 1903.

He played and arranged for Paul Whiteman for ten years before leaving to form his own band in 1935. Malneck occasionally played the ballrooms, provided musical accompaniment for several vocalists, recorded instrumentals on the Decca label under the name The Sophisticates, and performed on radio, television, and in motion pictures.

On radio Malneck waved his baton for such shows as Abbott and Costello, The Billie Burke Show, Campana Serenade, Bob Crosby and Company, Duffy's Tavern, and Stop or Go. He was also heard on his own Music by Malneck show which is described under that heading.

Matty Malneck died in March of 1981 at the age of seventy-seven.

FLORENCE MALONE

Actress Florence Malone was born on October 8th c.1891. Her career included stage, screen, and radio; however, credits indicate radio as her principal medium.

On the airwaves she played Mrs. Gilder on Amanda of Honeymoon Hill; Mrs. Scott on Against the Storm; Mrs. Diamond on both the Captain Diamond and Cape Diamond Light series; Miss Ellis on Mr. Keen, Tracer of Lost Persons; Mrs. Mogram on Pretty Kitty Kelly; and Martha on Young Widder Brown. She was also a cast member on such other radio series as Betty and Bob, By Kathleen Norris, Doc Barclay's Daughters, Horse and Buggy Days, Our Gal Sunday, and The Singing Lady. Florence Malone died on March 4, 1956. She was reported to be in her mid-sixties.

PICK MALONE (Andrew Pickens Maloney)

Performer Pick Malone was born on June 23, 1892 near Dallas, Texas. Pick moved to Oklahoma at the age of five, attended Oklahoma State Normal School, and later served in the Army during World War I. It was during his military service that Pick got his start in show business by clowning for the troops. After discharge he toured the vaudeville circuit, and in 1929 teamed with Pat Padget. Their long association as blackface acts known as Pick and Pat and Molasses 'n' January endured until 1952 when they split up, presumedly due to the current lack of popularity for blackface acts.

On radio they appeared on Friendship Town, Model Minstrels, Modern Minstrels, their own Pick and Pat show, Pipe Smoking Time, and the (Maxwell House) Show Boat.

Pick Malone died on January 22, 1962 at the age of sixty-nine.

TED MALONE (Frank Alden Russell)

Radio announcer Alden Russell was born in Colorado Springs, Colorado on May 18, 1908. His interest in radio began when he broadcast his high school basketball games, later he attended William Jewell College before embarking on a full time radio career. He joined the staff of Kansas City's station KMBC in 1929 and shortly thereafter was pressed into service reading poetry as a fill-in for absent talent. He agreed, but only if allowed to use a "nom de poetry." That day marked the airwaves birth of Ted Malone, one of radio's best known and enduring readers of poetical writings. By 1932 his Between the Bookends poetry series was a regular feature of KMBC. In 1935 he became program director of that station, but the following year he left Kansas City for New York and the CBS network. Although Malone was to continue as an announcer, storyteller, emcee, and was as a foreign news correspondent during World War II, his programs of poetry are what is best remembered. Other radio credits included: Crossroads, Leave It to the Girls, Lifetime of Living, Pilgrimage of Poetry, The Prudential Family Hour, Top of the Evening, Westinghouse Presents Ted Malone, and Yankee Doodle Quiz. As late as the 1980s Malone's poetry was still being heard by way of syndicated transcriptions.

On television he was seen on a video version of Crossroads and also on Freedom Flight, and Holiday Overseas.

In addition to appearing before radio microphones and television cameras,

Malone was busy with several other endeavors. He was poetry editor for Good Housekeeping and Pictorial Revue, recorded on the RCA Victor label, and was a continuity writer for New York's station WOR.

Ted Malone died of liver cancer on October 20, 1989 at the age of eighty-one.

MAMA BLOOM'S BROOD

Spot Sales of Hollywood syndicated the transcribed domestic drama Mama Bloom's Brood during the 1940s. The seventy-eight fifteen minute humorous episodes of Jewish family life never revealed the members of the cast and the announcer did not identify himself. The entire production was an obvious copy of the long and popular Goldbergs series.

MAN ABOUT HOLLYWOOD

Hollywood gossipmaster George McCall hosted a 1939 weekly half hour summertime sustainer over the CBS network titled Man About Hollywood.

McCall interviewed guests and delved into obscure human intrest stories taking place in filmland. The orchestra of Wilbur Hatch provided the music and Wendell Niles announced.

MAN AGAINST CRIME

Two reference sources indicate that the series Man Against Crime was both on radio and television; however, this information is incorrect. Before his death the show's star Ralph Bellamy confirmed to Archives of the Airwaves that Man Against Crime was only a television series.

MAN BEHIND THE GUN

Actual incidents of heroism in wartime were dramatized on Man Behind the Gun. The CBS network introduced the sustaining series on October 7, 1942 as a weekly half hour program.

During the major portion of 1943 Elgin National Watch Company was the sponsor; however, it then reverted to its sustaining status until leaving the air in February of 1944.

Jackson Beck served as narrator, Nathan Van Cleave composed and conducted the music, and Charles Pauls was the organist. A semi-regular dramatic cast included: Roger DeKoven, Robert Dryden, Carl Eastman, Larry Haines, Ed Latimer, Frank Lovejoy, Paul Luther, Jimmie McCallion, Myron McCormick, Bill Quinn, Elizabeth Reller, Everett Sloane, and Chester Stratton.

THE MAN BEHIND THE MASTERPIECE

The Man Behind the Masterpiece was a 1946 syndicated series produced under the auspices of The Masterpiece Reproduction Society.

The twenty-six half hour transcribed programs combined drama and commentary to depict the lives of great artists.

Dr. Bernard Myers, a New York University lecturer, was the host. Ann Leaf was the organist and a varied cast provided the dramatic sketch.

THE MAN CALLED X

Spies, intrigue, smugglers, globe hopping, and beautiful women were all ingredients of the thriller drama titled The Man Called X.

Ken Thurston, a government intelligence agent with the code name X, found adventure and danger wherever duty called. Radio listeners joined Thurston in such notorious cities as Beirut, Cairo, Istanbul, Saigon, Singapore, and Tangier.

The Man Called X was first heard on July 10, 1944 over the CBS network, sponsored by The Lockheed Aircraft Corporation. The thirty minute program filled one half of the time period vacated by the vacationing Lux Radio Theatre. These initial episodes were linked to the FBI, but soon Thurston's assignments came under the control of a vague fictional agency. When The Lux Radio Theatre returned to the air in September, The Man Called X moved his base of operations to the ABC network with Lockeed remaining as sponsor. The series left the air in March of 1945.

Starting on June 12th of 1945 and June 18th of 1946 the show became the summer replacement for Bob Hope. Both years assuming Hope's Pepsodent sponsor on the NBC network. On April 3, 1947 The Man Called X landed a regular season spot in the CBS network's schedule, sponsored by General Motor's Frigidaire Division. This run of programs endured until September 26, 1948.

Trurston's travels were revived during the 1950-51 season as a sustaining feature of the NBC network, and a final gasp of his globe girdling exploits were sustained by the Mutual network in 1951-52.

Screen actor Herbert Marshall was cast in the title role and Leon Belasco played Pagon Zeldschmidt, Thurston's world-wise side-kick with connections on both sides of the law. Others who were heard in weekly supporting casts included: Gloria Blondell, Hans Conried, Cy Kendall, Gee Gee Pearson, Lurene Tuttle, Theodore Von Eltz, and Will Wright. Music was under the direction of Johnny Green, Felix Mills, and Claude Sweeten. The announcers were Wendell Niles and John Storm.

THE MAN FROM COOK'S

See: Cook's Travelogue

THE MAN FROM G-2

See: Major North, Army Intelligence

THE MAN FROM HOMICIDE

"I don't like killers" was the motto of the tough and cynical Lieutenant Lou Dana, The Man From Homicide.

The NBC network auditioned a pilot broadcast of the police drama on

September 14, 1950; but it was not heard again until first airing as a sustaining summer series on June 25, 1951 over the ABC network.

Screen actor Charles McGraw was initially cast in the title role; however, he was very soon replaced by Dan Duryea.

Bill Bouchy appeared as Inspector Ed Sherman, music was under the direction of Buzz Adlam, and Orville Anderson announced.

The Man From Homicide left the air on September 24, 1951.

THE MAN I MARRIED

The daytime serial drama The Man I Married was the story of a woman whose good-for-nothing husband was the disinherited son of a wealthy father. The Monday through Friday fifteen minute episodes began on July 3, 1939 over the Red network and the Canadian Broadcasting Company, sponsored by Procter and Gamble's Oxydol.

The lead role of Evelyn Waring was played by Barbara Lee, Dorothy Lowell, Vicki Vola, Gertrude Warner, Betty Winkler, and Lesley Woods. Adam Waring, the man she married, was portrayed by Bud Collyer and Van Heflin. Other members of the cast included: Fanny May Baldridge, Jackson Beck, Spencer Bentley, Frances Carden, Jackie Grimes, Ed Jerome, Raymond Edward Johnson, Arnold Moss, Santos Ortega, Ethel Owen, Walter Vaughn, and Betty Worth. The announcers were Howard Petrie and Del Sharbutt.

On July 21, 1941 the serial moved to the CBS network where Campbell Soup assumed sponsorship, with actress Alice Yourman in the role of Mary Ann Miller delivering the commercials. The final episode of The Man I Married was broadcast on April 3, 1942.

MAN IN THE FRONT ROW

A mix of news and music was the format for Man in the Front Row. Clothing manufacturers Hart, Shaffner, and Marx were the sponsors of the weekly half hour program which aired over the CBS network during the 1931-32 season.

Newsman Edwin C. Hill reported "the news of today, and about the people in the news of yesterday." The orchestra of Victor Young and The Hart, Shaffner, and Marx Trumpeters provided the music.

MAN IN THE MOON

See: William McNeary

A MAN NAMED JORDAN

The familiar story line of an American's ownership of a cafe in some foreign crossroads of the world was the basis for a radio series initially called A Man Named Jordan.

It premiered over the CBS network on January 8, 1945 as a daily fifteen minute sustaining serial drama. The setting was Jordan's Cafe Tambourine located "on a narrow street off Istanbul's Grand Bazaar," a rendezvous for sinister prople engaged in shady activities. Naturally, Jordan always managed to become involved.

Jack Moyles was cast as Rocky Jordan, Paul Frees did his best to sound like Peter Lorre as Jordan's flunky named Ali, Jay Novello was heard as his sidekick Duke O'Brien, and Dorothy Lovett portrayed his girlfried Toni Sherwood.

A Man Named Jordan left the air in 1946.

During the 1949-50 season the series returned to the air as a weekly half hour adventure titled Rocky Jordan. It was aired on the west coast only over the CBS network, sponsored by The California Packing Company's Del Monte food products. In addition to the change from a daily serial to a weekly half hour, the location of Jordan's Cafe Tambourine was moved to Cairo. Moyles resumed his role of Rocky Jordan and Jay Novello returned, but as Captain Sabaaya of the Cairo police (sounding very much like Sidney Greenstreet). Richard Aurandt directed the music and Larry Thor announced.

On June 27, 1951 a new Rocky Jordan adventure was broadcast coast-to-coast over the CBS network as a summer replacement for Mr. Chameleon. Screen actor George Raft succeeded Moyles as Jordan. Dan Cubberly and Larry Dobkin were the announcers. Rocky Jordan closed the doors of his Cafe Tambourine forever when Mr. Chameleon returned from his vacation in the fall.

MAN ON THE FARM (QUIZ)

Questions rooted in the knowlege of agronomy was the format for Man on the Farm. The Saturday morning series started as a regional mid-west broadcast originating from Chicago, but eventually went coast-to-coast. On July 30, 1949 the Mutual network began carrying the program and and on August 27th The Quaker Oats Company came aboard as sponsor to promote their Ful-O-Pep Feed.

With the passage of time, less emphasis was put on the quiz and more of the program was devoted to interviews, farming tips, and entertainment. Chuck Acree served as emcee and George Menard announced. Also included in the rural ramblings was comedian Reggie Cross, songstress Ann Andrews, and livestock expert Dr. O.B. Kent.

Man on the Farm endured on the airwaves until 1954.

MAN ON THE MOON

See: Albert E. Sonn

MAN TO MAN SPORTS

The American Tobacco Company's Roi Tan Cigars sponsored a weekly fifteen minute series on sports. Man to Man Sports made its debut on April 5, 1937 over a limited numer (five) CBS affiliated ststions. Tom Hanlon and Mark Kelly reported the sports news and conducted interviews with people from the sport's world.

Man to Man Sports concluded its run on June 28, 1938.

FU MANCHU

Tales of the criminally brilliant Dr. Fu Manchu, based on the writings of Sax Rohmer, were adapted for radio and brodcast on four separate and distinct series. Dr. Fu Manchu, a Chinese psysician, contrived his bizzare and evil schemes as revenge for the accidental death of his wife and son at the hands of Dr. James Petrie.

The first of these Fu Manchu series aired as a segment of The Collier Hour. On September 26, 1932 a thirty minute weekly version premiered over the CBS network. It was sponsored by Campana Italian Balm and remained on the air until April 24, 1933. Next was a transcribed series that was syndicated by Radio Attractions. The fifteen minute serial was titled The Shadow of Fu Manchu and was heard three times weekly from May 8, 1939 through August 4, 1939. Finally, another transcribed Fu Manchu took to the air from the studios of WMCA in New York on March 18, 1940. The fifteen minute episodes were heard six times weekly and concluded on June 22, 1940 after seventy-seven broadcasts.

The role of Fu Manchu was played by John C. Daly, Arthur Hughes, and Harold Huber; Scotland Yard Inspector Nayland Smith by Hanley Stafford and Charles Warburton; Dr. James Petrie by Gale Gordon and Bob White; and French Detective Malik by Stanley Andrews. Peggy Davis, Robert Fiske, Sunda Love, Charlotte Manson, Norman McDonald, Isabel Randolph, and John Stamford completed the principal cast.

MANDRAKE THE MAGICIAN

Trained by wizards in Tibet at The College of Magic, Mandrake the Magician used his skills to fight evil. Uttering the words "invovo legem magicarum," he summoned his powers to do battle with sinister forces at work in the world.

The radio adaptation of Mandrake the Magician was based on the syndicated King Features comic strip drawn by Phil Davis and Lee Falk. The first of the fifteen minute radio episodes aired over the Mutual network on November 11, 1940.

Mandrake was played by Raymond Edward Johnson, the giant Lothar by Joseph Granby and Juano Hernandez, and Princess Narda by Francesca Lenni. Youthful actor Laddie Seaman was also a regular cast member.

The final broadcast of Mandrake the Magician was aired on February 6, 1942; however, World Broadcasting syndicated one hundred fifty-six transcribed episodes during the mid 1940s and a syndicated television version was distributed in 1954.

MANHATTAN AT MIDNIGHT

A weekly half hour of light drama was presented on the Manhattan at Midnight series. Cummer Products Company, makers of Energine, sponsored the program which made its debut over the NBC Blue network in September of 1940.

Narrator Jim Ameche was joined by such guest stars as Ted de Corsia, John Gibson, Milton Herman, Jackie Kelk, Jeanette Nolan, Alan Reed, and Tom Tully. They were just a sampling of the many who took part in the dramatic cast. The organists were John Gart and Charles Paul.

In the fall of 1942 sponsorship was assumed by The Sterling Drug Company.

Manhattan at Midnight failed to make the network's 1943 fall schedule and faded from the airwaves.

MANHATTAN MERRY-GO-ROUND

The Manhattan Merry-Go-Round became a Sunday evening musical tradition to radio listeners of the NBC network, enduring for nearly two decades.

The carousel of music premiered on the Sunday afternoon of November 6, 1932 over the NBC Blue network, sponsored by The R.L. Watkins Company's (later Sterling Products) Dr. Lyon's Tooth Powder. In the fall of 1933 the program was moved to its familiar position in the Sunday evening lineup of NBC's Red network.

Produced by the Hummerts of daytime serial drama fame, the premise was that of an imaginary tour of New York City's famous night spots. A sampling of the current popular and show tunes were "Sung so clearly you can understand every word and sing them yourself." Each musical session was introduced by a singing theme that invited the listener to "Jump on the Manhattan Merry-Go-Round. We're touring alluring old New York town. Broadway or Harlem, a musical show, be our guest as you rest at your radio. We're serving music, songs, and laughter. A happy heart will follow after. And we'd like to have you all with us on the Manhattan Merry-Go-Round."

A long list of talent paraded before the show's microphones during its seventeen seasons on the air. Vocalists included: The Boys and Girls of Manhattan, Rachel Carlay, Glen Cross, Alan Holt, Rodney McClennan, Marian McManus, The Men About Town, Lucy Monroe, Ona MunsonDick O'Connor, David Percy, Barry Roberts, Dennis Ryan, Oliver Smith (Pierre LeKreune), Tamara, Conrad Thibault, Thomas L. Thomas, Bea Wain, and Robert Weede. During the 1935 season comic impersonator Jerry Mann was included in the cast as an added feature. Several orchestras provided the music, but initially the house name of Don Donnie was used. The actual conductors included Victor Arden, Abe Lyman, Jacques Renard, Alfred Rickey, Gene Rodemich, and Andy Sanella. Ford Bond and Roger Krupp were the announcers.

The imaginary Merry-Go-Round put away the brass ring and came to a stop after the broadcast of February 27, 1949.

MANHATTAN MOTHER

Marriage, estrangement, and love triangles permeated the story line of life in New York City on the daytime serial drama Manhattan Mother. The announcer introduced the saga with the statement "Cities are made of steel, but human hearts are of a different stuff. We give you Manhattan Mother." The series was first heard as a half hour pilot program broadcast over the CBS network in April of 1938.

The first of the weekday fifteen minute episodes aired over the CBS network on March 6, 1939, sponsored by Procter and Gamble's Chipso Soap Powder. Two days later Variety described the series as "magnificently tawdry." The lead role of Patricia Locke was played by Kaye Brinker and Margaret Hillas, her husband Tony was portrayed by Dan Sutter. For only a year-long series a long list of familiar radio voices appeared in the supporting cast. They included: John Brown, Eric Dressler, Louise Fitch, Ken Griffin, Arnold Moss, Ethel Owen, Effie Palmer, Ed Prentiss, Elizabeth Reller, James Van Dyke, and Vicki Vola. The announcers were James Fleming and Ed Roberts, Milton Charles was at the organ.

Manhattan Mother left the air on April 5, 1940.

MANATTAN PEE-RADE
See: Arthur Godfrey Programs

MANHATTAN PLAYHOUSE
Manhattan Playhouse was a transcribed sustaining series of weekly half hour plays broadcast over the Mutual network. It premiered on December 4, 1948 with the production of Mr. Wolf Steps Out. The format was very similar to the more familiar First Nighter series. Screen actor John Harvey was cast in the permanent male lead role, heading a varied supporting cast. Sylvin Levin directed the orchestra and Jack O'Reilly announced.

Manhattan Playhouse ran only a short time into 1949 and was then cancelled.

MANHUNT
Ziv Radio Productions first syndicated the detective series Manhunt in 1945.

Detectives Drew Stevens, played by Maurice Tarplin, and Bill Morton, played by Larry Haines, left no stone unturned as they hunted down their man.

There were seventy-eight rapid fire fifteen minute complete manhunts in the transcribed series.

GLORIA MANN
Youthful radio actress Gloria Mann was born in 1928 and was already performing before the microphone by the age of twelve.

She portrayed Veronica Lodge on the Archie Andrews series for several seasons and was heard as Marilyn Chandler on The Life and Love of Dr. Susan. Her other airwave credits included: Death Valley Days; The Johnny Morgan Show; The Story of Bess Johnson, and We, The People.

Gloria Mann died on April 21, 1961 at the age of thirty-three.

JERRY MANN (Jerome Mann)

Comedian and writer Jerry Mann was born in New York City on August 1, 1910. Young Jerry began performing on the vaudeville stage at the age of nine and received his education at The Professional Children's School.

He made his radio debut in 1934 over station WMCA on Nick Kenny's Scandals. As a comedian and impersonator his later radio credits included: Broadway Varieties, Hammerstein Music Hall, Lum and Abner, Manhattan Marry-Go-Round, Stairway to the Stars, and The Alan Young Show.

In addition to performing on radio Mann wrote music and scripts for radio, motion pictures, and television. He also appeared in several film shorts.

MARION MANN (Marion Bateson)

Singer Marion Mann was born on September 9, 1914 in Columbus, Ohio. After finishing school she sang with the bands of Emerson Gill, Jan Garber, and Bob Crosby in that order.

She vocalized with Crosby's band on radio and the Decca record label. She was also a regular on The Breakfast Club Club Matinee, and The Danny Thomas Show.

PAUL MANN

Actor Paul Mann was born on December 2, 1915 in Toronto, Canada. He studied acting at several studios in New York City and made his stage debut in 1934.

On radio he played George Kirby on Topper and Perry "Quiz" Quisinberry on Passport for Adams. He also appeared in roles on such other dramatic shows as Columbia Presents Corwin and The Philip Morris Playhouse.

Mann was seen in several motion pictures, founded his Paul Mann Actors Workshop, and during the 1970s he served as a professor in the Theatre Arts Department of City College of New York.

PEGGY MANN (Margaret Germano)

A native of New York City, vocalist Peggy Mann sang with several bands during the 1930s and 40s. She performed with such bands as Larry Clinton, Gene Krupa, Enoch Light, Henry Halstead, Ben Pollack, and Teddy Powell. She was heard with these bands in the ballrooms, on radio, and records. Additional radio credits included: Name the Movie, The RCA Victor Show, and her own sustaining fifteen minute program of songs aired Monday through Friday over the ABC network during the 1944-45 season.

Peggy Mann mostly faded from the performing spotlight by the 1950s. She then turned to writing novels, plays, and songs.

LUCILLE MANNERS

Singer Lucille Manners was born in Newark, New Jersey c.1912.

The soprano vocalist made her radio debut in 1932, but her main claim to fame on radio was as the replacement for the popular Jessica Dragonette on The Cities Service Concert. She filled-in for Miss Dragonette during the summer of 1936, but remained with the show for nearly a decade follwing Jessica's defection to the CBS network's Palmolive Beauty Box Theatre.

KNOX MANNING

The radio career of Knox Manning encompassed duties as an announcer, narrator, emcee, actor, and commentator.

He was born on January 17, 1904 in Worcester, Massachusetts. After receiving his education at Allen Military Academy and The University of Vermont he began his show business career as a stage actor, he later appeared in motion pictures and made his radio debut in 1930 over his hometown station WORC.

Manning's tenure on the airwaves extended through radio's heyday and into the television era. He was heard on such radio series as Behind the Scenes, Blondie, The Euclid Ballot Box, Ford Festival of American Music, Front Page Features, Get That Story, Hollywood Preview, Sherlock Holmes, I Was There, Melody and Madness, and Stars Over Hollywood.

In addition to coast-to-coast exposure, Manning was even more well-known on New England's Yankee Network and the CBS Pacific network. For example, he broadcast Knox Manning and the News six nights weekly for thirty years and announced for The Union Oil Program, both heard only on the West Coast.

On television he announced for several shows and was the voice who introduced then vice presidential candidate Richard Nixon's "Checkers" speech on September 23, 1952.

He was also active in The American Federation of Radio and Television Artists, serving as both Los Angeles and national president and later on its board of directors.

In 1979 Manning was involved in a serious auto accident that claimed the life of Annette Whiting, his wife of forty-six years. After hospitalization, he retired to The Motion Picture and Television Country House. He died there at the age of seventy-six on August 26, 1980.

TOM MANNING

Announcer and sportscaster Tom Manning was born 1903. His later aspiration to become a professional athelete was dashed when he broke his arm. As a result he became a pioneering fixture on Cleveland, Ohio radio; a career that lasted for decades.

Manning's long association with Cleveland's station WTAM started in 1928 with play-by-play broadcasts of Cleveland Indians baseball. Since WTAM was owned and operated by NBC's Red network (the station was later owned by Westinghouse and Gannett under different call letters), he was also assigned to cover network events. They included football, political conventions, The Soap

Box Derby, and World Series broadcasts. He was also one of many announcers on the RCA Magic Key programs. With the coming of the television era in 1948, Tom Manning was seen on local video programming in the Cleveland area.

MANOR HOUSE PARTY

The W.F. McLaughlin Company, makers of Manor House Coffee, sponsored a program of music and song over the NBC network during 1947.

The Manor House Party featured the song stylings of Skip Farrell and the orchestra of Freddie Aune.

CHARLOTTE MANSON

Actress Charlotte Manson was born on January 21, 1921 in New York City. At the same time she was attending New York University, she was also a member of the dramatic staff at The Dalton School.

Her first radio appearance took place in February of 1939 as the Glamour Girl on the obscure Parade of Progress series; however, it was to launch into a whirlwind acting career on the airwaves. Her many roles and striking beauty, combined with her love of parties and glamourous clothes, made her the "talk of the town."

She played Patsy Bowen on Nick Carter, Master Detective; the dual role of Carol Douglas and Gillian Gray on Nora Drake; Karameneh, the slave girl on Fu Manchu; Rose Kransky on

The Guiding Light; Doc on Hotel for Pets; Randy on King's Row; Marcelle Betrand on Mary Noble, Backstage Wife;

Dr. Carson McVicker on Road of Life; Marjorie Claiborne on The Romance of Helen Trent; and Kay Fairchild, the stepmother on Stepmother. She was also heard in the cast of such series as Amanda of Honeymoon Hill; Aunt Jenny; The Brighter Day; Cavalcade of America; Counterspy; The Joe Dimaggio Show; Gangbusters; Grand Central Station; Mike Hammer; Her Honor, Nancy James; Hilltop House; MGM Screen Test; Modern Romances; Myrt and Marge; My True Story; Arch Oboler's Plays; Michael Shayne; The Sheriff; Tales of Tomorrow; Top Guy; True Confessions; and Whispering Streets. In addition she narrated the American Woman series; she was the "Ronson Girl" who spoke on behalf of Ronson Cigarette Lighters on programs they sponsored; and also served as the CBS network's "Good Will Ambassador".

On television Charlotte Manson was seen on the video version of Famous Jury Trials, Strike it Rich, and The Paul Winchell Show.

In later years severe eye problems curtailed her activity.

MANY HAPPY MOMENTS

See: Horace Heidt Shows

MAPLE CITY FOUR

In 1925 a male quartet drove their rickety automobile from LaPorte, Indiana to Chicago. Bass Pat Patterson, baritone Art James, second tenor Bob Bender (later replaced by Al Rice), first tenor Fritz Meissner, and pianist Rege Peel were determined to "make it big" on radio in the "Windy City." Arriving in Chicago, they were first heard on several local shows aired over station WLS. They performed on their own Show Boat series and Songs of Home Sweet Home; howevwer, when The National Barn Dance program made its debut over the NBC network in 1933, The Maple City Four achieved their goal of nationwide recognition.

The group was also heard on The National Farm and Home Hour and as The Sinclair Quartet on The Sinclair Minstrels.

JOSEF MARAIS

Singer and composer Josef Marais was born in Sir Lowry Pass, South Africa on November 17, 1905. After studying music at The South African College of Music and The Royal Academy in London, he was heard as a violinist on BBC network. He came to the United States in 1939 and later premiered his radio series called African Trek over the NBC Blue network.

The program was on the air from 1940 to 1942. He also served with OWI (Office of War Information) during World War II and broadcast over the Voice of America.

Marais composed many songs and instrumental works, performed concerts with his wife Miranda, and recorded much of his music. In later years he and his wife taught in the Southern California area.

Josef Marais died on April 27, 1978 at the age of seventy-two.

MARATHON MELODIES

Marathon Melodies was a program of music and song aired over a limited number of NBC Blue network stations (eleven) in the midwest during the 1939-40 season. The Ohio Oil Company, producers of Marathon Petroleum products, sponsored the weekly half hour series; it premiered on September 1, 1939.

Josef Cherniavsky conducted the orchestra and the vocalists included: Steve Merrill, Sylvia Rhodes, and The Thrasher Sisters. The announcing duties were handled by Fred Foster and Charles Woods.

Marathon Melodies was hardly a marathon series; it left the air on May 24, 1940 after only a nine month run.

HARRY MARBLE

Announcer and newscaster Harry Marble was born in the state of Maine in 1905. He began his first radio career with an announcing job at Boston's station WORL, and in 1941 joined the CBS network in New York. His long association with that network included: newscasting on The CBS News of the World and The World Today; he announced for Margaret Arlen, Columbia Presents Corwin, The Columbia Workshop, and Eric Sevareid's newscasts; he acted in the role of a reporter on As Others See Us and You Are There; and was the narrator of Up For Parole.

In 1955 Marble left CBS to return to his home state. There he was employed by station WGAN radio and television in Portland for many years before retiring.

Harry Marble died on August 1, 1982 after a long illness. He was seventy-seven years old.

HAL MARCH (Harold Mendelson)

Actor and emcee Hal March was born on April 22, 1920 in San Francisco, California. During his high school days young March became interested in acting and was determined to make show business his career.

He began as a straight man in a vaudeville act, but military service during World War II postponed his climb up the ladder of success. After discharge he returned to San Francisco as a radio announcer, but shortly thereafter he teamed with Bob Sweeney on the Sweeney and March comedy series heard over the CBS network. March's other radio credits included playing the role of Mr. Cook on Too Many Cooks and as a cast member on Much About Doolittle, My Favorite Husband, The Alan Young Show, and Young Love.

He was also a frequent guest on radio shows with Jack Benny, Burns and Allen, Perry Como, and Bob Hope.

March became a household name as the emcee of the popular, but scandal ridden, television quiz show The Sixty-Four Thousand Dollar Question. He was also seen by television viewers on Burke's Law, Burns and Allen, The Imogene Coca Show, Laughs for Sale, The Lucy Show, The Monkees, My Friend Irma, The Soldiers, and What's it For?

In addition to radio and television, March achieved a measure of recognition on the stage and in motion pictures.

In 1956 he married actress Candy Toxton Torme, the former wife of singer Mel Torme.

Hal March died on January 19, 1970 at the age of forty-nine. He had a lung removed several months before due to lung cancer and was unable to survive a bout of pneumonia..

THE MARCH OF GAMES

The March of Games was a juvenile quiz show with contestants, the quizmaster, and the assistant all drawn from the moppet set.

The fifteen minute program first aired over the CBS network in the spring of 1938 as a late afternoon offering of "school-housey" entertainment. The sustaining broadcasts were heard on Mondays, Tuesdays, and Wednesdays. Fourteen year old Arthur Ross presided over the festivities, with ten year old Sybil Trent serving as his assistant. The entire production was presented under the watchful eye of Nila Mack, well known for creating and directing the Let's Pretend series.

The March of Games left the air in the fall of 1938, but returned a year later as a weekly half hour Sunday program. The final broadcast aired in the spring of 1940.

THE MARCH OF TIME

The March of Time format pioneered the dramatized reenactment news actualities. Then, as today, simulated news caused some problems. For example, in July of 1937 a March of Time broadcast featured a story about the disappearance of flyer Amelia Earhart. During the course of the dramazation a conversation between Earhart and naval vessels led many radio listeners to believe it to be the real thing. The concept of dramatized news events was the brainchild of broadcast pioneer Fred Smith. His pilot program called Newsdrama would become The March of Time series.

The initial series of March of Time broadcasts were first aired over the CBS network on March 6, 1931, sponsored by Time Magazine (also Life and Fortune). The show was later carried as a sustainer under the title A Parade of Current Events.

Time resumed sponsorship on November 4, 1932 and the program was again known as The March of Time. During 1933-35 Time was displaced as sponsor by Remington Rand, in 1936 Wrigley Gum underwrote the series, and for three months in 1938 Servel's Electrolux Refrigerators paid the bills; however, Time continued its involvement with the production.

Westbrook Van Voorhis, who also narrated The March of Time films, is best remembered as "the voice of time; however, Ted Husing and Harry Von Zell also served in that capacity on the earlier brodcasts. During that time Van Voorhis was heard as the "Voice of Fate." The voices of the great and infamous newsmakers of the world were imitiated by a host of radio actors. Among them were Bill Adams, Art Carney, and Staats Cotsworth as Franklin D. Roosevelt, Marion Hopkinson, Nancy Kelly, Agnes Moorehead, and Jeanette Nolan as Eleanor Roosevelt, Edwin Jerome as Halie Selassie and Josef Stalin, Dwight Weist as Adolph Hitler, Ted de Corsia as Benito Mussolini, and Maurice Tarplin as Winston Churchill. Still more familiar radio voices heard in the dramatic casts were Georgia Backus, Kenny Delmar, Peter Donald, Martin Gabel, Ted Jewett, William Johnstone, Adelaide Klein, Myron McCormick, John McIntire, Gary Merrill, Claire Niesen, Frank Readick, Patricia Reardon, Elliott Reid, Everett Sloane, J. Scott Smart, Lotte Stavisky, Karl Swenson, Orson Welles, and Agnes Young.

Assisting in the gathering of material used in producing the current event dramas were foreign correspondents from the four corners of the globe.

Music for the program was under the direction of Howard Barlow, Victor Bey, and Donald Voorhees. From March 30, 1936 to September 25, 1936 the series departed from its normal weekly half hour presentations and was heard for fifteen minutes on Monday through Friday. It moved from the CBS network to the NBC Blue network on October 14, 1937 and was off the air from the summer of 1939 to the fall of 1941 due to war restrictions. It remained on NBC following the split of the Red and Blue networks, but shifted to the ABC (Blue) network for its final season on the air.

The March of Time marched off the airwaves and into radio history after the broadcast of July 26, 1945.

ADRIENNE MARDEN

Character actress Adrienne Marden appeared in a limited number of supporting roles on stage, screen, radio, and television. She also directed and produced several stage productions.

On radio she played Patricia Jordan on The Story of Bess Johnson and was a cast memeber on The Aldrich Family; Helen Hayes Theatre; Light of the World; Lincoln Highway; Manhattan at Midnight; Philip Morris Playhouse; The Kate Smith Show; and We, The People.

Her only regular television appearance was on Matinee Theatre where she was seen in the role of Geraldine.

Adrienne Marden died of a heart attack at the age of sixty-nine on November 9, 1978.

MARDI GRAS

See: The Packard Hour

MARGO (Maria Margarita Guadalupe Teresa Estela Bolado Castilla y O'Donnell)

Actress and singer Margo as born in Mexico City, Mexico on May 10, 1917. She moved to the United States as a youngster to live with her grandmother and aunt. She first performed professionally as a dancer at the age of ten.

Margo's subsequent career encompassed stage, screen, radio, television, recordings, and the nightclub circuit (often performing with her bandleader uncle Xavier Cugat).

Her radio credits included: The Dreft Star Playhouse, played the role of Tanya on the daytime serial drama Into the Light, sang on Uncle Xavier's show Romance and Rhumbas, and was a guest star on other dramatic and musical productions.

Margo was married to actor Francis Lederer in 1937, a union that ended in divorce in 1942; three years later she became the wife of actor Eddie Albert.

In later years she was a civic activist and was involved with several societies that endowed the arts.

Margo Albert died on July 17, 1985 at the age of sixty-eight.

MARGO OF CASTLEWOOD

The saga of Margo Carver, the seventy-nine year old family matriarch, unfolded on the daytime serial drama Margo of Castlewood.

Quaker Oats began sponsoring the fifteen minute Monday through Friday episodes over the NBC Blue network at the start of 1938.

Barbara Luddy was cast in the title role with support from Francis X. Bushman. The announcer was Charles Lyon.

The brief series came to an end on March 18, 1938.

MARIA'S CERTO MATINEE

An afternoon program of music and song was the format of Maria's Certo Matinee sponsored by Certo Sure Jell homemade jelly additive. Tenor Lanny Ross was the star of the show, he was joined by baritone Conrad Thibault and Gus Haenschen's orchestra.

The show aired over the NBC Red network during the 1934-35 season. It became the basis for the 1935 summer replacement for Jack Benny titled State Fair Concert which is described under that heading.

MARIE, THE LITTLE FRENCH PRINCESS

Marie, The Little French Princess was the first of the daytime serial dramas offered to a coast-to-coast radio audience by the CBS network. It took to the airwaves on March 7, 1933 sponsored by Louis Phillipe.

The story line revolved around a princess from a mythical kingdom who forsook her regal heritage for life among the common folk.

Ruth Yorke played the title role and James Meighan was heard as Richard Collins, her commoner love interest. The supporting cast included: Porter Hall, Alma Kruger, and Allyn Joslyn.

The announcer was Andre Baruch.

The final chapter of the princess to pauper tale was heard in October of 1935.

THE MARINO FAMILY

See: Little Italy

CHARLES MARKS

See: Charlie Dale

GARNETT MARKS

The well traveled radio personality Garnett Marks began his career on the airwaves during the early 1930s. With time out for service in the Navy during world war II, he was heard on both network and local radio.

His diverse assignments included: acting, announcing, newscasting, singing, and sportscasting. He was also associated with such stations as KGFN in Grass Valley, KFWB and KNX in Hollywood, KMPC in Los Angeles all in

California; KMOX in St. Louis; WENR in Chicago; WKRC in Cincinnati; WMCA and WOR in New York City; and WSAY in Rochester, New York. On network radio he was heard on Dr. Christian, Echoes of New York, Gangbusters, The General Electric Hour, newscasts, and play-by-play sports.

SHERMAN MARKS

Actor, director, and writer Sherman Marks brought these talents to bear on both radio and televison.

As an actor on radio Marks was one of three to play the Captain's sidekick Ichy (Ichabod Mudd) on Captain Midnight and was also heard as Joe Binney on Mary Noble, Backstage Wife. Other acting credits included: American Novels, Meet the Meeks, The Peabodys, and The World's Great Novels.

He directed such series as Cloak and Dagger and The Whistler.

On television Marks directed The Bill Goodwin Show, The Ghost and Mrs. Muir, Many Happy Returns, and others. As a writer he penned scripts for The Freewheelers and Toni Twin Time.

Serman Marks died on April 4, 1975.

(THE STORY OF) MARY MARLIN

The Story of Mary Marlin was one of a handfull of classic daytime serial dramas that enjoyed such popularity it endured for many years on the radio airwaves. The series creator and writer Jane Crusinberry sold her story idea to Chicago's station WMAQ in 1934 where it made its radio debut on October 3rd. The serial was so well received in the Chicago area that the NBC Red network began carrying it coast-to-coast on January 1, 1935 under the sponsorship of International Cellucotton Company's (later Kimberly-Clark) Kleenex Tissues. In the fall of 1935 the series shifted to the CBS network over a flap regarding commercials for Quest Deodorant, but returned to NBC on September 14, 1936.

Procter and Gamble's Ivory Soap took over sponsorship on March 29, 1937 when listening demands were very high. Subsequently this led to two airings the same day, NBC's Blue network in the morning and the Red in the afternoon.

The Story of Mary Marlin contained all the ingredients necessary for the quintessential serial. Mary and her husband Joe moved from their hometown of Cedar Springs, Iowa to Washington, D.C. following Joe's election to the U.S. Senate; (POWER); Joe's plane later crashed in Tibet while he was on a mission to Russia (TRAGEDY); Joe survives, but has amnesia and roams the world searching for his identity (PATHOS); Mary assumes her missing husband's seat in the Senate (FEMINISM); love triangles abound as lustful desires are revealed (SEX); and finally, Joe and Mary are reunited (JOY).

The cast list was long, due to the legions of characters that came and went over the years. Not uncommonly some in the cast played more than one role. Actresses Joan Blaine, Linda Carlon, Betty Lou Gerson, Muriel Kirkland,

Eloise Kummer, and Anne Seymour at one time or another all appeared in the title role. Senator Joe Marlin was played by Robert Griffin; Joe and Mary's son Davey by Delores Gillen, Bobby Dean Maxwell, and Jerry Spellman; Joe's law partner David Post by Carlton Brickert and Arthur Jacobson; Washington's "upper crust" social climber Bunny Mitchell by Fran Carlon and Templeton Fox; Bunny's husband Frazier by Phil Lord and Fred Sullivan; private detective "Never Fail" Hendricks by Frank Dane and William Lee; President of the United States Rufus Kane by Rupert LaBelle; and a Chinese man named Oswald Ching, who befriended Joe on his global trek, by Peter Donald.

More familiar radio voices who portrayed other characters included: Bill Adams, Charme Allen, Francis X. Bushman, Betty Caine, Eddie Firestone Jr., Murray Forbes, Elinor Harriot, Mary Jane Higby, Raymond Edward Johnson, Arthur Kohl, Bill Lipton, Judith Lowry, June Meredith, Bret Morrison, Arnold Moss, Arthur Peterson, Isabel Randolph, and Anne Stone.

Pianists Allan Grant and Joe Kahn played the melancholy strains of the theme song Calir de Lune. The announcers were Truman Bradley, Bob Brown, Nelson Case, Tibbits "Tip" Corning, Bill Farren, Les Griffith, Howard Petrie, and John Tillman.

During 1941 the serial was again broadcast twice daily over different networks, this time NBC and CBS. When Procter and Gamble cancelled as sponsors in 1943, Mary was then heard exclusively over the CBS network for Tenderleaf Tea for the next two seasons. Mary Marlin left the air on April 13, 1945, probably due in no small part to the anticlimactic story line following the return of Joe Marlin. After a six year hiatus, a last ditch effort to revive interest in her story brought Mary Marlin back to the air in 1951 over the ABC network. The revival failed to gain a sponsor or acceptable ratings and departed after the final chapter aired on April 11, 1952.

MARY MARLOW

Singer Mary Marlow (not to be confused with actress Mary Marlo [aka Ada Orlando]) was born in 1925 in Philadelphia, Pennsylvania. Her father, "Uncle" Jim Harkins, was a well-known vaudevillian and sidekick to Fred Allen. He was adamant in discouraging Mary from seeking a career in show business. She studied to be a stenographer, but continued her interest in singing professionally. She made a home recording which later led to a fifteen minute daily program of songs she broadcast over New York City's station WMCA. Still later she became a page at the NBC studios before winning a job as a vocalist with Sammy Kaye's band in January of 1946. Mary appeared with Kaye on such radio shows as So You Want to Lead a Band? and Sunday Serenade.

HUGH MARLOWE (Hugh Herbert Hipple)

Actor Hugh Marlowe was born in Philadelphia, Pennsylvania, on January 30, 1911. Marlowe made his radio debut in 1931 as an announcer for station

WHO-WOC in Davenport, Iowa; in 1936 he appeared in his first New York stage production, and the next year in his first motion picture.

Although he began his radio career as an announcer, that phase of his tenure on the airwaves was of little importance.

Marlowe is best remembered for his portrayal of the title role on the Ellery Queen series. He also played Queen in both the motion picture and television versions of the famous detective's adventures. Other radio acting credits included being one of several to play the lead role of Dr. Benjamin Ordway on Crime Doctor, Jim Curtis on the Brenda Curtis serial and Gann Murray on the Our Gal Sunday daytime drama. He was also a cast member on Amateur Gentleman, Hollywood Hotel, and Shell Chateau.

On television he portrayed Jim Matthews on the daytime serial Another World for thirteen years. He was also seen as a guest star on numerous video dramas and as the aforementioned star of the Ellery Queen mysteries.

Hugh Marlowe succumbed to a heart attack on May 2, 1982. He was seventy-one years old.

PHILIP MARLOWE

Author Raymond Chandler's private detective Philip Marlowe was first adapted for radio as a 1947 summer replacement show for the vacationing Bob Hope.

The weekly half hour adventure series signed on over the NBC network on June 17, 1947, sponsored by Lever Brothers' Pepsodent Tooth Paste.

Van Heflin played the title role, Lynn Murray directed the orchestra, and announcer Wendell Niles deliverd the dentifrice commercials. Heard in the supporting cast were Harry Bartell, William Conrad, Olive Deering, and Lurene Tuttle.

Marlowe gave way to Hope's return in the fall.

Philip Marlowe's hard driving crime capers reappeared on the airwaves on September 26, 1948 over the CBS network with new adventures and and a new cast. Gerald Mohr took over as the tough investigator, opening each program with the following warning to those who would break the law: "Get this and get it straight, crime is a sucker's road, and those who travel it wind up in the gutter, prison, or an early grave." Music was directed by Richard Aurandt and Roy Rowan announced. Others in the cast included: Parley Baer, Joan Banks, Edgar Barrier, Gloria Blondell, Lois Corbett, Jeff Corey, John Dehner, Larry Dobkin, David Ellis, Laurette Fillbrandt, Paul Frees, Virginia Gregg, Wilma Herbert, Vivi Janiss, Lou Krugman, Jack Kruschen, Peter Leeds, Howard McNear, and Jack Noyles.

For the most part, the latter day series was sustained by CBS except for a beief period when The Ford Motor Company assumed sponsorship.

The last of Philip Marlowe's radio mysteries was broadcast on January 28, 1950. A video version was seen during the 1959-60 season with Philip Carey portraying Marlowe.

EDDIE MARR

Character actor Eddie Marr was born on February 14, 1900 in Jersey City, New Jersey. He was seen on the motion picture screen beginning in the 1930s and was heard in diverse radio roles during the 1940s.

Eddie "Tell you what I'm Gonna Go" Marr was the star of Fun and Mirth with Eddie Marr, an obscure radio series aptly described by its title. The show aired over the ABC network in 1945, sponsored by The Signal Oil Company. He also played a salesman and Carson's press agent on The Jack Carson Show, served as the quizmaster on Win, Place, And Show, and was the first to play the crook on Jack Benny's show who demanded of Benny "Your money or your life." Marr was also heard on such other radio shows as Five Star Jones, Bob Hope, The Kraft Music Hall, The Lux Radio Theatre, Meet Corliss Archer, Murder Will Out, Radio Hall of Fame, The Damon Runyon Theatre, and Suspense.

On television he was the barker on Circus Boy and frequented the video version of Bob Hope's show.

THE MARRIAGE

The Marriage was a light hearted drama revolving around the lives of the Marriott family. The husband and wife acting team of Hume Cronyn and Jessica Tandy, best known for their stage and film work, were cast as Ben anad Liz Marriott. Daughter Emily was played by Susan Strasberg and son Peter by Malcolm Brodrick.

The sustaining series was aired over the NBC network starting on October 4, 1953. The final radio episode of The marriage was broadcast on February 4, 1954; but a short lived video version was seen from July 1st to August 19th of 1954 with the same cast.

MARRIAGE CLUB

See: Your Marriage Club

MARRIAGE FOR TWO

Plans for marriage between a stable young woman and her irresponsible fiance was the story line for the daytime serial drama Marriage for Two.

The initial episode was broadcast on February 9, 1948 as a sustaining feature of the CBS network; however, it quickly left the air in March. On July 11, 1949 it returned to the air over the NBC network, and by October 3rd had attracted The Kraft Foods Company as a sponsor.

Vikki Adams, the perspective bride, was played by Fran Lefferty and Amzie Strickland. Roger Hoyt, her husband to-be was played by Staats Cotsworth. The supporting cast included: Marion Barney, House Jameson, Evelyn Varden, and Gertrude Warner. The organist was Fred Feibel and Rosa Rio. The announcer was John Tillman.

The Marriage for Two went on the rocks and was last heard on March 31, 1950.

MARRIAGE LICENSE (BUREAU)(ROMANCES)

A unique concept in interview show formats was first aired locally in the Chicago area over station WMAQ in 1935. Titled Marriage License Bureau, couples applying for their marriage licenses were asked questions as how they met and to describe their wedding plans. Quin Ryan was the interviewer and Jeff Sparks announced.

Beginning on June 27, 1938 the show was carried by a limited number of Mutual network stations under the title Marriage License Romances. It was heard as a sustaining fifteen mnute series broadcast three times weekly. Marriage License Romances ended in 1939.

MARRIED FOR LIFE

Married for Life premiered on March 3, 1946 over the Mutual network, claiming to be dedicated to "patience, loyalty, love, and understanding!!" A happy couple about to wed was interviewed and a dramatization of their courtship was presented by a cast of actors. Also included in the weekly half hour was a shower of gifts for the perspective bride and groom and also a description of the wedding ceremonies of couples who had been on the show before their marriage.

Bill Slater presided over the festivities. The dramatic cast included: Bryna Raeburn, Eleanor Shernon, Johnny Sylvester, and Lawson Zerbe. The announcer was Don Frederick.

On April 22nd the show expanded to a Monday through Friday schedule, but too many starry eyed expectant brides were more than listening audiences could tolerate. The show returned to its weekly Saturday schedule after only two weeks.

Married for Life left the air for the summer of 1946, but returned in the fall with a new lineup of talent. Bert Parks was the emcee, tenor Keith David serenaded the engaged couple with wedding songs, and the dramatic cast was comprised of Polly Bester, Mitzi Gould, John Larkin, and Joan Lazer.

Married for Life was last heard in the spring of 1947.

AUDREY MARSH

Singer and actress Audrey Marsh was born in the New York City area in 1912. She started to sing when she was only a year old, and since her father was a singer and her mother a pianist, little Audrey was encouraged during her childhood to pursue her desire to enter show business.

She began her career on the stage, but in 1930 radio beckoned her towards that medium.

On the airwaves she was cast in the title role on Dance With Countess D'Orsay, played Esther on the Harv and Esther series, and sang with her sister Beverly on Johnny Presents. She was also heard on such shows as The Ford Summer Hour, Fox Fur Trappers, Jeddo Highlanders, Necco Surprise Party, and (Maxwell House) Show Boat.

Audrey Marsh's appearances on radio waned by the close of the 1930s.

HOWARD MARSH

Musical comedy star Howard Marsh was born in Bluffton, Indiana c. 1895. Howard studied law and finance at Perdue University, but later opted for a show business career. He subsequently performed on stage, radio, and in nightclubs during the 1920s and 30s. His limited appearances on radio in the 1930s included: acting, conducting, and singing. Among his airwave credits were such musical series as Buick Presents, Evening in Paris, and The Frigidaire Program.

In later years Marsh returned to the world of finance and banking, although he maintained his ties to show business by operating nightclubs in New Jersey.

Howard Marsh died on August 7, 1969.

JOAN MARSH (Nancy Ann Rosher)

Actress and singer Joan Marsh was born on July 10, 1913 in Porterville, California. She first appeared on the motion picture screen as a baby and subsequently grew into adult film roles. By the mid 1930s her reputation as Hollywood's playgirl led her briefly away from films and into radio. The exotic blond bombshell exploded onto the airwaves as a regular cast member of The Flying Red Horse Tavern. However, her career on radio was limited and of short duration as she soon returned to the "fast lane" of filmdom.

By the close of the 1950s Joan Marsh retired from the field of entertainment and started Paper Unlimited, a successful stationery business.

MYRA MARSH

Character actress Myra Marsh was born on October 29, 1894. She appeared in several motion pictures and radio series, mostly during the 1930s and 40s. On radio she played Dora Foster on A Date With Judy, Hilda, the maid, on Junior Miss, and Mrs. Rhinelander on My Friend Irma. She was also in the cast of The First Hundred Years.

Myra Marsh died in 1964 at the age of seventy.

EVERETT MARSHALL

Baritone vocalist and actor Everett Marshall was born in Lawrence, Massachusetts on December 31, 1901. He studied at The Cincinnati Conservatory of Music and at similar schools in London, England and Milan, Italy. He made his stage debut in 1926 in Milan.

Although not a major part of his career, he made his first radio appearance on The Atwater Kent Hour in 1928. He would subsequently become familiar to radio audiences during the 1930s as the star of Broadway Varieties.

HELEN MARSHALL

Vocalist Helen Marshall was born in Joplin, Missouri c. 1914. She studied music at Juilliard, and while there, was selected to be a guest star in Columbia

University's Morningside Players production of The Beggar's Opera. During one of the performances Helen was "discovered" by composer Sigmund Romberg.

Billed as "The Lady in White," and with Romberg as her mentor, Helen Marshall became a radio sensation during the mid 1930s. She was heard on such programs of that era as Fireside Recitals, Sigmund Romberg's Concert, and Swift's Studio Party.

HERBERT MARSHALL

Suave actor Herbert Marshall was born in London, England on May 23, 1890. After a brief period in the business world, Marshall made his acting debut on the stage in 1911. Despite the loss a a leg during military service in World War I, he would continue to portray roles on stage and screen on both sides of the Atlantic.

Marshall's unique manner and voice became well known to radio listeners for his portrayal of secret agent Ken Thurston on The Man Called X series. Less recalled airwave credits included: The Chase and Sanborn Program in the summer of 1937, was one of several to emcee Hollywood Hotel, he played the permanent male lead on Hollywood Playhouse (replacing Charles Boyer, who joined the French Army), and The Old Gold Show. He also appeared as a guest star on such other series as The CBS Radio Workshop, Hallmark Playhouse, Hollywood Startime, The Lux Radio Theatre, Screen Gild Theatre, Skippy Hollywood Theatre, Suspense, Theatre of Romance, and This Is My Best.

On television he appeared as a regular on Ken Murray's show, hosted Times Square Playhouse and The Unexpected, and was a cast member on other dramatic presentations and specials.

Actor Barry Sullivan played Ken Thurston on the video version of The Man Called X.

Marshall was married five times. His wives in chronological order were Molly Maitland, Edna Best, Lee Russell, Patricia "Boots" Mallory, and Dee Kahmann.

Herbert Marshall suffered a fatal heart attack at the age of seventy-five on January 22, 1966.

NANCY MARSHALL (Nancy MacGregor)

Actress, and Georgia native Nancy Marshall was born in the "Peach State" c. 1912. She studied acting at dramatics school in Washington and attended Columbia University.

Nancy first appeared on the stage before turning to radio in the late 1930s. Her limited career on the airwaves endured only a few years into the 1940s. She was one of five to play the lead role of Ruth Evans in the daytime serial drama Big Sister. She was also heard as Natalie Holt on The Story of Bess Johnson and Francesca Maguire on Lone Journey.

During the summer of 1965 Nancy Marshall appeared on a television comedy pilot titled Young at Heart. However, the show never became a regular series.

MARTIN AND LEWIS

The team of (Dean) Martin and (Jerry) Lewis first made an impact on the world of entertainment during the late 1940s on the nightclub circuit. Subsequently they expanded their horizons to include motion pictures, radio and television.

The Martin and Lewis radio show first aired over the NBC network on April 3, 1949 as a weekly half hour of sustaining comedy. Later the show attracted sponsorship by such products as Anacin, Chesterfield Cigarettes, and Chiclets.

Although both dabbled in each other's specialty, Martin was basically the foil/singer and Lewis the wacky comic. A weekly list of well-known guest stars augmented the banter between Dean and Jerry. Regulars on the show included Flo McMichael, The Skylarks singing group, and the orchestra of Dick Stabile. The announcers were Ed Herlihy, Johnny Jacobs, Marvin Miller, and Jimmy Wallington.

Despite consistently poor ratings, and less than enthusiastic reviews by the critics, the series remained on the air until 1953. By then the lure of television for both the performers and the audience led Martin and Lewis to call it quits on radio. The final broadcast was aired on July 14, 1953.

DEAN MARTIN (Dino Paul Crocetti)

Singer and actor Dean Martin was born in Steubenville, Ohio on June 17, 1917. Martin worked at such diverse jobs as a boxer, gambler, and steel worker before starting his career as a nightclub singer. He first teamed with zany comedian Jerry Lewis in 1946. Together they toured the nightclub circuit, appeared on the motion picture screen, radio and television before splitting up in 1956.

On radio Dean and friend cavorted on their own show for several seasons. He also performed as a guest, both as a team and solo, on other shows.

As a recording artist Martin was mostly associated with the Capitol label. He made numerous records, several of which became popular hits.

On television Martin and Lewis hosted The Colgate Comedy Hour and after going their separate ways, Martin became the star of his own very successful variety show that remained on the air for nearly a decade. Dean Martin created the image of a heavy drinking womanizer, a reputation he carried into motion pictures and as a member of Frank Sinatra's "Rat Pack" (a group that also included: Joey Bishop, Sammy Davis, Jr., and Peter Lawford). Martin also appeared in over fifty other films, the last in 1984.

Dean Martin died of respiratory failure on December 25, 1995. He was seventy-eight years old.

DR. DOLPHE MARTIN

Musician and physician Dr. Dolphe Martin was born in Poland in 1890. He came to the United States as an infant when his family immigrated and settled near Boston, Massachusetts. Dr. Martin was a graduate of both Harvard University and Massachusetts Institute of Technology. He received his musical training at Ecole Cesar Franck in Paris.

Dr. Martin's medical specialty was psychiatry, while his expertise in music was composing and conducting. He often combined music and psychiatry in the treatment of his mental patients.

On the show business side of his career he was a conductor, won a Pulitzer Prize for his collaboration with Paul Green in composing the score for Roll Sweet Chariot, and applied his musical talents to the medium of radio.

His first association with radio began in Boston at stations WEEI and WNAC. He served as associate musical director for a regional New England network (Yankee) and conducted the orchestra on The Tydol Jubilee (later called Music on the Air) which aired over the CBS network during 1933. During the 1940s he presided over Youth on Parade, a juvenile talent show heard over the CBS network originating from the Boston studios of WEEI, and led a children's choir on Rainbow House. On television, he produced a local video version of Youth on Parade seen locally during the 1960s in the Boston area.

Dolphe Martin died on October 3, 1974 at the age of eighty-four.

FRANK MARTIN (J. Frank Martin)

Announcer and actor Frank Martin served in one or the other of these capacities on several radio series during the 1940s and the early 1950s.

As a network announcer he was associated with such shows as Danger Assignment; Everything for the Boys; The Dick Haymes Show; His Honor, the Barber; I Love a Mystery; Lights Out; Mayor of the Town; The Merry Life of Mary Christmas; The Roma (Wine) Show; Sara's Private Capers; The Penny Singleton Show; Suspense; Tales of the Texas Rangers; and Your Luck Strike.

As an actor he played the title role on Hashknife Hartley. He also heard in the supporting cast on Big Town, Dear John, Dr. Christian, Red Ryder, and Silver Theatre.

Martin was also listed as a staff announcer on several local stations. They included: WICS in Springfield, Illinois; WIIK in Erie, Pennsylvania; WKY in Oklahoma City, Oklahoma; and KFI and KFWB in Los Angeles, California.

During his lifetime Martin not only appeared before the radio microphone, but was also an active attorney.

Frank Martin died on December 22, 1994 at the age of eighty.

FREDDY MARTIN (Frederic A. Martin)

Bandleader and saxophonist Freddy Martin was born in Cleveland, Ohio on December 9, 1906. He was reared in a Columbus, Ohio orphanage, but returned to Cleveland at the age of sixteen to live with his aunt. It was during his high school days in Cleveland that he began his musical career. He continued to play with several bands after graduation until he organized his own dance band in October of 1931.

Martin's band played the hotels and ballrooms (he became a fixture for a quarter century at Ambassador's Coconut Grove in Los Angeles), recorded on a half dozen labels, was heard on radio, appeared in a few motion pictures, and was seen occasionally on television.

His radio achievements included several of his own shows. Martin's music was the catalyst for Maybelline cosmetic's spokeswoman Dorothy Hamilton to promote their products over the NBC Red Network on Penthouse Serenade. In 1942 his music was featured over the CBS network on a show that also included dramatic vignettes associated with the musical numbers. The announcer was Pierre Andre. Still at it in 1954, The Freddy Martin Show took to the air over the CBS network with a weekly half hour of music and song. Other airwave credits included: American Revue, The Jack Carson Show, The Cass Daley Show, dance band remote broadcasts, The Fitch Bandwagon, Fray and Braggiotti, Going Places, Lady Esther Serenade, and Vick's Open House. Martin's orchestra was also syndicated on such transcribed series as The RCA Thesaurus Library, The Freddy Martin Show, and Ziv's Showtime from Hollywood.

Undismayed by the decline for big bands and the rise of rock and roll, Martin continued to play to ballroom dancing enthusiasts until a series of strokes forced him off the air.

Freddy Martin died on September 30, 1983 of complications from his latest stroke. He was seventy-six years old.

H. GILBERT MARTIN

Announcer H. Gilbert Martin (not to be confused with newscaster Gilbert Martyn) attracted little notice during his tenure on the network airwaves in the 1940s. The almost anonymous announcer was heard on such series as Behind the Mike, Charles Courboin Organ Concerts, Deadline Drama, Gangbusters, and Star Spangled Theatre.

IAN MARTIN

A native of Scotland, actor Ian Martin was born in Glasgow in 1912. He made his stage debut at the age of three, and after coming to the United States as a boy, continued to pursue acting as a career.

He performed in stage productions, motion pictures, and was heard on radio and seen on television both in dramatic casts and commercials. In addition, he penned scripts and was an accomplished dialectician.

On radio he played Dr. Reed Bannister on Big Sister, Ian McLaughlin on John's Other Wife, Hank Briston on Life Can Be Beautiful, Addison Smith on When a Girl Marries, Steve Holbart on Woman of Courage, and Horace Sutton on Young Dr. Malone. He was also one of many appearing as Dr. Watson on the Sherlock Holmes series and served as host/actor on Mystery Playhouse.

Martin's other airwave credits included: Against the Storm, Archie Andrews, Cavalcade of America, Chandu the Magician, Doc Rockwell's Brain Trust, Easy Aces, Helen Hayes Theatre, Land of the Lost, Light of the World, Manhattan Mother, Murder by Experts, The Mysterious Traveler, Pretty Kitty Kelly, The Right to Happiness, Romance, The Kate Smith Show, Thunder Over Paradise, True Detective Mysteries, and Wheatena Playhouse.

On television he played Uncle Bill on the video version of The O'Neills and wrote scripts for The Doctors. He was also in the cast of The Edge of Night, Search for Tomorrow, and The Wonderful John Action.

Ian Martin died of a heart attack on July 25, 1981. He was sixty-nine years old.

MARY MARTIN

Singer and actress Mary Martin was born on December 1, 1913 in Weatherford, Texas. She began her career in nightclubs, subsequently rising to superstardom on the Broadway musical stage. To a lesser degree she also performed in motion pictures, on radio, records, and television.

On radio she appeared on such shows as Good News of 1938, The Kraft Music Hall, Maxwell House Coffee Time, Stagedoor Canteen, The Telephone Hour, Tex and Jinx, Tuesday Night Party, and Twin Stars.

As a television star she was seen on several specials, most notably recreating her stage triumph in the title role on a video presentation of Peter Pan.

Mary Martin died of cancer on November 3, 1990 at the age of seventy-six.

MARY HALE MARTIN

Mary Hale Martin was the "house" name of Libby Foods' home economist. She was created in 1919 and first appeared in women's magazines in 1923.

Mary Hale Martin took to the radio airwaves on March 3, 1924 over Chicago's station WMAQ with what Libby claimed to be the very first talk program beamed at homemakers. In 1930 the series became a regular feature of NBC's Blue network under the title Mary Hale Martin's Kitchen Chatter. It aired as a weekly fifteen-minute program, naturally sponsored by Libby Foods.

Several home economists in Libby's employ assumed the role of Martin; however, the two heard on radio were Vernetta Battle and Dorothy Knight.

The program was on network radio for only a single season, but other Mary Hale Martins have continued to plug Libby products in commercials on radio and television.

THE ADVENTURES OF SANDRA MARTIN

The Adventures of Sandra Martin (aka Lady of the Press) was a daytime serial drama with a romantic mystery storyline. Originating from Hollywood, it was broadcast over the CBS network for a brief time during the 1944-45 season, sponsored by Miles Laboratories' Alka Seltzer.

The series followed the vaguely recalled exploits of Sandra Martin, an investigative reporter for The Los Angeles Daily Courier and her romantic involvement with detective Hack Taggart.

The title role was played by Mary Jane Croft, Hack Taggart by Howard Culver and Ivan Green, reporter Eddie Dalton by Bob Latting, gangster Steve Heywood by Howard McNear, and Daily Courier editor Wilson by Grif Barnett. The announcer was Dick Hudding.

TONY MARTIN (Alvis Morris)

Singer and actor Tony Martin was born in Oakland, California on December 25, 1912. While still in his teens, young Martin began playing the saxophone and singing with obscure West coast bands. Early in his career he played the nightclubs and had a bit part in a motion picture, but it was exposure on radio that established him as a versatile entertainer. He appeared in a few more films, recorded on several labels, toured the nightclub circuit, and was a popular performer on both radio and television.

Martin made his radio debut on March 28, 1932 on The Lucky Strike Orchestra program. He later starred in his own radio shows and was heard vocalizing on such programs as Burns and Allen, The Carnation Contented Hour, Listen to a Love Song, The Rexall Parade of Stars, and as both singer and emcee on Tune Up Time.

On television he hosted The Tony Martin Show from 1954 to 1956 and was a frequent guest on other shows, especially with Bob Hope. Martin was married to singer/actress Alice Faye in 1937, a union that ended in divorce in 1940. After military service in World War II, he we entertainer Cyd Charisse in 1948.

THE TONY MARTIN SHOW(S)

Tony Martin, singer of popular songs, was heard on several radio shows, including his own. On January 1, 1941 The Tony Martin Show premiered over the NBC Red networked sponsored by Woodbury Soap. The quarter hour of music and song was broadcast weekly with the orchestra of David Rose providing the accompaniment. This series gave way to The Thin Man in the summer of 1941 and did not return.

Following a career hiatus for military duty in World War II, a new Tony Martin Show (aka The Texaco Star Theatre) hit the radio airwaves in 1947. The initial program aired over the CBS network on March 30, 1947, sponsored by Texaco products. Joining Tony were Jeff Alexander's Chorus, Evelyn Knight, Alan Young, weekly guest stars, and Victor Young's orchestra.

The announcer was Jimmy Wallington. The show switched to the ABC network in the fall of 1947.

A sustaining musical series title Tony Martin Time was heard over the NBC network during the 1953 season, with Al Sack's orchestra providing the music.

NINO MARTINI

Tenor Nino Martini was born in Verona, Italy on July 8, 1904. He arrived in the United States in 1929, made his American operatic debut in 1931, and joined The Metropolitan Opera Company in 1933.

In addition to opera, Martini also performed on radio and in motion pictures.

His radio credits included Metropolitan Opera broadcasts, his own twice weekly programs of songs aired over the CBS network during the early 1930s, The Chesterfield Program, Four to Go, Seven Star Revue, and guest appearances on many of the music and variety shows of the 1930s. Martini retired from "The Met" in 1946 and retired from performing in 1948.

Nino Martini died of a heart attack at the age of seventy-two on December 9, 1976.

GILBERT MARTYN

Newscaster Gilbert Martyn, not to be confused with actor H. Gilbert Martin, delivered the news on both radio and television during his tenure on the airwaves from the 1930s to the 1950s.

The best remembered, and longest running of Martyn's news programs, was Kellogg's Home Edition. This Monday through Friday fifteen minute daytime newscast was first broadcast on August 9, 1943 over the ABC network. As the title suggested, it was sponsored by Kellogg's Cereals. The series was on the air until 1947. Martyn then began his association with KTLA in Los Angeles. eventually becoming that station's news director and tele- vision news anchor. Gilbert Martyn died of throat cancer at the age of fifty- three on January 24, 1959.

MARVELOUS MELODIES

See: Powder Box Revue

JOHNNY MARVIN

Country music singer and song writer Johnny Marvin was born in Butler, Oklahoma on July 11, 1897 and first appeared on the vaudeville stage at the age of ten. He later sang and accompanied himself on guitar or ukulele on stage, records. radio, and in nightclubs.

During the late 1920s and early 1930s he was the star of his own radio show broadcast over the NBC network from New York. Marvin then migrated west to California where he composed music for Gene Autry films and wrote a number of songs such as Goodbye Little Darlin'.

Johnny Marvin died of a heart attack on December 20, 1944. He was forty-seven years old.

TONY MARVIN

Radio announcer and newscaster Tony Marvin was born in New York City on October 5, 1912. He attended St. John's University and then set out to pursue a radio career. Initially he tried acting and singing but later decided that wag not his calling. He became chief of special events at New York's station WNYC, and by 1939 advanced to the network level with CBS, reporting on the New York World's Fair. Marvin later became a fixture on Arthur Godfrey's various radio and television shows. He was also the announcer for Casey, Crime Potographer; Cinderella, Inc.; Fun With Dunn; Radie Harris; Bill Henry Newscasts; Hobby Lobby; Men of Vision; Now and Forever; The Original Amateur Hour; Rosemary; The Sparrow and the Hawk; Stage Door Canteen; This Life is Mine; Vox Pop; Wilderness Road; and Winner Take All. In addition, he broadcast the news over the CBS and Mutual networks and occasionally returned to acting in minor roles on such series as Columbia Presents Corwin. Tony Marvin died on October 10, 1998 at the age of eighty-six.

THE MARX BROTHERS

The Marx Brothers comedy team, led by Groucho, began their climb to stardom as early as 1907. Their major mediums were the vaudeville stage and motion pictures, but Groucho occasionally accompanied by one or more brothers, was heard on radio. Much later Groucho became a hosehold name as the zany host of the quiz/interview show You Bet Your Life.

Groucho (Julius Henry) Marx was born on October 2, 1890 and died from a respiratory ailment on August 19, 1977 at the age of eighty-six. Chico (Leonard) Marx was born on March 22, 1887 and died on October 11, 1961 at the age of seventy-four. Harpo (Arthur) Marx was born on November 23, 1888 and died on September 28, 1964 at the age of seventy five. Zeppo (Herbert) Marx was born on February 25, 1901 and died on November 30, 1979 at the age of seventy-eight. Gummo (Milton) Marx, who died in 1977, left the act following World War I and was not included in any radio appearances. Zeppo quit the group in 1933, and those who were left went their separate ways in 1949.

On radio Groucho and Chico starred on a comedy series titled Flywheel. Shyster, and Flywheel. On his own Groucho presided over Blue Ribbon Town and served as quizmaster on You Bet Your Life. Groucho was also heard frequently as a guest on many other shows.

On television Groucho Marx continued his antics as the host of the video version of You Bet Your Life and was also seen on Dupont's Show of the Week, The Bob Hope Show, Show Biz, Tell it to Groucho, Time for Elizabeth, and others.

GROUCHO MARX (AND COMPANY) (SHOW)
See: Blue Ribbon Town
Flywheel, Shyster, and Flywheel

LLOYD MARX

Composer and Conductor Lloyd Marx both led the orchestra and directed Major Bowes' radio shows on The Capitol Family Hour and The Original Amateur Hour. On the latter series his tenure extended from 1935 through the video version hosted by Ted Mack. Marx also served as a staff conductor for the CBS network.

Lloyd Marx died on May 26, 1988 of complications from a heart attack suffered in November of 1987. His age at the time of death was reported to be seventy-two; however, in that case he would have been only nineteen years old as a network conductor in 1935!

MARY AND BOB'S TRUE STORY HOUR
See: True Story Hour

ALICE G. MASLIN
See: Nancy Craig

JAMES MASON

Actor James Mason was born in Hudderfield, England on May 15, 1909. He studied architecture at Marlborough College and Cambridge University before abandoning the design of buildings for an acting career. He made his stage debut in 1931 and his first film in 1935. In 1939 he married actress and writer Pamela Kellino, a union that endured until divorce ended it in 1961.

Although most notable for his dramatic roles on the motion picture screen, he was not unfamiliar to radio and television audiences.

On radio he was a frequent guest star on such programs as The Fred Allen Show, The Lux Radio Theatre, and Suspense. Also, during the summer of 1949 he and wife Pamela were the stars of their own show. They were divorced in 1964. On television Mason hosted The Lux Video Theatre and, as on radio, performed in guest star roles. Included among these appearances was A.D. (televised after his death), The Alcoa Theatre, Playhouse 90, and The Schlitz Playhouse of Stars. In 1982 he authored his autobiography titled Before I Forget. James Mason died of a heart attack on July 27, 1984 at his retirement retreat in Switzerland. He was seventy-five years old.

His former wife Pamela died on June 29, 1996 at the age of eighty.

THE JAMES AND PAMELA MASON SHOW

Film star James Mason and his actress/writer wife Pamela (Kellino) played the lead roles on a 1949 summer program of dramas sustained over the NBC network.

The initial show aired on July 14, 1949 as a replacement for The Sealtest Variety Theatre. The announcer was Frank Barton. James and Pamela concluded their warm weather series in September.

LOUIS MASON

Character actor Louis Mason was born in Danville, Kentucky on June 1, 1888. He specialized in rural roles in many motion pictures during the 1930s and 40s, but also saw limited exposure on the airwaves.

On radio he played Clem on the serial drama Moonshine and Honeysuckle and co-starred with Arthur Allen on The Schrader-town Band comedy series.

Louis Mason died on November 12, 1959 at the age of seventy-one.

MARY MASON (Betty Ann Jenks Wharton)

Actress Mary Mason (not to be confused with the women's program hostess), was born in 1911 in Pasadena, California. She made her acting debut at age seven and would subsequently perform on stage, screen, radio, and television.

Plagued with eye problems throughout her life, Mary quit the bright lights of motion pictures in 1934 to concentrate on stage and radio. She migrated east to New York where she appeared on several network radio series and in Broadway stage productions.

Her airwave accomplishments included the title role of Maudie Mason on Maudie's Diary. She was also one of several to play Mary Aldrich on The Aldrich Family, she was heard as Nancy Chandler on The Life and Love of Dr. Susan, Penny Bartlett on My Best Girls, Jinny Roberts on The Strange Romance of Evelyn Winters, and appeared in supporting roles on Grand Central Station and The Lux Radio Theatre.

In 1936 she married theatrical manager Carl Fisher which ended in divorce. In 1949 she wed theatrical attorney John F. Wharton and was widowed in 1977.

Mary Mason died of cancer on October 13, 1980 at the age of sixty-nine.

MARY MASON (Vella Reeve)

Mary Mason (not to be confused with the actress of the same name) was associated with several women's programs on radio. On network radio she hosted Women's Review and Women's Magazine of the Air and assisted on Ida Bailey Allen's Home-maker's Club. She also presided over local programs aired in Boston over stations WBZ and WNAC and in Washington on WRC.

PAMELA MASON

See: James Mason

PERRY MASON

Perry Mason, the legendary infallible defense attorney, created by lawyer/author Erle Stanley Gardner, was first heard on the radio airwaves in 1943.

Unlike its later television counterpart, the radio version of Perry Mason was a fifteen minute daytime serial drama aired on Monday through Friday. The initial episode was broadcast on October 18, 1943 over the CBS network, sponsored by such Procter and Gamble products as Crisco and Camay. The title role was played by Don Briggs, John Larkin, Santos Ortega, and Bartlett Robinson. His secretary and assistant Della Street was played by Joan Alexander, Jan Miner, and Gertrude Warner; private investigator Paul Drake by

Matt Crowley and Charles Webster; and police Lieutenant Arthur Tragg by Frank Dane and Mandel Kramer. Others in the cast included Susan Douglas, Jean Ellyn, Maurice Franklin, Betty Garde, Ruth Gilbert, Mitzi Gould, Mary Jane Higby, Ge Ge James, Lamont. Johnson, Jack Smart, and Arthur Vinton. Organist William Meeder provided the mood music. Later in the series Paul Traubman served as musical director. Bob Dixon, Don Hancock, Alan Kent, and Richard Stark announced.

The verdict in the final transcribed case of radio's Perry Mason was handed down on December 30, 1955 and the series was gaveled off the air.

The popular televison series was broadcast from 1957 to 1966 and again during the 1973-74 season. Thereafter there were syndicated reruns and made-for-television movies. Although many of the principal characters remained on the video versions, the cast was completely different.

SYDNEY MASON

The well traveled announcer and actor Sydney Mason occupied the radio airwaves during the 1930s and 40s before turning his talents to motion pictures and television. He was associated with radio stations KECA, KFAC, KFI and KFVD in Los Angeles; WEAF, WJZ, WMCA, and WOR in New York; WXYZ in Detroit; WLW in Cincinnati; and WIBC in Indianapolis. Mason's credits on the network included Famous Jury Trials, The Gibson Family, Home Sweet Home, Johnny Presents, Masquerade, The O'Neills, Roses and Drums, and True Detective Mysteries.

On television he played Sheriff Downey on My Friend Flicka and hosted stump the Authors. Sydney Mason died on April 11, 1976 at the age of seventy- one.

MASQUERADE

Masquerade was a daytime serial drama broadcast over the NBC network during the 1946-47 season, but for the record, there was a one time only program aired under the same title in late summer of 1935. The latter was an hour long special sustained over the CBS network that featured an array of novelty impressions. For example: Agnes Moorehead appeared as Bea Lillie, Dwight Weist as Fred Allen, Paul Douglas as W.C. Fields, and Alice Frost as Gracie Allen. The orchestra of Mark Warnow played well known arrangements of other bands. Ted Husing, as himself, served as emcee.

The Masquerade serial drama made its debut over the NBC net- work on January 14, 1946. The Monday through Friday fifteen minute episodes were sponsored by General Mills products. Initially it was broadcast from Chicago, but moved its point of origination to the west coast by the summer of 1946. The vaguely defined story line of post war life in Fairfield, Iowa was one of a quartet of serials created by Ira Phillips whose plots were loosely intertwined. The title was derived from the description of people who "hid behind the mask of their true emotions and identity."

The cast (both east and west) included: Marguerite Anderson, Grif Barnett, Conrad Binyon, Francis X. Bushman, Jack Edwards, Sondra Gair. Nancy Gates, Carlton KaDell, Geraldine Kay, Ned LeFevre, Sydney Mason, Ted Maxwell, Jack Petruzzi, Herbert Rawlinson, Janet Scott, Art Seltzer, Ruth Shames, Jack Swingford, and Beryl Vaughn. The organist was Dick Aurandt and Vincent Pelletier announced. Masquerade left the air on August 29, 1947.

CURT MASSEY (Curtis D. Massey)

Singer and musician Curt Massey was born in Midland, Texas on May 3, 1910. After attending Homer Conservatory of Music, he fronted a band in Kansas City until 1930. He then joined his sister Louise as a soloist with her group known as Louise Massey and the Westerners, making his radio debut over KMBC in Kansas City.

By the mid 1940s Massey decided to shed his image as a country singer and thereafter became better known as a baratine crooner of popular music.

On radio he sang with The Westerners and on his own shows. He also performed on such other radio series as The Andrews Sisters N-K Musical Showroomw, Avalon Time, Plantation Jubilee, (Maxwell House) Show Boat , and Sunday on N-K Ranch. On record he teamed with The Westerners, Martha Tilton, and others on a host of both well-known and obscure labels. Massey hosted his own show on television and served as the music director for The Beverly Hillbilies, Green Acres, and Petticoat Junction. He composed and sang the theme song for the latter series.

Curt Massey died on October 20, 1991 at the age of eighty- one.

THE CURT MASSEY (AND COMPANY) (AND MARTHA TILTON SHOW)

Singer, and occasional musician, Curt Massey was the star of his own radio show titled Curt Massey and Company during the 1943-44 season. The weekly quarter hour of songs was aired over both the NBC and CBS networks. The Schutter Candy Company's Old Nick and Bit-O-Honey candy bars sponsored the program.

In 1949 Curt Massey was joined by vocalist "Liltin' " Martha Tilton on a Monday through Friday fifteen minute show heard over the CBS network. The series (aka Alka-Seltzer Time) was sponsored by Miles Laboratories. In 1951 the show was cloned as a second daily songfest broadcast over the Mutual network for the same sponsor.

Others participating in these series were The Cheerleaders, The Dinning Sisters, and Marian Morgan; the orchestras of Jack Fascinato and Country Washburn; and announcers Charles Lyon, Jack Narz, and Fort Pearson. Maasey and Tilton left the air in 1954.

ILONA MASSEY (Ilona Hajmassy)

Actress and singer Ilona Massey was born in Budapest, Hungary on June

16, 1912. After coming to America, Ilona Maasey made her Hollywood film debut in 1937. She would also add to her credits the mediums of stage, radio, and television. As a singer she co-starred with Nelson Eddy on the motion picture screen, but audiences seemed to prefer Jeanette MacDonald as his duet partner. She also appeared on the Broadway stage with Milton Berle during the 1943 - 44 Ziegfeld Follies.

As a radio actress, her Hungarian accent led to portrayals of mysterious characters. To that end she was cast in the role of Baroness Karen Gaza on Top Secret. She was also heard in similar roles as a guest on other series. On television Ilona Massey hosted her own music show and played dramatic roles on Holiday Hotel, Rendezvous, Studio One, and many others.

Following her retirement from show business, she became active in charitable and political causes. Ilona Massey died on August 20, 1974. She was sixty-two years old.

LOUISE MASSEY AND THE WESTERNERS

Louise Massey and the Westerners was a group of country singers and musicians. They performed on tour, on records, and on radio from 1930 through the 1940s. Louise Massey was joined by her husband Milt Mabie; Larry Wellington; and her brothers Curt, Dott, and Allen.

On radio they were heard on local stations in Kansas City and Chicago. Their exposure on the network airwaves included: The Log Cabin Dude Ranch, The National Barn Dance. Plantation Party, and Reveille Roundup.

They also had a series of fifteen minute transcribed shows packaged for syndication by Morton Radio Productions and Neblett Radio Productions of Chicago.

RAYMOND MASSEY

Actor Raymond Massey was born on August 30, 1896 in Toronto, Canada, He received his higher education at Oxford University in England, served in the Canadian Army in both World Wars I and II, made his acting debut on the London theatre stage in 1922, and first performed on the New York stage in 1931. In 1944 Massey became an American citizen.

For much of his career on stage, screen, radio, and tele- vision Raymond Massey's name was linked with his critically acclaimed portrayals of Abraham Lincoln.

On radio his credits included Cavalcade of America, Norman Corwin Plays, The Doctor Fights, The Eternal Light, Every- man's Theatre, Inner Sanctum Mysteries, The Lux Radio Theatre, The Philip Morris Playhouse, Arch Oboler's Plays (Plays for Americans), Pursuit of Happiness, and The Kate Smith Hour. He served as the emcee on Harvest of Stars. On television he is well remembered as Dr. Gillespie on the video version of Dr. Kildare. He was also seen on The Clock, I Spy, The Kraft Television Theatre, and Lights Out. He penned two autobiographies: When I Was Young, published in 1976, and A Hundred Lives, published in 1979.

Raymond Massey was in failing health for several years prior to his death from pneumonia on July 29, 1983. He was eighty six-years old.

MASTER OF MYSTERY
See: Majestic's Master of Mystery

MASTER RADIO CANARIES
Master Radio Canaries (aka The Canary Pet Shop) was broadcast over the Mutual network during the 1944-45 season sponsored by Hartz Mountain Pet Food.

For some reason this era spurned not one, but two radio series starring the singing of canaries! (also see American Radio Warblers).

The fifteen minute show featured such feathery soloists as Sonny Boy and Frankie, accompanied by organ and violin. Jess Kirkpatrick hosted the chirp fest and also sang along.

FRANKIE MASTERS
Bandleader Frankie Masters was born on April 12, 1904 in St. Marys, West Virginia. He quit Indiana University to play with a theatre band in Chicago. In the late 1920s he formed his own dance band using a cascading choral gimmick he called "Bell Tone Music."

Masters played the ballrooms and hotels; he recorded on the Columbia, Mercury, Okeh, RCA Victor, and Vocalion labels; and he performed on radio and television. On radio the Masters' band was heard on the late night dance band remote broadcasts. He also supplied the music for such shows as The Fitch Band Wagon, It Can Be Done, Master's Music Room, One Night Stand, and Show of the Week. On television he was seen locally in the Chicago area.

After a brief retirement, Frankie Masters returned to the bandstand to occasionally wave his baton for private parties and convent ions.

JACK MASTERS
See: Treasure Adventures of Jack Masters

MONTY MASTERS (Montgomery Mohn)
Actor and producer Monty Masters was born on January 28, 1912 in New Haven, Connecticut.

Monty first appeared on radio in 1930, subsequently using both the name Mohn and Masters (the latter his mother's maiden name).

Based in San Francisco, Masters played the role of Mel Sherwood on the serial drama Hawthorne House. Also in the cast was Natalie Park, whom he later married. He appeared in several obscure series originating from the studios of KGO in San Francisco. They included Santa Claus Time, Sonia's Party, The Sperry Sunday Special, and Winning the West. He also co-starred with his wife on the situation comedy The Mad Masters, a show Masters wrote and produced. Other more familiar shows on which he was a cast member were Death Valley Days, Dr. Kate, I Want a Divorce, and Professor Puzzlewit.

Later Masters created the detective series Candy Matson, which starred his wife in the title role.

THE MASTER'S MUSIC ROOM

Three obscure radio series aired under the title The Master's Music Room.

The first was a program of classical music performed by violinist Jan Rubini and pianist Salvatore Santelli during the 1935-36 season.

Next were broadcasts of dance band music led by Frankie Masters.

Finally, Spot Sales of Hollywood syndicated a transcribed series of semi-classical music during the mid-1940s.

NATALIE MASTERS (Natalie Park)

A native of California, Natalie Park Masters appeared in commercials and as an actress on radio during the 1930s and 40s.

She was playing the role of Lois Liston on the serial drama Hawthorne House when she met fellow cast member Monty Masters (Montgomery Mohn). Several years later they were married.

Natalie was also heard in the title role on Candy Matson, a radio series created by her husband, and co-starred with Monty in the situation comedy The Mad Masters. On television she was seen on Alice, A Date With the Angels, Dragnet, and Noah's Ark.

Natalie Masters died on February 9, 1986.

JACK MATHER (John E. Mather)

Actor and dialectician Jack Mather played character roles in several motion pictures, was heard on radio, and seen on tele- vision.

On radio he is best remembered for his portrayal of the Cisco Kid. He was also in the cast of such shows as The Jack Benny Show; The Chase and Sanborn Hour; Speed Gibson; The Grouch Club; Al Jolson's Lifebuoy Show; Meet Me at Parky's; Jack Oakie's College; Paducah Plantation; Red Ryder; Jonathan Trimble, Esquire; and Tuesday Night Party.

On television Mather was seen in supporting roles on Bonanza, Death Valley Days, Dragnet, and M Squad.

Jack Mather succumbed to a heart attack on August 16, 1966 at the age of fifty-eight.

MATHEWS

See: Matthews

MATINEE AT MEADOWBROOK

A Saturday afternoon dancing party was broadcast on the radio series known as Matinee at Meadowbrook. Frank Dailey's Meadow- brook was a dance hall located on The Pompton Turnpike in Cedar Grove, New Jersey. The hour long program of music and chatter first took to the air on January 18, 1941 over the CBS network.

Initially Wheeler Jackson served as emcee and, for the first program only, Bobby Byrne's band provided the music. Thereafter various bands and talent shared the spotlight. This series of Matinee broadcasts was on the air for only one year and then was absent during World War II.

It returned in May of 1946 with John Tillman as emcee. Later Ross Mulholland and even Frank Dailey himself presided over the festivities. The bands of Tommy Dorsey, Glen Gray, Stan Kenton, and Ray McKinley all took their turn on the band-stand. Also such other vocalists and performers as Chris Adams, Art Carney, Richmond Gale, Bernie Gould. Helen Lewis, Monica Lewis, Kay Little, Teddy Norman, Jerry Wayne, and Orson Welles shared their talents with the listening and dancing audience.

Matinee at Meadowbrook faded from the air as the 1940s drew to a close.

MATINEE THEATRE
See: Dangerously Yours

MATINEE WITH BOB AND RAY
See: Bob and Ray

CANDY MATSON

Candy Matson was a pioneeing female in the parade of private detective dramas on radio. Operating from her San Francisco apartment on Telegraph Hill, she took calls for her services over the telephone number Yukon 2-8209.

The sustaining series originated from the studios of KNBC in San Francisco. It was first heard over west coast stations of the NBC network on June 29, 1949.

Natalie Masters was cast in the title role, while her husband Monty wrote and produced the sagas of murder and mayhem. Candy's assistant was Rembrandt Watson played by Jack Thomas and her love interest was San Francisco homicide inspector Ray Mallard played by Henry Leff. Eloise Rowan rendered the theme song Candy on the organ and also provided the ominous mood music. The announcer was Dudley Manlove.

Candy Matson's last case aired on May 21, 1951.

RUTH MATTESON (Ruth Anne Matterson)

Actress Ruth Matteson was born in San Jose, California on December 8, 1909. After attending Columbia University, she began her acting career. In 1929 Ruth Matteson first appeared professionally on the stage and in 1934 made her Broadway debut. Later she also performed on radio and television.

On radio she played the role of Nicole Scott on Against the Storm. Further airwave credits included Lighted Windows, The Lux Radio Theatre, and This Life is Mine. On television she was seen on Fair Meadows, U.S.A.; The Kate Smith Show; and in dramatic roles on several CBS network product ions.

Ruth Matteson died on February 5, 1975 at the age of sixty-five.

GRACE MATTHEWS

Actress Grace Matthews was born in Toronto, Canada. She made her acting debut there with The Hart House Theatre. She would Subsequently perform on stage, radio, and television in Canada, England, and the United States. In 1939 she made her radio debut in Canada and in 1946 began amassing a long list of airwave credits on shows originating from New York. She played the lead role of Ruth Evans on the daytime serial drama Big Sister, was cast as Liz Dennis on The Brighter Day, portrayed Julie Erickson on Hilltop House, and was one of several heard as Margo Lane on The Shadow. Still more radio shows on which she appeared included: Aunt Jenny, The Big Story, Call the Police, Cavalcade of America, The Columbia Workshop, Counterspy, Stella Dallas, Front Page Farrell, Gangbusters, The Greatest Story Ever Told, The Guiding Light, Just Plain Bill, Perry Mason, Mr. District Attorney, My True Story, Portia Faces Life, Ellery Queen, The Right to Happiness, Road of Life, The Second Mrs. Burton, Tennessee Jed, Theatre of Romance, Valiant Lady, Wendy Warren and the News, When a Girl Marries, Whispering Streets, You Are There, and Young Dr. Malone.

On television she was seen on the video versions of The Brighter Day, The Greatest Story Ever Told, and The Guiding Light. She was also seen on As the World Turns, City Hosp- ital, Lamp Unto My Feet, and Look Up and Live. Grace Matthews and actor Court Benson were married in 1940; she was widowed in 1995.

JUNIUS MATTHEWS

Radio actor Junius Matthews kept his personal life private, however, he was heard in a wide range of diverse roles on radio from the 1930s through the 1950s.

He played Ling Wee on Gasoline Alley, Grandpa on David Harum, Wille on Buck Rogers, and shared the role of Red Lantern with Art Carney on The Land of the Lost. Matthews was also in the cast of Frontier Gentleman, Sherlock Holmes, Hawk Larabee, Leonidas Witherall, and a serialized radio adaptation of The Wizard of Oz.

BILLY AND BOBBY MAUCH

Youthful performers Billy and Bobby Mauch were identical twins born on July 6, 1924 in Peoria, Illinois. The brotherly duo was heard on the radio airwaves and seen in several motion pictures during the 1930s and 40s. On the latter medium Billy continued alone appearing into his young adult years.

On radio the Mauch twins' credits included The Children's Hour, Coast-to-Coast On a Bus, The Gibson Family, The Lady Next Door, Let's Pretend, and Robinson, Crusoe Jr. In later years both continued in the entertainment business in behind the scenes positions. Billy as a sound editor for Warner Brothers Studios, and Bobby as a television production editor.

MAUDE AND COUSIN BILL

The juvenile adventures of Maude and Cousin Bill were written for radio by the well known author Booth Tarkington. The scripts were penned under the watchful eye of The Atlantic and Pacific Tea Company (A&P), the series' sponsor. The fifteen minute transcribed episodes were broadcast over the NBC Blue network during the 1932-33 season. The stories were about the everyday lives of typical American kids named Maude Ricketts, Bill Ricketts, and their friend Henry Hooker.

Members of the cast were not credited on the program, but it is speculated they may have been the same cast heard on Penrod, another of Tarkington's radio scripts. It is also possible the characters in Maude and Counsin Bill used their real names.

MAUDIE'S DIARY

The comedy series Maudie's Diary made its debut over the CBS network on August 14, 1941, sponsored by Continental Baking Company's Wonder Bread. The weekly half hour show revolved around entries in the diary of teenager Maudie Mason, a student at Sullivan High School.

The title role was First played by Mary Mason and later by Charita Bauer. Maudie's boyfriend Davie Dillion was played by Bob Walker (subsequently better known as Robert Walker), her parents by William Johnstone and Betty Garde, sister Sylvia by Marjorie Davis, and friend Pauly by Caryl Smith. Music was under the direction of Elliot Jacoby and Art Millet was the announcer.

The last entry in Maudie's Diary aired on September 24, 1942.

THE SOMERSET MAUGHAM THEATRE

Prolific writer W. Somerset Maugham hosted his own radio and television programs during the early 1950s. The thirty minute radio dramas were first broadcast over the CBS network in January of 1951 on Saturday mornings. Bymart-Tintair was the sponsor of the radio version of The Somerset Maugham Theatre, which concluded in 1952.

The television version was initially titled Teller of Tales. but was shortly changed to The Somerset Maugham Fireside Theatre. The video series was on the air from October of 1950 to December of 1951.

Novelist Somerset Maugham died of a stroke at the age of ninety-one on December 16, 1965.

REX MAUPIN

Musician and orchestra leader Rex Maupin was born in St. Joseph, Missouri on November 25, 1886. He studied at Kansas State University and furthered his musical education at The American Musical College and Chicago Musical College. Maupin taught in the music department of Kansas State and played with nearly a dozen orchestras, including Chicago's station KYW orchestra led by Jules Herbuveaux.

As a conductor, Rex Maupin led the orchestra for a long list of radio shows that included: The Big Hand, Black Night, The Breakfast Club, Club Matinee, Johnny Desmond's College Show, Hour of Music, I Fly Anything, Jamboree, Kaltenmeyer's Kindergarten, Listen to This, Musical Memos, The National Farm and Home Hour, The NBC Minstrel Show, Public Hero Number One, The Ransom Sherman Show, Shopper's Special, Smile Parade, The Danny Thomas Show, Those Sensational Years, and Wake Up and Smile.

He also aired a musical show under his own name over the NBC Blue network during the 1941-42 season and a weekly half hour of music called Solo and Soliloquy heard over the ABC network during the 1952-53 season.

On television Maupin directed the orchestra for The Little Revue, Music in Velvet, The Benny Rubin Show, and Tin Pan Alley.

Rex Maupin died on July 28, 1966 at the age of seventy-nine.

EDWIN MAX

Born in 1909, character actor Edwin Max appeared in several motion pictures and in support ing roles on at least a dozen radio series. Research reveals little else about the life and career of MAX.

His airwave credits included: Big Town, Calling All Cars. Cinnamon Bear, Hollywood Hotel, Hollywood Showcase, The Lux Radio Theatre, The Ken Murray Show, Jack Oakie's College, Joe Penner, Strange as it Seems, Voyage of the Scarlet Queen, and Wheatenaville.

BOBBE DEANE MAXWELL

See : Ted Maxwell

ELSA MAXWELL

Internationally known party hostess Elsa Maxwell was born in Keokuk, Iowa on May 24, 1883. She quit school at the age of fourteen to become a piano accompanist and a vaudeville performer. Later she penned blunt and revealing articles about society's inner circle. However, it remains a mystery just how she became the dowager queen of high society. She was also seen on the motion picture screen in several films, presided over Elsa Maxwell's Party Line on radio, and was heard and seen as a guest on both radio and television shows.

Her Party Line broadcasts premiered over the NBC Blue network on January 2, 1942 sponsored by The Ralston Purina Company's Ry-Krisp. The sponsor's diet cracker was used as a "tie-in" with Miss Maxwell's ongoing battle against being overweight. The weekly fifteen minute show was a vehicle for Elsa to divulge her vast reservoir of society and celebrity gossip. The announcer was Graham McNamee. This short-lived series left the air in 1943, but in 1945 she returned with more of the same aired over the Mutual network. Norman Brokenshire announced this series which also left the air after a short run.

Elsa Maxwell died on November 1, 1963 at the age of eighty.

MAXWELL HOUSE COFFEE SHOW(S)

Several radio series were broadcast under the sponsorship of Maxwell House Coffee. Among them were Burns and Allen, Good News, The Frank Morgan Show, The Charlie Ruggles Show, Show Boat, (which are described under those headings), and others bearing the sponsor's name.

The Maxwell House Hour took to the newly formed NBC Blue network in 1926 with a weekly sixty minute program of concert music. Later tenor Richard Crooks added vocalizing to the orchestra's accompaniment.

In 1929 the program was retitled Maxwell House Melodies and underwent a change to a musical variety format. The half hour featured an orchestra under the direction of Harold Sanford, various singers and vocal groups, and announcer/emcee Edmund (Tiny) Ruffner. The format returned to a classical concert for the 1930-31 season under the title Maxwell House Coffee Revue. Kenn Sisson directed the orchestra.

Maxwell House Coffee Time (aka The Fanny Brice-Frank Morgan Show) made its debut on September 5, 1940 over the NBC Red network. The lavish half hour of comedy and variety followed a similar format of the earlier series titled Good News. Gary Breckner, John Conte, Dick Powell, and Robert Young all took their turn as emcee; Frank Morgan performed his comedy routines; and Fanny Brice was heard in her precocious Baby Snooks skits. Others on the show were Alan Reed and Hanley Stafford as Snooks' daddy, Cass Daley as Frank Morgan's niece, vocalists Mary Martin and Carlos Ramirez, and the orchestras of Albert Sack, Frank Tours, and Meredith Willson. The announcers were Harlow Wilcox and Don Wilson. During the 1944-45 season Maxwell House Coffee Time's principal acts went their separate ways, leaving the show without its stars. This dealt the show a lethal blow and it left the airways.

Maxwell House Coffee Time returned as a summer series in 1946 with Ben Gage as the singing emcee. Joining him were The King Sisters vocal group and Meredith Willson's orchestra. The defunct Maxwell House Coffee Time format again returned to the air in 1947 as a replacement for the vacationing Burns and Allen show. The Maxwell House Summer Show first aired on June 5, 1947 starring popular singer Frances Langford. Carmen Dragon's orchestra provided the music, a male chorus augmented Miss Langford's vocalizing, and Tobe Reed announced.

MAXWELL HOUSE ICED COFFEE TIME

See: The Charlie Ruggles Show

MAXWELL HOUSE SHOW BOAT
See: Show Boat

MAXWELL HOUSE SUMMER HOUR
See: The Frances Langford Show

MARILYN MAXWELL (Marvel Marilyn Maxwell)
Singer and actress Marilyn Maxwell was born in Clarinda, Iowa on August 3, 1921. As a child she traveled with her mother, a piano accompanist, and first performed as a dancer at the age of three. During her teenage years Marilyn sang with several bands, such as Buddy Rogers and Ted Weems. In 1942 she made her motion picture debut, eventually graduating from bit parts to star in blonde bombshell roles.

On radio Marilyn Maxwell was a regular vocalist on The Abbott and Costello Show and Beat the Band. She was also frequently a guest on radio and televison with Milton Berle, Bing Crosby, Jimmy Durante, Bob Hope, Frank Sinatra, and Red Skelton.

The cast of several dramatic series featured her on tele- vision, most notably as Grace Sherwood on Bus Stop. She also appeared in a few stage productions, toured the nightclub circuit, and later in her career was the star of a burlesque show.

Her three marriages, the first to actor John Conte, all ended in divorce.

Marilyn Maxwell died from complications of high blood pressure on March 20, 1972. She was fifty years old.

RICHARD MAXWELL
Singer and radio host Richard Maxwell was born in Mansfield, Ohio on September 12, 1897. He made his singing debut in his church choir at the age of two! He later used his singing talent to earn his way through Kenyon College and aviation school. Maxwell served in the Air Corp during World War I before embarking on a career in the entertainment field. He subsequently appeared on the musical stage, was heard on radio, and organized "Good Neighbor Clubs." These clubs offered assistance to the needy in eighteen states and in Canada.

On radio Richard Maxwell is best remembered as the host of A Friend in Deed, a program that saluted and dramatized stories of individual acts of kindness. He was also heard on Cheer and Comfort, a fifteen minute show of song and talk aired over the CBS network from 1936 to 1939 sponsored by Baume Bengue (Ben-Gay). Dale Kennedy and John Harper were the announcers. During the 1937-38 season he presided over The Garden of Memories, a series broadcast over the Mutual net- work sponsored by The Serutan Company. In addition, he was one of the song leaders on Community Sing. he was in the cast of Seth Parker, and vocalized on National Youth Conference. In later years he worked with the Fred Waring organization as the director of the sacred music division of Shawnee Press. Richard Maxwell died after a long illness at the age of fifty- seven on September 4, 1954.

TED MAXWELL (Edward H. Maxwell)

Actor and writer Ted Maxwell was born in Oakland. California on January 9, 1899. He received his education at The Univer- sity of California and authored several stage plays before making his radio debut as a cast member in one of his own plays. He joined the NBC network in 1928 as an actor and writer.

On the airwaves he was heard as Captain Russ on Flying Time, Leo Warner on Girl Alone, Chic Morgan on Hawthorne House, Fred Nino on Masquerade, and the skipper on Out of the Deep. He also appeared on such other radio series as Death Valley Days, First Nighter, Grand Hotel, Lights Out, and Welcome Valley. He served as the emcee on My Secret Ambition and penned scripts for Hawthorne House, Lights Out, Out of the Deep, and Holly Sloan.

His wife, actress Bobbe Deane Maxwell, joined him in the cast of Hawthorne House playing the character Marietta Sherwood. She was also heard in the role of the child Davy Marlin on the Mary Marlin daytime serial and appeared with Ted on numerous obscure West Coast radio series.

Ted Maxwell was left a widower when Bobbe died at the age of fifty-nine on July 15, 1959.

BILLY MAY

Multi-talented musician Billy May was born in Pittsburgh, Pennsylvania on November 10, 1916. May played piano, trumpet, and trombone; he also arranged, conducted, and composed. He was associated with such bands as Charlie Barnet, Les Brown, Woody Herman, Glenn Miller, and Alvino Rey. Early in the 1950s May fronted his own band; however, in 1954 Ray Anthony took over the band and selected Sam Donahue as its leader.

May conducted studio orchestras for such radio shows as Bing Crosby, Forever Ernest , Stan Freberg, Ozzie and Harriet, Red Skelton, and You Bet Your Life.

May's work in the television medium was mostly confined to composing and arranging, but he did lead the orchestra for Milton Berle and Let's Dance.

MAYBELLINE MUSICAL ROMANCE

See: Musical Romance

EDDIE MAYEHOFF

Bandleader and comedian Eddie Mayehoff was born in Baltimore, Maryland on July 7, 1911. He graduated from Yale University's School of Music in 1932, but spent two years as a magazine salesman before beginning a six year stint fronting his own dance band.

By the end of the 1930s Mayehoff exchanged his baton for a typewriter. He became a writing associate of Norman Corwin, a career change that eventually led him to perform as a comedian.

On radio he presided over the Eddie Mayehoff on the Town variety show which aired over the Mutual network during the 1940-41 season. Tommy Dorsey's band provided the music. Mayehoff was also heard as a regular on The Edgar Bergen Show and replaced Hildergarde as emcee of Beat the Band during its last three months on the air in 1944.

Eddie Mayehoff's credits in other media included several mot ion picture appearances, stage performances, nightclub tours, and television. On the latter he was cast in the title role on Doc Corkle, emceed Hour Glass, and played "Jarring" Jack Jackson on That's My Boy.

At the close of the 1950s Mayehoff all but abandoned show business in favor of sales and advertising, performing only occasionally.

JOHN MAYO

Announcer John Mayo was born in Providence, Rhode Island on July 31, 1899. He was educated at Culver Military Academy and Brown University. He saw action with the Army during the pursuit of Mexican bandit Pancho Villa and and later in World War I.

Mayo was in both the cosmetic and oil businesses before an audition in 1930 led to a staff announcing position with the CBS network.

In 1934 he shifted his announcing duties to the NBC network. but by 1940 there is no indication that John Mayo was still pursuing a career in radio announcing.

MAYOR OF THE TOWN

The essence of small town life in the 1940s was captured on the Mayor of the Town series. The mythical town in question being Springdale, located seventy-five miles from Capitol City and twenty miles from Crescent City, whose bustling factories turned out the materials to fight World War II. The low Key weekly half hour of homey drama premiered over the NBC Red network on September 6, 1942, sponsored by Lever Brothers' Rinso. However, after only one month on the air the

Mayor moved his constituents to the CBS network. Late in 1943 the show left the air, but returned on March 11, 1944 with Noxzema Skin Cream as its new sponsor. On October 8, 1947 the Mayor was on the move again! This lime to the ABC network with Noxzema continuing to underwrite the series. The Mutual Benefit Health and Accident Association of Omaha took over as the sponsor on January 2, 1949 and shifted the program to the Mutual network.

The likable, but irascible Mayor (he was never called by name), was played by veteran actor Lionel Barrymore. Others in the cast included: Agnes Moorehead as Marilly Jones, the housekeeper; Conrad Binyon as the Mayor's ward Butch (his mother had died and his father was serving with the Navy's Construction Battalion [seabees]); Claire Trevor as the Mayor's secretary; Gloria McMillan as Batch's girlfriend Sharlee; and Priscilla Lyon as the

Mayor's granddaughter Holly-Ann. Music was under the direction of Gordon Jenkins, Bernard Katz, and Frank Worth. The announcers were Warren Cook, Carlton KaDell, Frank Martin, Ken Peters, and Harlow Wilcox. The final Mayor of the Town drama aired on July 3, 1949.

THE MAYTAG RADIO HOUR

The Maytag Radio Hour was a weekly thirty minute broadcast of music and song. It aired over the NBC Blue network beginning in the fall of 1930, sponsored by the manufacturers of Maytag Washing Machines.

The Maytag Dance Orchestra was initially conducted by Victor Young, and later by Roy Bargy. Also featured on the program was the vocal trio Tom, Dick, and Harry, the piano duo of Retting and Platt, tenor Pedro Espino, and baritone Lawrence Salerno. The announcer was Ted Pearson. The series left the air in 1932.

MBS

See: The Mutual Broadcasting System

DE WITT McBRIDE

Radio actor DeWitt McBride played supporting roles on several series during the 1930s and 1940s.

He was the narrator of Famous Jury Trials, played Mal Tanner on Lone Journey, Mark Mathews on Ma Perkins, and Arthur Adams on Mary Marlin. Other airwave credits included: First Line; Knickerbocker Playhouse; Tom Mix; Mary Noble, Backstage Wife; Painted Dreams; and Road of Life.

MARY MARGARET McBRIDE

Radio interviewer and hostess Mary Margaret McBride was born in Paris, Missouri on November 16, 1899. She briefly attended The University of Missouri, but left after the first year to pursue a career as a writer and newspaper reporter. In 1934 Mary Margaret made her radio debut with a "grandmotherly" styled talk show. Later the same year she was chosen by New York's station WOR to portray Martha Deane (a WOR "house name") on a women's radio series. She premiered as Martha Deane on May 3, 1934 and continued with that "nom de radio" until 1940. However, in 1937 she cast off total anonymity when she also hosted another homemaking series on which she broadcast under her own name.

The Mary Margaret McBride program became a radio institution among homemakers for the next seventeen years (CBS 1937-1941, NBC 1941-1950, and ABC 1950-1954). She relished recipes for good food; could pitch a sponsor's product as few could; and conducted interesting interviews with the great, near great, and the downright unknown. Her homey and frank style was often likened to Arthur Godfrey and was frequently referred to as his female counterpart. Despite the fact that Miss McBride was never married, she was able to project the image of a mother or close relative to her vast radio following. She was held in such high regard by so many, that her 10th and 15th anniversary broadcasts were held in Yankee Stadium! After retiring from network radio in 1954, she moved to her upstate New York Catskill retreat. However, she could still be heard on local radio airwaves three times weekly over WGHO with Your Hudson Valley Neighbor program.

In addition to radio, she presided over a video version of her interview broadcasts during the late 1940s. She also penned magazine articles for several publications and authored autobiographical reminiscences of her tenure on radio under the titles A Long Way From Missouri and Out of the Air.

Mary Margaret McBride succumbed to cancer on April 7, 1976. She was seventy-six years old.

JOHN K.M. McCAFFERY

The diverse career of John K.M. McCaffery included radio and television broadcasting, advertising, writing, editing, and public relations. McCaffery was born in Moscow, Idaho on November 30, 1913 and raised in Madison, Wisconsin. After completing his education he was employed in the publishing business before launching that portion of his life that embraced broadcasting. On radio he hosted The Author Meets the Critics and What Makes You Tick?. He was also the moderator of the We Take Your Word series.

On television he reported the news in the New York City area and presided over such network shows as The Nation's Future, One Minute Please, Take a Guess, Television Screen Magazine, What's the Story?, and the video versions of The Author Meets the Critics and We Take Your Word.

John K.M. McCaffery died on October 3, 1983 at the age of sixty-nine.

GEORGE McCALL
See: Hollywood Screen Scoops
Man About Hollywood

JIMMY McCALLION

Youthful actor Jimmy McCallion grew to adulthood during the time he was performing before the microphone on numerous radio shows.

He was born in Glascow, Scotland on September 27, 1918 and was already a veteran actor of stage and screen before reaching his teens.

On radio he worked his way from singing and juvenile roles in the 1930s to the portrayal of more mature characters in the 1940s. He was heard as Billy White on Billy and Betty, Caruso on City Desk, Skeezix on Gasoline Alley, Sidney Lawrence on One Man's Family, Little Ulysses on Sandy and Lil, David Weston on Wilderness Road, Jimmy Davis on Young Widder Brown, and Sam Williams on Penrod. McCallion's other airwave credits included: Arabesque, The Children's Hour, Coast-to-Coast on a Bus, Death Valley Days, Dixie's Circus, Eno Crime Clues, The Fat Man, Gangbusters, Jolly JunKeteers, The Lady Next Door, The Light of the World, The Man Behind the Gun, My True Story,

The Parker Family, Joe Palooka, Raising Junior, Ellen Randolph, Theatre Guild on the Air, Uncle Don, and Pepper Young's Family.

On television McCallion was seen on The Best in Mystery, National Velvet, Rear Guard, and made guest appearances on several dramatic series.

Jimmy McCallion died on July 11, 1991. He was seventy-two years old.

MERCEDES McCAMBRIDGE (Carlotta Mercedes Agnes McCambridge)

Actress and singer Mercedes McCambridge was born in Joliet, Illinois on March 17, 1916. While a student at Mundelein College she made her radio debut on June 4, 1936 as a member of the speaking choir. Later the same year she inked a contract with the NBC network. Subsequently she would make her presence well known for many years on stage, screen, radio, and television.

On the radio airwaves she played Rosemary Levy on Abie's Irish Rose; Betty Drake on Betty and Bob; shared the lead role of Ruth Evans with four others on Big Sister (she also portrayed other characters on that series); was Mitzi on A Date With Judy; attorney Martha Ellis Bryant on Defense Attorney; Peg Martinson on Nora Drake; Sarah Ann Spencer on Family Skeleton; Mary Ruthledge on The Guiding Light; Joyce Jordan, Girl Interne on the pre-network episodes; Midge Meredith on Midstream; and Flora Little on A Tale of Today. Other shows in her lenghty list of radio credits included: Affairs of Anthony, Avalon Time, Carrington Playhouse, Bulldog Drummond, Everything for the Boys, First Nighter, The Ford Theatre, Girl Alone, Grand Central Station, Grand Hotel, Arnold Grimm's Daughter, Dan Harding's Wife, Hollywood Playhouse, I Love a Mystery, Inner Sanctum, Inside Story, Bill Lance, Mary Marlin, Fibber McGee and Molly, Murder at Midnight, One Man's Family. Passport for Adams, Plays for Americans, Screen Director's Playhouse, Suspense, There Was a Woman, The Thin Man, Dick Tracy, Uncle Walter's Doghouse, The Rudy Vallee Show, Don Winslow of the Navy, and Your Health.

On television she was seen in the video versions of Defense Attorney, The Guiding Light, and One Man's Family. Other credits in this medium included: The Chevrolet Theatre, The Doctors, Fireside Theatre, Front Row Center, Studio One, Toast of the Town, Two for the Money, Jane Wyman Presents, and The Loretta Young Theatre.

In her autobiography titled The Two Of Us, Miss McCambridge chronicled her life as a survivor. She endured marriage and divorce to William Fifield and Fletcher Markle, serious injuries to herself and son, alcoholism, and a fire that ravaged her home.

BESSIE McCAMMON

Radio actress Bessie McCammon was born in Cincinnati, Ohio in 1884. During her early years she received some training in the theatre, but until the untimely death of her husband in 1932, she committed full time to being a wife and mother. With the sudden need to support herself and two sons, she was hired to teach at The Schuster-Martin School of Drama. This position shortly led to a six year association with station WLW in Cincinnati. Later Bessie McCammon appeared on several network radio series originating from Chicago and New York. She was mostly cast in matronly roles on the daytime serial dramas. She played Alice Sanders on The Life of Mary Sothern; Jessie King on Lone Journey; Mrs, Dubois on Mary Noble, Back-stage Wife; Aunt Agatha Anthony on The Romance of Helen Trent; Mother Fairchild on Stepmother; and Olivia McEvoy on Young Widder Brown. She was also in the cast of Hot Copy: Huckleberry Finn; Joyce Jordan, M.D.; Mary Marlin; My True Story; Road of Life; and Woman in White.

Bessie McCammon died of a heart attack on March 2, 1964. She was eighty years old.

ALFRED AND DORA McCANN

The husband and wife team of Alfred and Dora McCann hosted The McCann Pure Food Hour. Alfred McCann, Sr. first aired a radio series about food during the 1920s over New York's station WOR following a bout of food poisoning. McCann became a whistle blower on food products that failed to pass the strict standards of his food testing laboratory.

Alfred McCann, Jr. took over the program after his father's death in 1931 and was joined by his wife Dora in 1947. At that time the title of the series was changed to The McCanns at Home.

Alfred McCann died in December of 1972, but Dora continued on the air with assistance from daughter Patricia.

Dora McCann died on August 14, 1975 at the age of sixty.

THE McCANN PURE FOOD HOUR

See: Alfred and Dora McCann

THE McCANNS AT HOME

See: Alfred and Dora McCann

CHARLIE McCARTHY

See : Edgar Bergen

CLEM McCARTHY (Charles L. McCarthy)

Sportscaster Clem McCarthy was born on September 9, 1882 in East Broomfield, New York. His father was a horse dealer and auctioneer, so naturally young Clem was raised around horses.

His ambition to become a jockey was foiled when he grew too tall; however, he went on to become the legendary voice of the Kentucky Derby and countless other horse races. McCarthy first broadcast racing in 1928 over the facilities of station KYW in Louisville, Kentucky. The following year he began his long association with the NBC network. His distinctive gravel throated voice described horse racing events and boxing matches until 1947. He was also heard as a sportscaster in the New York area over stations WINS and WMCA during the 1930s.

On television he covered harness racing during 1949-50 and was the commentator on The Gillette Summer Sports Reel in 1953.

In 1954 the illness and subsequent death of his wife Vina from cancer left him in severe financial difficulty. Clem McCarthy sadly died alone and penniless from Parkinson's disease on June 4, 1962. He was seventy-nine years old.

GRACE McCARTHY
See: The Doring Sisters

JACK McCARTHY

The voice of more than one Jack McCarthy was heard over the radio airwaves.

Announcer Jack McCarthy was featured on The Chamber Music Society of Lower Basin Street series under the name of Dr. Giacomo. He also announced for Tales of Willie Piper and hosted The Museum of Modern Music using his own name.

Another Jack McCarthy was associated with Detroit's station WXYZ beginning in 1938. He served as chief announcer and appeared as an actor on local programs. On network shows originating from WXYZ he was one of several to play the Green Hornet and was cast in the title role on Ned Jordan, Secret Agent. In 1955 he left "The Motor City" for New York. There he was a television newscaster for WPIX-TV. He broadcast using the name John E. McCarthy to differentiate between him- self and the aforementioned NBC announcer Jack McCarthy.

JIMMY McCLAIN

Announcer and emcee Jimmy McClain was associated with Texas stations KABC, WFAA, and WOAI and the Texas State network. Later he worked in radio advertising in Chicago before beginning his studies for the ministry at Seabury-Western Theological Seminary.

While a seminary student he served as the quizmaster of the Dr. IQ Jr. juvenile series in 1942. Later the same year he took over the adult Dr. IQ show, replacing Lew Valentine who was called to military duty. In 1946 McClain left radio to devote full time to his ministry in the Episcopal Church. Rev. Jimmy McClain took a leave of absence from his pastoral duties during the 1953-54 season to preside over the video version Dr. IQ.

JOYCE McCLUSKEY

Radio actress Joyce McCluskey was heard in supporting roles on a lengthy list of airwave credits. She began her acting career before the microphone during the late 1940s, and extended that career into the early 1950s.

She was a member of the cast of such shows as Alias Jane Doe; Broadway is My Beat; Dr. Christian; Dragnet: Family Theatre; Gunsmoke; Halls of Ivy; Pete Kelly's Blues; The Lux Radio Theatre; Stars Over Hollywood; Suspense; This Is Your FBI; The Whistler; and Yours Truly, Johnny Dollar. On television she was associated with stations KTLA-TV in Los Angeles and WBKB-TV in Chicago.

KATE McCOMB

Stage and radio actress Kate McComb was born in Sacramento, California on November 25, 1871. Kate's early ambition to become a singer and concert pianist was curtailed by illness. After recovering, she married John McComb, but he fell ill which further frustrated Kate's goal to be a performer. John later died and Kate moved to New York where she made her acting debut on the Broadway stage in 1926. Her initial radio appearance was on the February 8, 1930 broadcast of The Silver Flute. Subsequently her acting roles on the airwaves included: Mrs. Kerrigan on The Goldbergs, Nannie on Lora Lawton, Mother O'Neill on The O'Neills, Hattie on Snow Village Sketches, Maggie on The Strange Romance of Evelyn Winters, Mrs. Grover on Two on a Clue, and Mrs. Evans on Valiant Lady. She was also heard on Big Town, Cavalcade of America, The Gibson Family, The March of Time, and The Kate Smith Hour.

Kate McComb died on April 15, 1959 at the age of eighty-seven.

LU LU McCONNELL

Comedienne Lu Lu McConnell was born in Kansas City, Missouri on April 8, 1882. She began her professional career on the stage in both repertory theatre and vaudeville. Later she performed in Broadway and Winter Garden productions, on radio, and television.

She is best remembered on radio as a regular panelist on the wacky It Pays to be Ignorant series. Less memorable airwave appearances were on the 1933 version of The Big Show with Paul Douglas and Gertrude Niesen.

On television she was seen in the video version of It Pays to be Ignorant.

Lu Lu McConnell died of cancer on October 9, 1962 at the age of eighty. She had been married to vaudeville performer Grant Simpson who died in 1932.

ED McCONNELL

Performer Ed McConnell was born on January 12, 1892 in Atlanta, Georgia. The son of a preacher, young Ed was the song leader for several evangelists. However, he soon left the sawdust trail for the more secular vaudeville stage and radio airwaves. He sang songs, played the piano and banjo, and told stories on several local stations before his Smilin' Ed McConnell Show premiered on network radio in 1932. In 1944 he began a long association with The Brown Shoe Company who sponsored his Buster Brown Gang series.

Smilin' Ed continued to occupy the airwaves until his death in 1954 at the age of sixty-two.

JOHN McCORMACK

Tenor John McCormack was born on June 14, 1884 in Athlone, Ireland. McCormack won international recognit ion for his performances with several opera companies, his RCA Victor recordings, personal concert tours, and on the radio. On the latter medium he thrilled radio audiences on opera broadcasts with William Daly's orchestra, The RCA Victor Hour, and other NBC network musical productions from the 1920s to the mid 1930s.

Due to failing health, John McCormack returned to his native Ireland. He died there of bronchial pneumonia at the age of sixty-one on September 16, 1945.

MYRON McCORMICK (Walter Myron McCormick)

Actor and comedian Myron McCormick was born in Albany, Indiana on February 8, 1908. A Phi Beta Kappa graduate of Princeton University, McCormick decided on a career in show business and made his Broadway debut in 1932. He subsequently added the mediums of film, radio, and televison to his scope of performing.

On radio he was heard as Private Steve Mason on Buck Private (And His Girl); Robert Shallenberger on Central City; Dan Dodge on Crime Letter from Dan Dodge; Steve Harper on Help- mate; Paul Sherwood on Joyce Jordan, Girl Interne; Adams on A Passport for Adams; Walter Manning on Portia Faces Life: and the title role on Christopher Wells. Other airwave credits included: Gangbusters, Inner Sanctum, Listening Post, The Man Behind the Gun, The March of Time, and Mr. District Attorney. On television he appeared as a guest star on several dramatic productions.

Myron McCormick died of cancer on July 30, 1962 at the age of fifty-four.

ROBERT McCORMICK

Two Robert McCormicks were heard on the radio airwaves. Colonel Robert R.McCormick was born in Chicago. Illinois on July 30, 1880. His colorful career was launched following graduation from Yale University in 1903. He was a newspaper war correspondent, rose to the rank of colonel during service in World War I, authored several books, was a military historian, radio personality, and most importantly served as editor and publisher of The Chicago Tribune.

On radio he appeared weekly on The Chicago Theatre of the Air broadcasts with talks on current topics and historical events.

Colonel McCormick died on April 1, 1955 following several years of failing health. He was seventy-four years old. Newsman Robert McCormick was born in Danville, Kentucky in 1911. A graduate of George Washington University, he entered the field of broadcasting in 1942 as a news correspondent for the NBC network. In 1948 he covered the Democratic National Convention on television. This was the first ever convention to be aired on this medium.

Robert McCormick died of a heart attack on September 4, 1985 at the age of seventy-four.

THE McCOY
See: Pilot/Audition

JACK McCOY
Announcer Jack McCoy was employed at WOAI in San Antonio, Texas during the mid 1940s before elevation to the network level.

Among his network announcing credits during the 1940s and 50s were The Steve Allen Show, Breakfast in Hollywood, Escape, The Life of Riley, Art Linkletter's House Party, Maisie, My Mother's Husband, and The Dinah Shore Show, He also served as the emcee of Live Like a Millionaire.

On television he hosted Glamour Girl and the video version of Live Like a Millionaire.

Jack McCoy died on March 18, 1991 at the age of seventy-two.

JEAN McCOY
Radio actress Jean McCoy played supporting roles on several series during the 1940s. She played Margie on Scattergood Baines; Sue on Chick Carter, Boy Detective: Mary Crowell on Four Corners, U.S.A.; Abby Matson on Lorenzo Jones; Margie on Snow Village Sketches; and Marcella on Pepper Young's family. She was also heard in the cast of The Aldrich Family.

MARY McCOY (Laura Townsley McCoy)
Singer Mary McCoy was born in Great Bend, Kansas. She first performed at a party when she was only three years old. Later, while singing on a local Kansas City radio station, she was discovered by the famous diva Madame Ernestine Schumann-Heink. As her protege, Mary studied with her and was soon appearing on stage and radio.

Mary McCoy's vocal talent was heard on such radio series as Fred Allen's Town Hall Tonight, The Camel Pleasure Hour, The Chase and Sanborn Choral Orchestra, The Country Club, The Cuckoo clock (as Eugenia Skidmore), Evening in Paris, and Tea Time Tunes.

MARGARET McCRAE
Band vocalist Margaret McCrae sang wit Benny Goodman's band and was also featured on a few radio shows. Those shows included: The Joe E. Brown Show, (Maxwell House) Show Boat, and from May to July of 1936 she sang on Your Hit Parade.

TEX McCRARY (John Reagan McCrary)

The diverse life of Tex McCrary began on October 13, 1910 when he was born in Calvert, Texas. After attending Yale University he worked as a newspaper reporter, columnist, and was chief editorial writer for The New York Daily Mirror. During World War II he rose to the rank of Lt. Colonel in the Air Force.

McCrary was employed as a radio producer when he met Jinx F'alkenburg; they were married on June 10, 1945.

On radio Tex and Jinx were heard together on such talk series as Hi Jinx, Meet Tex and Jinx, and Tex and Jinx. On television they were seen on video versions of their radio format under the titles At Home With Tex and Jinx, Preview, and The Swift Home Service Club.

Tex McCrary also authored several books and covered the Korean conflict for The Daily Mirror. With wife Jinx he co- wrote a daily column for The New York Herald Tribune titled New York Close-Up and a weekly column for Variety called Radio Activity.

CATHERINE McCUNE

Radio actress Catherine McCune was born in Honolulu, Hawaii on August 20, 1917. She made her radio debut over station WDAF in Kansas City in 1929 at the age of twelve. She was subsequently heard in supporting roles on a number of rad io series broadcast during the 1930s and 40s. She played the role of Clara Potts for several seasons on Scattergood Baines. Her other radio credits included Calling All Cars, Hollywood Hotel, The Lux Radio Theatre, The Ken Murray Show, Jack Oakie's College, and The Joe Penner Show. For a brief time she also penned scripts for Calling All Cars.

HATTIE McDANIEL

Actress and singer Hattie McDaniel was born in Wichita, Kansas on June 10, 1895. She began singing professionally at the age of sixteen with her brother's traveling tent show. She was later a vocalist with George Morrison's band.

In 1931 Hattie made her radio debut on a local variety show called The Optimistic Do-Nut Hour aired over station KNX in Los Angeles. The following year she appeared in the first of many motion pictures. In 1939 she was the first black actress to win an Academy Award for her support ing role of Mammy in Gone With the Wind. On radio Hattie McDaniel is best remembered in the title role on the Beulah series. She was also heard over the air- waves on Amos 'n' Andy, The Billie Burke Show. The Eddie Cantor Show, and (Maxwell House) Show Boat.

In 1952 she was scheduled to resume her role of Beulah on the video version of that show, but ill health prevented her from appearing,

Hattie McDaniel died of cancer on October 26, 1952 at the age of fifty-seven.

ARCH McDONALD

Sportscaster and announcer Arch McDonald (not to be confused with Boston newscaster Arch MacDonald) was born in 1901 in Hot Springs, Arkansas.

He began his radio career in 1930 with station WDOD in Chattanooga, Tennessee. Four years later he moved to WJSV (now WTOP) in Washington, D.C. where he broadcast Washington Senators baseball and Washington Redskins football. In 1939 he shifted his base of operations to WABC in New York for a single season association with New York Yankees and Giants baseball and then returned to the Washington sports teams. Arch McDonald died of a heart attack on October 16, 1960 at the age of fifty-nine. He succumbed while returning to Washington on a train following a broadcast of a Redskins football game.

CRAIG McDONNELL (Craig McDonnell Kenney)

Radio actor Craig McDonnell was born in Buffalo, New York on June 8, 1907. After completion of his education at Culver Military Academy, McDonnell made his radio debut in 1927 as a singer.

During his subsequent three decades on the airwaves as an actor, singer, and announcer he amassed a lengthy list of credits. He played both Irish and Harka on Bobby Benson. Dinty Moore on Bringing Up Father, Daddy on Daddy and Rollo. Peter on The Greatest Story Ever Told, the title role on David Harum, Lieutenant Dan Britt on Official Detective, Judge Watson on The Second Mrs. Burton, Story Man on The Story Shop, The Captain Drake on Under Arrest, Jolly Rogers on Valiant Lady, and Elmer the Bull on Ed Wynn's Happy Island Show.

Other radio credits included: Alias Jimmy Valentine; Charlie Chan; Destiny's Trails; Gangbusters; Gramps; Kay Kyser's Kollege of Musical Knowledge; The March of Time; The Mighty Show; Mr. District Attorney; Mr. Keen, Tracer of Lost Persons; News of Youth; Our Gal Sunday; The Jack Pearl show; Pretty Kitty Kelly; Raising Junior; Renfrew of the Mounted; Sky Blazers; Kate Smith's A&P Bandwagon; Dick Tracy; Jerry Wayne's show; When a Girl Marries; and Young Dr. Malone. He also served as the announcer for The O'Neils serial drama.

Craig McDonnell retired from radio in October of 1956 due to ill health. He died on November 24, 1956 at the age of forty- nine.

JACK McELROY

Vocalist Jack McElroy was born on October 21, 1913 in the state of Kansas.

On radio he sang and announced on the Bride and Groom series and serenaded the ladies on Breakfast in Hollywood. Later he took over as emcee of the latter program, remaining in that capacity after the title was changed to Welcome to Hollywood. In 1956 he was seen in his one and only motion picture. Holly- wood or Bust.

Jack McElroy died of lung cancer on March 2, 1959 at the age of forty-five.

DAVE McENERY
See: Red River Dave

BRASS McGANNON
See: Pilot/Audit ion

McGARRY AND HIS MOUSE

McGarry and His Mouse, based on characters created by Matt Taylor in This Week Magazine, was adapted for radio as a 1946 summer replacement for Eddie Cantor's show.

The comedic adventures of bumbling third grade detective Dan McGarry and his "mouse" (girlfriend Kitty Archer) made its debut over the NBC network on June 26, 1946. The warm weather series was sponsored by Bristol Myers' Ipana Toothpaste and Trushay Hand Lotion.

The show was sufficiently well received to warrant a reprieve over the Mutual network starting on January 6, 1947 with General Foods' products as sponsor. However, the return was short lived and McGarry disappeared for good from the air. Taking their turn in the lead roles were Wendell Corey, Ted de Corsia, and Roger Pryor as Dan McGarry and Patsy Campbell, Peggy Conklin, and Shirley Mitchell as "the mouse". Also in the cast were Jack Hartley and Jerry Macy as the police inspector (McGarry's Uncle Matthew), Carl Eastman, Betty Garde, and Thelma Ritter. Peter Van Steeden led the orchestra and Bert Parts announced.

FIBBER McGEE AND MOLLY

One of a handful of classic long running radio comedy shows. Fibber McGee and Molly entertained listening audiences for twenty-two seasons.

The husband and wife team of Jim and Marian Jordan appeared together on several radio series before making their debut as Fibber McGee and Molly (aka The Johnson's Wax Program) over the NBC Blue network on April 16, 1935. The following year they moved to NBC's Red web where they remained throughout radio's "golden age."

From their familiar address at 79 Wistful Vista, Fibber and Molly applied their unique and successful comedy format to living room loudspeakers from coast-to-coast. Each week the half hour show featured various regular characters dropping in at the McGee's front door to trade conversation and tongue-in-cheek insults about Fibber's latest scheme. Occasionally the McGees strayed from home and hearth, but mostly the scene was set in their living room. The scripts were laced with such catch phrases as Fibber's "dad rat the dad ratted" or Molly's "heavenly days." There were also such recurring situations as opening the hall closet door which always resulted in an avalanche of its contents pouring down on Fibber's head.

Two of the best remembered of the regular visitors to the McGees were Hal Peary as Throckmorton P. Gildersleeve and Marlin Hurt as Beulah, the maid.

Both were later catapulted to stardom on their own spin-off series. Versatile performer Bill Thompson was heard as the Old Timer (Cliff Arquette was also cast in this role and others) who always had an unrelated joke to tell prefaced by "that's purty good Johnny, but that ain't the way I heerd it." Thompson also played the henpecked bird watcher Wallace Wimple, con man Horatio K. Boomer, Molly's Uncle Dennis (also played by Ransom Sherman), and Greek restaurateur Nick Depopolous. Arthur Q. Bryan as Doc Gamble invariably engaged Fibber in a contest of trading insults. Gale Gordon as Mayor Latrivia always became so enraged at McGee chat speech failed him. The character was supposedly a good natured verbal take-off on New York's Mayor LaGuardia. When LaGuardia died in 1947, the character was retired from the cast. Gordon also played Otis Cadwallader, Foggy Williams (the weatherman), and other minor roles.

Isabel Randolph played the snobbish Mrs. Uppington, Shirley Mitchell was their wartime boarder Alice Darling, and Bea Benaderet was Mrs. Carstairs. Fibber often carried on a one way conversation with Myrt, the telephone operator, but her voice was never heard. Marion Jordan often stepped out of her co-starring role as Molly to portray Teeny, the little girl next door. Using a high pitched squeaky voice, she bombarded McGee with the incessant query of "Whatcha doin' mister, whatcha doin', huh? huh?". Marian's voice was also heard as Geraldine, Old Lady Wheelock, Mrs. Waddington, and Lady Vere de Vere.

From November 15, 1937 to April 11, 1939 Marian Jordan was ill and did not appear on the show. During that time the program was retitled Fibber McGee and Company. Actress Betty Winkler filled the void, but never assumed the role of Molly. A long list of other radio voices and guest stars paraded through the McGee's front door over the years. Some of them included: Elvia Allman, Jim Backus, Parley Baer, Mel Blanc, Ken Christy, Mary Jane Croft, Mary Lou Harrington, Jess Kirkpatrick, Dick LeGrand, Tyler McVey, Frank Nelson, Gil Stratton, Hugh studebaker, and Herb Vigran.

Music was provided by the orchestras of Jimmy Grier, Ulderico Marcelli, Billy Mills, and Ted Weems. The vocalists were Clark Dennis, The Four Notes (Lee Gillette. Lee Gotch, Bob James, and Marjorie Whitney), The King's Men (Ken Darby, Jon Dodson, Bud Linn, and Rad Robinson), Peter Leeds, The Master Singers Quartet, Donald Novis, Gale Page, Ronnie and Van, Jimmy Shields, Martha Tilton, and Kathleen Wells. During the time Harlow Wilcox was the announcer for the show, he was also considered one of the cast. Other announcers were John Wald, Don Wilson, and Harry Von Zell.

On May 23, 1950 Johnson's Wax severed their long association as sponsor, but Fibber and Molly quickly rebounded with Pet Milk taking over sponsorship. After Pet had "milked" all they could from the McGee's antics, they cancelled after the broad- cast of June 10, 1952. On October 7, 1952 the McGees returned to the airwaves for Reynolds Aluminum. Following their usual summer hiatus in 1953, the show premiered on October 5th with an abbreviated fifteen minute format which aired on Monday through Friday. After a few weeks

Reynolds was replaced with Richard Hudnut products, Miles Laboratories, Papermate, and Prudential Insurance who all shared in the underwriting of the show.

At this point Fibber and Molly began to agonize with the reality that the marathon series was winding down. However, they held on until March of 1956. After that they still continued to provide skits for NBC's Monitor series through the summer of 1959.

Marian Jordan died two years later, ending once and for all the legendary radio life of Fibber McGee and Molly. An unsuccessful attempt to bring Fibber and Molly to the television screen, with a totally different cast, aired from September of 1959 to January of 1960.

PATRICK McGEEHAN

Radio announcer and actor Patrick McGeehan was born in Steelton, Pennsylvania on March 4, 1907. Young McGeehan left home at the age of fourteen. He went to sea, toured the vaudeville circuit, and was a tightrope walker's assistant with Barnum and Bailey's Circus before embarking on a radio career in 1935.

He was subsequently associated with such series as Abbott and Costello, Aunt Mary, The Joan Davis Show, Bill Lance, The Life of Riley, Maisie, The Red Skelton Show, and Stars Over Hollywood. He also served as narrator of Ceiling Unlimited, The Hour of St. Francis, and Strange as it Seems. Patrick McGeehan died of a cerebral hemorrhage at the age of eighty on January 3, 1988.

JOHN McGOVERN

Actor John McGovern (not to be confused with youthful actor Johnny McGovern) was heard on numerous radio series during the 1930s and 40s.

He played supporting roles on Amateur Gentleman; Big Sister; The Casebook of Gregory Hood; East of Cairo; The Gibson Family; The Goldbergs; Highway Patrol; Lorenzo Jones; Just Plain Bill; Mrs. Wiggs of the Cabbage Patch; My True Story; Mysteries in Paris; Mary Noble, Backstage Wife; The Orange Lantern; Our Gal Sunday; Pages of Romance; Pretty Kitty Kelly; Ellen Randolph; Second Husband; The Shadow; The Kate Smith Show; Society Girl; and Tennessee Jed.

JOHNNY McGOVERN

Juvenile actor Johnny McGovern (not to be confused with adult actor John McGovern) was first heard on the radio airwaves during the late 1940s.

He was one of several to play the role of Little Beaver on the Red Ryder series. His other credits included: The Bob Burns Show, Doorway to Life, One Foot in Heavenand smilin' Ed McConnell's Buster Brown Gang.

OLIVER McGOWAN

See: Sherling Oliver

PAUL McGRATH

Actor Paul McGrath was born on April 11, 1904 in Chicago, Illinois. He attended Carnegie Institute of Technology. but in 1924 he left before graduating to go on tour with a theatre company. For the next half century McGrath performed on stage, screen, radio, and television.

On radio he shared the role of host and keeper of the squeak- ing door on Inner Sanctum Mysteries, Dr. John Wayne on Big Sister, and the title role on The Casebook of Gregory Hood. Also included in his impressive list of other airwave credits were The Affairs of Dr. Gentry, The Brighter Day, Crime Doctor, A Date With Judy, Lora Lawton, My Son Jeep, Studio One, Theatre Guild on the Air, This Life is Mine, When a Girl Marries, and Young Dr. Malone.

On television McGrath was equally at home on both prime time drama and daytime serials. Among his video credits were The Armstrong Circle Theatre, The Edge of Night, First Love, The Guiding Light, The Hallmark Hall of Fame, Love is a Many Splendored Thing, Love of Life, Play of the Month, The Secret Storm, and The United States Steel Hour.

Paul McGrath died in his sleep of heart failure at the age of seventy-four on April 13, 1978.

FRANK McHUGH (Francis Curray McHugh)

Character actor Frank McHugh was born on May 23, 1898 in Homestead, Pennsylvania. Although McHugh's claim to fame was mostly for his work on the motion picture screen, he enjoyed limited exposure on radio and television.

He played Finnegan on the brief radio series That's Finnegan, and frequently appeared with Bing Crosby on Crosby's radio and television shows.

Frank McHugh died on September 11, 1981 at the age of eighty- three.

JOHN MC INTIRE

Actor and radio announcer John McIntire was born in Spokane, Washington on June 27, 1907. McIntire began his radio career in 1928 as an announcer at station KMPC in Los Angeles, California. He later became a well established radio actor, appearing in a long list of shows spanning many years. It was not until 1948 that he was first seen on the motion picture screen, and 1955 before making his first appearance on television.

On the radio airwaves McIntire was one of a quartet of actors to play the title roles on Crime Doctor and Jack Packard on I Love a Mystery. He was also heard in the title roles on Bill Lance and Phone Again Finnegan. He played John Abbott on We, The Abbotts; he hosted Hall of Fame and Lincoln Highway; he served as the narrator for A Man Called X; and announced for Wings Over America. Additional radio credits included: Big Sister, Cavalcade of America, Brenda Curtis, Frontier Gentleman, Glamour Manor, The March of Time, Meet Mr. Meek, Mercury Theatre, On Stage, One Man's Family, Philip Morris Playhouse, Sam Spade, Suspense, Ellen Randolph, Tarzan, This is My Best, Orson Welles' Almanac, and The Ed Wynn show. His initial television appearance was on The

General Electric Theatre. Subsequently he was seen on American Dream, Aspen, The Naked City, Shirley, The Virginian, and Wagon Train. McIntire and his wife, actress Jeanette Nolan, appeared together on several radio and television series. John McIntire died of cancer and emphysema at the age of eighty-three on January 30, 1991.

FRANK McINTYRE

Actor Frank McIntyre was born in Ann Arbor, Michigan on February 25, 1879.

He made his stage debut in 1901, the medium for which he was best known for more than three decades. However, to a lesser degree, he also performed on the motion picture screen and radio.

He is best remembered on the airwaves as Captain Henry on the (Maxwell House) Show Boat series. A role he played for three seasons.

Frank McIntyre died on June 8, 1949 at the age of seventy.

HAL McINTYRE

Bandleader and alto saxophonist Hal McIntyre was born in Cromwell, Connecticut on November 29, 1914. He fronted his first band at the age of sixteen and later played with several dance bands, most notably with Glenn Miller.

McIntyre returned to waving his baton in 1941 with help and encouragement from former boss Miller. He took his music makers on tour of the big name ballrooms, theatres, and hotels. He also recorded on a half dozen labels and was heard on the radio airwaves.

On the latter medium he appeared on his own show during the 1942-43 season over the Mutual network and during 1945 over the ABC network. Other radio work included: dance band remote broadcasts and such shows as Let's Go to Town, The National Guard Show, One Night Stand, and Spotlight Bands. Hal McIntyre was severely burned in an apartment fire when he fell asleep while smoking. He died as a result of those burns three days later on May 5, 1959. He was forty-four years old.

THE McKESSON MUSICAL MAGAZINE

Products manufactured by McKesson (and Robbins) sponsored a weekly half hour of concert music.

The pages of The McKesson Musical Magazine came to life on the weekly half hour series broadcast over the NBC Red net- work from 1930 to 1932. The orchestra was initially under the direction of Frederick

Fradkin, who was later replaced by Erno Rapee. The featured tenor Fred Hufsmith was joined by various guest artists.

BARRY McKINLEY

Baritone vocalist Barry McKinley was born on November 1, 1913 in Ft. Wayne, Indiana.

He made his radio debut in 1933 over Cincinnati's station WLW and later serenaded radio audiences on several network shows. He was the principal star of Dreams Come True and entertained on his own sustaining fifteen minute series. The latter was aired over the NBC Blue network twice weekly during the 1937- 38 season and over NBC's Red web on a weekly basis during 1938-39. Other regular radio appearances included: Bicycle Party, Gray Gordon's Tic Toc Rhythms, Radiotron Party, Romantic Rhythms, and the 1937 version of Time to Shine. Before his career waned during the 1940s McKinley sang with the bands of Al Donahue and Emery Deutsch. He also led the band of Joe Haymes.

VICTOR McLAGLEN

Actor Victor McLaglen was born in Tunbridge, England on December 10, 1886. The son of an Anglican clergyman, the rebellious young man ran away from home to serve in the military during the Boer War and later sailed to Canada where he prospected for gold. Failing to strike it rich in the gold fields, he became a professional prizefighter and wrestler until World War I beckoned him back into the armed forces. Finally, in the early 1920s, McLaglen decided to make acting his career. His first Hollywood film in 1925 led to many subsequent major roles on the motion picture screen, which included his memorable portryal of Captain Flagg in What Price Glory.

On the radio airwaves he was cast as a Canadian Mountie in Red Trails and recreated his film role of Captain Flagg on the Captain Flagg and Sergeant Quirt series.

Victor McLaglen died of congestive heart failure at the age of seventy-two on November 7, 1959.

TOMMY McLAUGHLIN

Baritone vocalist Tommy McLaughlin was heard on several radio series during the 1930s. Among those airwave credits were (Major Bowes) Capitol family Hour, Threads of Happiness, and Vick's Open House.

Tommy McLaughlin died of tuberculosis on July 28, 1936. He was only twenty-seven years old.

MURRAY McLEAN

See: Jimmy Allen

GORDON McLENDON

Native Texan Gordon McLendon was a pioneer broadcaster, film producer, and activist in Democratic politics. Following service in the Navy during World War I, he founded station KLIF in Dallas, Texas. Nicknamed "The Old Scotsman," he organized the Liberty network and beginning in 1947 aired major league baseball's Game of the Day and professional football games. The Liberty network grew to a peak of four hundred and fifty-eight stations before it was dismantled in 1952.

After the demise of Liberty, McLendon was involved with many radio stations. He developed the Middle of the Road (MOR) and Beautiful Music (BM) radio formats, authored several books, ran for political office, and was considered an expert in the field of metallurgy.

Gordon McLendon died of cancer at the age of sixty-five on September 14, 1986.

MARIAN McMANUS

Singer Marian McManus first appeared on radio as a young hopeful on Metropolitan (Opera) Auditions of the Air. Subsequently she became one of the mainstay regulars on The Manhattan Merry-Go-Round for several seasons. She also sang on the ethereal carousel's spinoff series, The Monday Merry-Go-Round.

Other than this, there seams to be a drouth of information concerning Marian McManus' life and career.

GLORIA McMILLAN

Juvenile actress Gloria McMillan was born in Portland, Oregon in 1933.

She began her Los Angeles based acting career at the tender age of seven in 1940.

Although she played uncredited youthful roles on hundreds of radio shows, she is remembered most for her portrayal of Harriet Conklin on both the radio and television versions of Our Miss Brooks.

GRAHAM McNAMEE

One of the best known of the pioneering radio announcers was Graham McNamee. He was born on July 10, 1888 in Washington, D.C. McNamee worked his way through music school as a sales- man and railroad clerk. He made his professional debut as a singer in 1920. Three years later he first appeared on radio over New York's station WEAF as a vocalist; however, on August 23rd of the same year he abandoned singing in favor of sportscasting. Subsequently he would expand his horizons as the announcer on a long list of radio programs, serve as an emcee, cover the most memorable special events of the era, tour the lecture circuit, and narrate newsreels for Paramount and Universal studios. His salutation of "Good evening ladies and gentlemen of the radio audience" became the McNamee trade- mark. The New York Times described him as a "Voice to Remember."

Numbered among the radio series on which his voice was heard were The All Colored Revue, Along the News Front, Atwater Kent (Auditions), Behind the Mike, Broadway Hits, Cities Service Concerts, The Coca Cola Program, The Eveready Hour, Fireside Recitals, The Fleischmann Sunshine Hour, Four Star News, The Gold Dust Twins, The Hudson Terraplane Travelcade, Elsa Maxwell's Party Line, Millions for Defense, (Major Bowes) Original Amateur Hour, Parade of the States, The RKO Hour, The Royal Crown Revue, Rubinoff,

Time of Your Life, Rudy Vallee's shows, Vox Pop, and Ed Wynn's shows. Graham McNamee was heard on the radio for the last time on the April 24, 1942 broadcast of Elsa Maxwell's Party Line. He died of a brain embolism on May 9, 1942. He was fifty- three years old.

HARRY McNAUGHTON

Actor and comedian Harry McNaughton was born in Surbiton, England on April 29, 1896. McNaughton began his career on the stage in his native England and served with the British Army in World War I before coming to the United States. In 1919 he made his American debut in the theatre, later expanding to the mediums of motion pictures, radio and tele- vision.

On radio his very British accent was put to use as a butler named Bottle on Phil Baker's show. He was a regular on Town Hall Big Game Hunt and also served as a panelist on both the radio and television versions of It Pays To Be Ignorant. Harry McNaughton died on February 26, 1967 at the age of seventy.

HOWARD McNEAR

Actor Howard McNear was born in Los Angeles, California on January 27, 1905. His career encompassed motion pictures, radio, and television.

On radio he played Doc Adams on Gunsmoke (the late Milburn Stone was cast in the role on the video version). McNear's other appearances on radio included: The Affairs of Ann Scot- land, The Casebook of Gregory Hood, The CBS Radio Workshop, Cinnamon Bear, The Count of Monte Cristo, Speed Gibson, Bill Lance, The Lineup, Maisie, Philip Marlowe, Sandra Martin (Lady of the Press), Night Beat, On Stage, One Man's Family, Rogers of the Gazette, and Twelve Players.

On television McNear played barber Floyd Lawson on The Andy Griffith Show. He was also in the cast of such video series as The Brothers, Burns and Allen, The George Gobel Show, The Donna Reed Show, and was the voice of several characters on the Jetsons cartoon.

Howard McNear died on January 3, 1969 at the age of sixty-three.

WILLIAM McNEARY

William McNeary pioneered radio programming aimed at a juvenile audience. As early as 1923 he presided over the Man in the Moon series aired over station WOR (then located in Newark, New Jersey). McNeary was also an announcer for WJZ in New York before leaving the field of broadcasting to become advertising manager for The Equitable Life Assurance Company. William McNeary died of a kidney ailment on August 26, 1934.

DON MC NEILL (Donald Thomas McNeill)

Radio announcer and emcee Don McNeill was born in Galena, Illinois on December 23, 1907. While attending Marquette University he first appeared on the radio airwaves in the capacity of an announcer for station WISN in

Milwaukee. During his tenure at WISN he also became the radio editor for The Milwaukee Sentinel, the newspaper that owned the station.

In 1929-30 he announced for Milwaukee's WTMJ, and in 1930 it was on to WHAS in Louisville, Kentucky. There he and partner Van Fleming performed as Don and Van, The Two (Coo-Coo) Professors. After losing their sponsor in 1931, they moved their show to KGO in San Francisco.

In 1933 McNeill assumed the duties of emcee on a floundering Chicago based show called The Pepper Pot. It was renamed The Breakfast Club, and with McNeill at the helm, became one of the most listened to morning series on radio. It occupied a spot on the dial for the next thirty-five years, leaving the air in 1968.

Although most remembered for the long association with his Breakfast Club, McNeill was also heard on several other programs. They included: Avalon Time, Climalene Carnival, Jamboree, Sunset Dreams, and Tea Time at Morrell's. During the 1950s McNeill tried unsuccessfully to adapt the Breakfast Club format to television under the titles The Don McNeill Dinner Club and The Don McNeill TV Club. He was also seen on television on Bob Hope's show and as the host of Take Two.

After his long career on the air he taught communications at Marquette and Notre Dame Universities and was also associated with a Florida land development.

Don McNeill died on May 7, 1996 at the age of eighty-eight.

MAGGI McNELLIS (Maggi Newhouse)

Singer and gossip program hostess Maggi McNellis was born in Chicago, Illinois on June 1, 1918 (the name McNellis was from her first marriage, and Newhouse from her second). Maggi was a nightclub singer in Chicago and New York before turning her attention to radio in 1943. The Maggi McNellis Show first aired in New York over station WINS. In 1944 she signed a five year contract with WEAF and the NBC network to air a daily midday fifteen minute series. The program of confidential gossip and interviews was later titled Maggi's Private Wire and was introduced by her theme song When You and I Were Young Maggie. Herb Sheldon announced and chatted with Maggi. The series left the air in June of 1947 when she was granted a release from her contract.

Maggi was also heard on radio as one of several to serve as moderator of Leave It To The Girls and hosted Luncheon at the Latin Quarter. In 1959 she presided over a transcribed five minute "fill" series called Celebrity Talk.

On television she was seen on video versions of Leave It To The Girls and Maggi's Private Wire. She was also seen on The Crystal Room, Maggi's Magazine, Say it With Acting, and Talent Search.

Maggi McNellis died of heart failure on May 24, 1989. She was seventy-one years old.

DOROTHY McNULTY
See: Penny Singleton

BUTTERFLY McQUEEN (Thelma McQueen)
Actress Butterfly McQueen was born on January 7, 1911 in Tampa, Florida. Her long career began on the stage when she was thirteen years old. subsequently she also appeared on the motion picture screen, radio, and television. She is probably best remembered for her role as Prissey in the film Gone With The Wind.

On radio she was heard on The Fitzgeralds, The Danny Kaye Show, and Dinah Shore's Birdseye Open House. On television she played Oriole on the video version of Beulah and won an Emmy for the ABC Afterschool Special presentation of The Three Wishes of a Rich Kid. In later years Butterfly McQueen (who still answered to the name Prissey) devoted her time to community work in Harlem and in 1974 received her her Bachelor's degree from City College of New York at the age of sixty-four. Butterfly McQueen died on December 22, 1995 from burns she suffered when a kerosene heater in her home caught fire. She was eighty-four years old.

TYLER McVEY
Character actor Tyler McVey performed in supporting roles in motion pictures, on radio, and television during the 1940s and 1950s.

On radio he was heard in the cast of Gene Autry's Melody Ranch, Dear John, Dr. Christian, Glamour Manor, Maisie, Fibber McGee and Molly, One Man's Family, Screen Guild Theatre, and Today's Children. He also in the dual capacity of actor and announcer on The Smiths of Hollywood. On television he was seen on Men Into Space.

JIM McWILLIAMS
Vaudevillian Jim McWilliams went from the stage to the radio airwaves in 1930. His newly discoverd medium offered him the opportunity to become a radio quizmaster. As such he presided over The Ask-It-Basket, Correction Please, and Uncle Jim's Question Bee. After radio, Jim McWilliams inauspiciously faded into oblivion.

ME AND JANIE
First promoted under the title Behind the Eight Ball, the 1949 summer replacement for Alan Young took to the airwaves with the grammatically incorrect title of Me and Janie. The situation comedy revolved around a befuddled husband, his bossy wife, a precocious son, and a stern employer. The format very much resembled the popular Blondie series. Me and Janie premiered over the NBC network on July 12, 1949 sponsored by Lewis Howe's Tums Antacid Tablets.

George O'Hanlon played himself (Me), Lurene Tuttle played his wife Janie, Jeffrey Silver his son Tommy, and Willard Waterman his overbearing boss Mr. Lamb. Others in the cast were Lois Corbett, Hope Emerson, Verna Felton, and

Marvin Miller. Johnny Duffy provided the musical bridges on the organ and Don Wilson announced.

In the fall, Baby Snooks took over the weekly half hour in the network's new schedule.

MALCOLM R. MEACHAM

Character actor Malcolm R. Meacham played supporting roles on several radio series during the 1930s.

He appeared in the cast of such programs as Betty and Bob, Hall of Fame, Hollywood Hotel, Kitty Keene, The Lux Radio Theatre, Ma Perkins, Margot of Castlewood, Mary Marlin, and Road of Life.

THE MARTHA MEADE SOCIETY PROGRAM

California based home economist Martha Meade instructed radio listeners in the art of cooking. Her culinary expertise was aired over the Pacific Coast network of NBC's Red web. The weekly fifteen minute cooking classes premiered in the spring of 1931 sponsored by The Sperry Flour Company. The durable series ended on June 22, 1939.

JACK MEAKIN

Musician Jack Meakin was involved with radio in several capacities. After graduation from Stanford University in 1929, Meakin began his musical career as a pianist at the NBC studios of stations KGO and KPO in San Francisco. He was later the musical director of WOV in New York in addition to the aforementioned stations.

As a producer for the CBS and NBC networks he served in that capacity for such programs as The Hoagy Carmichael Show, The Chamber Music Society of Lower Basin Street, The Hedda Hopper Show, The Hour of Charm, Kay Kyser's Kollege of Musical Knowledge, and Your Hit Parade.

He composed and/or conducted music for Abbott and Costello; The Great Gildersleeve; Honest Harold; Arch Oboler's Plays; Silver Theatre; Summerfield Bandstand; Jonathan Trimble, Esq; and You Bet Your Life.

In later years Jack Meakin Enterprises provided music, sound effects, and commercials for radio and television. He also directed advertising and public relations for a company called Film Communicators.

Jack Meakin died of a heart attack on December 30, 1982 at the age of seventy-six.

MARTHA MEARS

Actress and songstress Martha Mears was born in Mexico, Missouri on July 18, 1910. She attended The University of Missouri and San Diego State Teachers College before giving in to the lure of show business. Her career would eventually encompass motion pictures, radio, television, and personal appearance tours.

She made her radio debut in 1931 over local stations in her home state (KFRU, KMOX, and WIL) . Two years later she was "discovered" by Gus Edwards, auditioned, and hired by the NBC network.

Her radio airwave credits included: The Phil Baker Show, Frances Lee Barton's (General Foods) Kitchen Party, Believe it or Not, Colgate House Party, It Happened in Hollywood, Al Pearce and His Gang, The Standard Symphony Hour, Ten-Two- Four Ranch, and The Texas Rangers. She appeared in several motion pictures and was also the singing voice for other actresses. The most notable of the latter was her dubbed-in vocalizing for actress Marjorie Reynolds in the 1942 film white Christmas.

On television she was seen on The Milton Berle show for several seasons before retiring in 1953.

Martha Mears died of Alzheimer's disease on December 13,1986 at the age of seventy-six.

BILL MEEDER

Radio and theatre organist Bill Meeder directed and provided mood and theme music for several radio series during the 1930s and 40s.

Among those shows were Against the Storm, Big Sister, The Brighter Day, The Gospel Singer, Life Can Be Beautiful, Lone Journey, Perry Mason, The O'Neills, The Open Door, The Right to Happiness, Road of Life, Snow Village, This Day is Ours, Truth or Consequences, Vic and Sade, and Pepper Young's Family.

MEET CORLISS ARCHER

Meet Corliss Archer was one of several situation comedies revolving around the lives of teenagers. The series was a radio adaptation of characters created by F. Hugh Herbert and the stage play Kiss and Tell.

Corliss, her family, and friends made their debut over the CBS network on January 7, 1943. The initial weekly half hour show met with mediocre reviews and lasted only a few weeks.

It returned to the air on July 2, 1943 as part of the CBS network's summer schedule, replacing the vacationing Kate Smith. The Archers were again absent from the airwaves from the fall of 1943 until January 8, 1944. They then took over a late Saturday afternoon CBS time slot with The Anchor-Hocking Glass Corporation sponsoring the program. However, the show's popularity soon warranted a move to a place in the network's prime time schedule.

Before leaving the air in 1955, Meet Corliss Archer had become a well traveled show. It was shuffled to different times, days, and networks to fill holes in the schedules and replace other shows during summer vacations.

On April 6, 1947 Campbell Soup took over sponsorship. It lasted off and on until March 28, 1948. Corliss moved to the NBC network as the 1948 summer replacement for Bob Hope. The following year she was hack on CBS to again serve as a warm weather fill in, this time for The Electric Theatre.

When the latter's star Helen Hayes declined to return in the fall, Meet Corliss Archer remained In the CBS schedule with the Electric Theatre's consortium of Electric Companies remaining as the sponsor. In 1952 Corliss and her sponsor moved to the ABC network. She had her final fling on the air during the 1954-55 season on the CBS and Mutual networks. Janet Waldo played the title role for most of the time the show was on the air. However, Priscilla Lyon was heard as Corliss on the initial brief series and Lugene Sanders took over during the final season. Her father Harry Archer was played by Bob Bailey and Fred Shields; her mother Janet by Helen Mack and Irene Tedrow; and boyfriend Dexter Franklin by Bill Christie, Sam Edwards, David Hughes, and Irving Lee. Others in the cast included: Arlene Becker. Scotty Beckett, Tommy Bernard, Dolores Crane, Mary Jane Croft, Louise Erick- son, Kenny Godkin, Eddie Marr, Virgina Sale, Barbara Whiting, Mary Wickes, and Bebe Young. The orchestra was led by Charles "Bud" Dant , Lud Gluskin, Wilbur Hatch, and Felix Mills. The announcers were Ken Carpenter, John Hiestand, Wendell Niles, and Del sharbutt.

MEET MARGARET MAC DONALD
See: Margaret MacDonald

MEET ME AT PARKY'S
Dialectician and comedian Harry Einstein, better known as Nick Parkyakarkas, managed his mythical Greek restaurant on the variety series Meet Me at Parky's. The gags came thick and fast, involving the various patrons of Parky'a "beanery."

Since 1932 Einstein's Parkyakarkas had appeared on radio as a guest on other shows, but in 1945 he became the star of his own series. Meet Me at Parky'a premiered over the NBC network on June 17, 1945 sponsored by Old Gold Cigarettes. Originally scheduled as a summer replacement, Parky's received enough listener support to remain on the air for three seasons. P. Lorillard's Old Golds bailed out as sponsor in the spring. of 1947 causing the show to leave the air. It returned in the fall of the same year over the Mutual network with co-op commercials.

Joining parky's ethnically Greek oriented comedy/variety show was a dramatic cast and a parade of vocalists. Elaine Arden was heard as his sister Shakyakarkas, Joan Barton as the cashier, Sheldon Leonard as Orville Sharp, Ruth Perrott as Prudence Rockbottom, and Minerva Pious as Parky's wife. Other roles were played by Arthur Q. Bryan, Leo Cleary, Elliott Lewis, Wally Maher, and Frank Nelson. The vocalists included Patty Ballon, Peggy Lee, Jane Rhodes, The Short Order Chorus, Dave Street, and Martha Tilton. Music was under the direction of Opie Cates and the announcers were Art Gilmore and Bob Willaims.

Parky closed the doors of his Greek eatery on July 11, 1948.

MEET ME IN MANHATTAN

A short lived audience participation series, Meet Me in Manhattan was sustained by the ABC network during August and September of 1946.

The Monday through Friday half hour matinee was reviewed by Variety as a "fumbling format that never jelled." The show augmented its contrived chats with members of the studio audience with such features as an amateur poet contest judged by a guest star, plus the give away of a one-of-a-kind prize. Walter Kiernan served as emcee and Gene Kirby announced.

MEET ME IN ST. LOUIS

Characters created by Sally Benson in her novel and on the motion picture screen were heard on the radio adaptation of Meet Me in St. Louis. Set at the turn of the century in 1900, the lives of St. Louis' Smith family provided the story line for the situation comedy.

The weekly half hour program made its debut over the NBC network on September 16, 1950. Reviews by the critics were enthusiastic, but the show never caught on with the radio audience. The final episode aired only a few weeks later on November 5, 1950.

The principal teenage Smith daughter was played by youthful film actress Peggy Ann Garner. Her mother and dad were portrayed by Agnes Young and Vinton Hayworth. Other members of the cast included: Brook Byron, Raymond Edward Johnson, Billy Redfield, and Ethel Wilson. The orchestra was conducted by Vladimir Selinsky.

MEET MILLIE

Meet Millie, the misadventures of Brooklyn secretary Millie Bronson, was a weekly half hour situation radio comedy of the 1950s.

Millie took to the CBS network's airwaves on July 2, 1951. For most of its tenure the show was a sustaining feature, but was sponsored for brief periods of time. Some of those underwriting the series included General Motors, Murine, Nash-Kelvinator, and Wrigley's Gum.

The title role was played by both Audrey Totter and Elena Verdugo; Johnny Boone, her boss' son and love intrest, by Rye Billsbury (Michael Rye); and her mama by Bea Benadaret and Florence Halop. Isabel Randolph and Earle Ross were also heard in the cast. Music was under the direction of Irving Miller and the announcer was Bob Lemond.

Meet Millie's final radio broadcast aired in September of 1954. The video version was seen from 1952 to 1956.

MEET MISS JULIA

Meet Miss Julia was a transcribed daytime serial drama that first aired over the Mutual network an October 2, 1939. The fifteen minute episodes were heard on Monday through Friday sponsored by Flit Insect Spray.

The setting for the story was a boarding house located in the Gramercy Park section of New York City. Actress Josephine Hull was cast in the title role as the "seventy year young" landlady, also described as the "keeper of her little brood."

When 1940 came to an end, so did the obscure serial Meet Miss Julia.

MEET MISS SHERLOCK

A weekly half hour of tongue-in-cheek detective drama aired during the summer of 1946 under the title Meet Miss Sherlock. Jane Sherlock, a department store buyer and amateur sleuth blundered her way through solving crimes. The show was heard over the CBS Pacific Coast network.

Miss Sherlock was played by an obscure actress named Monty Margetts (Betty Moran was heard in the title role on the initial broadcast). William Conrad played NYPD Captain Dingo. An uncredited actor was cast in the role of Peter Blossom who was both Miss Sherlock's attorney and love interest. Charles Milron led the orchestra and Murray Wagner announced.

MEET MR. MC NULTY

Film star Ray Milland often appeared on radio, but only once was he the star of a regular series. Milland played Professor Raymond McNulty on the weekly half hour situation comedy Meet Mr. McNulty. The storyline revolved around the amusing problems encounted by McNulty as a professor at Lynnhaven, a college for girls.

Actress Phyllis Avery played McNulty's wife Peggy. Gordon Jones and Jacqueline deWit were heard as their friends Pete and Ruth Thompson. The supporting cast included Joan Banks, Mel Blanc, Ken Christy, and Joseph Kearns. Del Sharbutt was the announcer.

Meet Mr. McNulty aired over the CBS network's airwaves from September of 1953 to June of 1954. The series was sponsored by General Electric.

MEET MR. MEEK

The comedic lifestyle of the Meek family was heard on the weekly half hour titled Meet Mr. Meek. The show premiered over the CBS network on July 10, 1940 sponsored by Lever Brothers' Lifebuoy Soap.

The wimpish Mortimer Meek was played by Budd Hulick and Frank Readick, his shrewish spouse Agatha by Adelaide Klein, his sympathetic daughter Peggy by Doris Dudley, and his parasitic brother-in-law Louie by Jack Smart. Rounding out the cast were Bill Adams, Charlie Cantor, Marjorie Davies, Ian McAllister, John McIntire, Agnes Moorehead, Jeanette Nolan, Arnold Stang, and Ann Thomas. The announcer was Dan Seymour.

The series concluded on March 25, 1942; however, in 1947 a new cast was assembled and returned the Meek clan to the air under the new title of Meet the Meeks which is described under that heading.

MEET MR. MORGAN

See: Henry Morgan

MEET THE ARTIST

Radio personalities were interviewed by CBS publicist Bob Taplinger on Meet the Artist. The Columbia network series was first broadcast on May 28, 1931 with singer Morton Downey as the initial celebrity interviewed.

The theme When Good Fellows Get Together, and other music, was provided by an orchestra under the direction of Fred Berrens.

Meet the Artist was on the air spasmodically through the mid-1930s.

MEET THE BOSS

See: Gay Lombardo Shows

MEET THE COLONEL

See: Stoopnagle

MEET THE DIXONS

The brief saga of newspaperman Wesley Dixon and his wife Joan was chronicled an the daytime serial drama called Meet the Dixons. The first episode took to the air on July 31, 1939 over the CBS network, sponsored by Franco American Spaghetti. Richard Widmark and Barbara Weeks were cast as the Dixons and Charles Dingle as Wesley's skinflint boss who was responsible for the Dixon's financial problems. The announcer was Dan Seymour. The series concluded its run on October 6, 1939.

MEET THE MEEKS

Meet the Meeks was a revival of the situation comedy Meet Mr. Meek.

The latter day story of the Meek family employed a new cast and arrived on the NBC airwaves on August 23, 1947 for a sustaining trial run. On November 8, 1947 Swift & Company began sponsoring the weekly thirty minute Saturday morning show.

Mortimer Meek was played by Forrest Lewis and his wife Agatha by Fran Allison. Others in the cast were Jack Bivens, Sherman Marks, Elmira Roessler, Cliff Soubier, and Beryl Vaughn. Elwyn Owen was the organist and John Weigle announced.

The Meeks vacated their "little green house with the white shutters" and left the air on April 24, 1949.

MEET THE MENJOUS

The Meet the Menjous series added to the seemingly endless supply of husbands and wives eager to chat with each other on the airwaves. Actor Adolphe Menjou and (third) wife Verree Teasdale were occasionally joined in their conversations by their twelve year old adopted son Peter.

The Menjou family took to the air over New York's station WOR on April 25, 1949 with a fifteen minute Monday through Friday program. Topics of discussion included: books, fashions, motion pictures, and the human experience. It was all too obvious the chats were scripted and not extemporaneous. The announcer was Russ Dunbar.

The series expanded its circle of listeners beginning in the summer of 1949 when Ziv Radio Productions syndicated the transcribed programs for distribution to local stations. Meet the Menjous continued to circulate during the early 1950s.

MEET THE MISSUS

A women 's quiz and interview series titled Meet the Missus first aired in the Chicago area in 1936 over station WBBM. The fifteen minute weekday show was initially sponsored by Kitchen Klenzer and hosted by Tommy Bartlett and Harry Wismer.

In 1944 Meet the Missus began a run on CBS' Pacific Coast net- work. It originated from Earl Carroll's Theatre-Restaurant in Hollywood with a variety of sponsors. Added to the quiz and interview format were such features as gifts for longest married and newest newlywed. Ed East, Harry Mitchell, Jay Stewart, and Harry Von Zell all took their turn as emcee. Music was provided by Charles Milton at the organ and Maurie Webster announced.

Meet the Missus expanded to include the full coast-to-coast CBS network in 1951. It was sponsored by The Leslie Salt Company until 1953 when Rheem's Wedgewood Ranges took over. The series concluded later into the 1950s.

There were other local versions of Meet the Missus. Among them, a 1947 show broadcast in Detroit over station WJR. Russ Mulholland presided over the festivities in The Motor City.

MEET THE MORGANS

See: Pilot/Auditions

MEET THE MUSIC

A Sunday afternoon half hour of music that showcased seldom heard tunes was the format of Meet the Music (aka Composer's Corner).

The CBS sustainer was first broadcast on January 19, 1941. Lyn Murray's orchestra and chorus was augmented with vocals by Fredda Gibson (Georgia Gibbs) and Jack Leonard. The announcer was Julian Miller.

Meet the Music endured for only a few weeks, presumably because the music was unpopular and unfamiliar.

MEET THE PRESS

The radio version of Meet The Press preceded its more familiar television counterpart by about two years. It made its radio debut over the Mutual network on October 5, 1945 as a half hour series. It was sponsored by The American Mercury Magazine.

Free-lance writer Martha Rountree and American Mercury editor Lawrence Spivak created the weekly grilling sessions of news- makers by a panel drawn from the press corps. Bill Slater, Martha Rountree, and Albert Warner served as moderators. Permanent panelist Lawrence Spivak was joined by guest journalists each week, and the announcer was Michael Wayne. Meet the Press originated from the studios of WOL in Washington, D.C.

While the video version of Meet the Press aired unabated from 1947 into the 1990s, it was absent from radio during the 1951- 52 season. It returned over the NBC network in the fall of 1952, continuing to the point of outliving radio's "golden age."

MEET YOUR LUCKY PARTNERS

Meet Your Lucky Partners was a quiz program with an unusual twist. It united a contestant from the studio audience with a telephone partner selected at random from phone books. They worked as a team to answer questions, being rewarded with duplicate prizes for correct answers. Later in the program the partners competed against each other for a single prize for the answer to the "jackpot" question.

The sustaining series premiered over the Mutual network on May 20, 1948. Veteran quizmaster John Reed King was scheduled to be the emcee, but there was a conflict with another show he presided over. The last minute substitute for King was disc jockey Paul Brenner from Newark, New Jersey's station WAAT.

Meet Your Lucky Partners left the air in September of 1948 when Talent Jackpot, ironically emceed by John Reed King, took over the time in Mutual's fall schedule.

MEET YOUR MATCH

Another of the many uninspired quiz formats occupied a spot in the Mutual network's schedule under the title Meet Your Match. It was first broadcast on May 5, 1949 as a weekly thirty minute series with Tom Moore serving as quizmaster. Contestants competed for the correct answers to quest ions. Those failing to answer correctly were forced to retire from the game and only the surviving contestant was given the chance to answer the "jackpot" question. It was asked by a masked character identified only as "The Brain."

Meet Your Match was cancelled in the fall of 1949, but was to reappear on NBC's network in 1952 with Jan Murray assuming the quizmaster duties. Wayne Howell was the announcer. The program left the air early in 1953.

Jan Murray took Meet Your Match to the television screen on August 25, 1952. However, the ill fated video version lasted for only two shows.

MEET YOUR NAVY

A wartime variety show that featured talents drawn from the ranks of Navy personnel was the format for Meet Your Navy. The series, originating from The Great Lakes Naval Training Station, premiered in January of 1942. It was initially sustained by the NBC Blue network, but in August of the same year Hallmark Greeting Cards took over as sponsor. The show's slogan became "Keep 'em happy with mail."

The Bluejackets band, choir, and rhythm orchestra headlined the weekly half hour show. They were joined by nationally known banjoist Eddie Peabody, then officially known as Lieutenant Commander Edwin E, Peabody. There was also a dramatized skit of a war incident and a morale building talk by a Navy hero.

Durward Kirby and Jack Stillwell were the emcees and the band was under the direction of Frank Mettlach. Sponsorship was shifted to The Raytheon Manufacturing Company in the fall of 1944.

Meet Your Navy was last broadcast during the summer of 1945.

MEET YOUR NEIGHBOR
See: Alma Kitchell

LAL CHAND MEHRA
Character actor and lecturer Lal Chand Mehra began his career on the motion picture screen and on radio in 1931. Mehra specialized in Hindustani and Punjabi roles. He also lectured on the story of India.

On radio he was heard in the cast of such series as Calling All Cars, Cavalcade of America, Hollywood Playhouse, I Love a Mystery, It Happened in Hollywood, The Lux Radio Theatre, Passing Parade, Screen Guild Theatre, and The Silver Theatre.

JAMES MEIGHAN
Radio and stage actor James Meighan was born in New York City on August 22, 1905.

Although he appeared on Broadway in such productions as My Maryland and the revival of Under the Gaslight, Meighan was best known for his numerous radio roles.

He shared the title role with other actors on such series as Alias Jimmy Valentine, The Falcon, and Flash Gordon. He was heard as Reid Wilson on Against the Storm; Jack Winter on City Desk; Will Horton on Dot and Will; Eric Dale on I Love Linda Dale; Kerry Donovan on Just Plain Bill; Cullen Andrews on Lone Journey; Peter Carver on Lora Lawton; Richard on Marie, the Little French Princess; Larry Noble on Mary Noble, backstage wife; Michael on Orphans of Divorce; Dr. John McKeever on Peggy's Doctor; and Alan Drake on Special Agent (Gentleman Adventurer). Other radio credits included: Bambi; Burns and Allen; By Kathleen Norris; (True Story) Court of Human Relations; David Harum; Mr. Keen, Tracer of Lost Persons; The Romance of Helen Trent; Roses and Drums; Second Husband; The Shadow; The Singing Lady; and Young Widder Brown. He was also the emcee of The Mohawk Treasure Chest. James Meighan died on June 21, 1970 at the age of sixty-six.

FRITZ MEISSNER
See: The Maple City Four

ELAINE MELCHIOR

Actress Elaine Melchior was born on December 8, 1909 in New York City.

She saw limited duty on radio during the 1930s. She played villainess Ardala Valmar on the Buck Rogers serial and was also heard on The Eno Crime Club and Pretty Kitty Kelly.

LAURITZ MELCHIOR

Opera singer Lauritz Melchior was born on March 20, 1890 in Copenhagen, Denmark. He started singing as a boy and later went on to perform on the stage of Copenhagen's Royal Opera and sing Wagnerian roles in Berlin. In 1926 he made his debut with New York's Metropolitan Opera Company.

Melchoir was not only a great opera star, but also became well liked as a performer on radio and the motion picture screen. He was in demand on the airwaves as a guest on almost every music and variety show and was a regular on the Metro- politan Opera broadcasts. His other radio credits included: The Fred Allen Show, General Motors Concerts, The Kraft Music Hall, The Magic Key of RCA, The Radio Hall of Fame, and The Voice of Firestone.

Despite the rotund tenor's charismatic appeal, he also had a stormy side to his life. He left the Metropolitan Opera in 1950 over a dispute with that organization's management. He was married three times, and divorced twice.

Lauritz Melchior died two days before his eighty-third birth- day on March 18, 1973. Death was attributed to complications following an emergency gall bladder operation.

MELODIANA

A half hour of Sunday afternoon variety entertainment was initially titled The Big Hollywood Show when it premiered over the CBS network in the fall of 1933. In 1934 it was renamed Accordiana and moved into a weeknight position in the network's schedule. The following year the show finally settled on the title Melodiana. Sterling Drug Products' Phillips Milk of Magnesia was the sponsor.

The series featured the orchestra of Abe Lyman, soprano vocalists Bernice Claire and Vivienne Segal, and tenor Oliver Smith (Pierre LeKreune).

The Melodiana melodies ceased after the final broadcast in December of 1936.

MELODIES ORGANISTIC

See: Richard Aurandt

MELODIES OF HOME

See: Burl Ives

MELODIES TO REMEMBER

Melodies to Remember was a sustaining ABC network "filler" program broadcast during 1947. Bill "Skipper" Dawes hosted the fifteen minute show that skipped around the network's schedule where needed to fill a void. Organist Mel Spooner provided the musical accompaniment for The Coraleens, a chorus of teenage girls.

MELODY AND MADNESS

As the title suggests, Melody and Madness brought both music and comedy to radio audiences during the late 1930s.

The show made its debut on November 20, 1938 over the CBS network sponsored by The P. Lorrillard Company's Old Gold Cigarettes. The weekly half hour series moved to the NBC Blue network on May 23, 1939.

The melody portion of the program featured the orchestra of Artie Shaw, later replaced by Lennie Hayton. The melodies were augmented by vocalists Helen Forrest and Dick Todd. The madness was provided by host Robert Benchley's gags. The announcers were James Fleming, Warren Hull, and Del Sharbut.

Melody and Madness left the air on November 14, 1939.

MELODY CRUISE

The Cunard Steamship Company sponsored the Melody Cruise program. It was heard over the NBC Blue network during the 1933-34 season.

Music for the mythical ocean voyage was supplied by the Phil Harris band.

The title not only promoted the sponsor's maritime services, but the 1933 motion picture of the same name in which Phil Harris also appeared.

MELODY HALL

Melody Hall was the title of a Mutual network interim program of music. It was first aired on August 9, 1942 and lasted only until October.

The weekly sustaining thirty minutes featured the orchestra of Bob Stanley and the vocals of soprano Margaret Daum.

MELODY HIGHWAY

The orchestra of Bernie Green and host Milton Cross combined to occupy fifteen minutes of the ABC network's airtime on Melody Highway.

The brief weekly sustaining series was on the air from the fall of 1952 until January of 1953.

MELODY LANE

Another of the popular titles for little remembered music shows on radio was Melody Lane. "The Golden Tenor" Ben Alley vocalized on such a program in 1938.

Jerry Wayne's Melody Lane show was on the air in 1945 and is described in detail under that heading.

MELODY MAGIC

Hungarian gypsy musicmaker Emery Deutsch and a girl's trio teamed to present Melody Magic during 1931.

THE MELODY MASTER

Author and screenwriter Homer Croy penned scripts and starred in his 1935 series called The Melody Master. The "down home" storyline revolved around town oracle and newspaper editor Clem Clemens of Willow Heights.

MELODY MASTERPIECES

From October of 1934 to September of 1935, the CBS network sustained a thirty minute program of music titled Melody Masterpieces.

The weekly series featured soprano Mary Eastman, baritones Gene Baker, Norman Cordon, Evan Evans, and Hubert Hendrie.

The symphony orchestra was under the direction of Howard Barlow.

MELODY MATINEE

Fifteen minutes of Sunday afternoon music on the Melody Matinee program was first heard on January 5, 1936 over New York's station WEAF. The series was expanded to a half hour and carried over the NBC Red network beginning on November 15, 1936. sponsored by Smith Brother's Cough Drops. Songs were sung by Morton Bowe, The Cavaliers Quartet, and Muriel Dickson. Victor Arden led the orchestra and William Farren announced.

Melody Matinee concluded its four months on the network airwaves on March 28, 1937.

MELODY OF ROMANCE

Vocalist Charles Sears and Harry Kogen's orchestra serenaded Saturday morning radio listeners on a brief series called Melody of Romance. The announcer was Everett Mitchell.

The quarter hour program was first broadcast over the NBC Blue network on November 7, 1936 sponsored by The Jell-Sert Company's Maple-Mix Dessert.

The final romantic melody wafted over the airwaves on January 30, 1937.

MELODY PUZZLES

The musical quiz show Melody Puzzles was initially broadcast on November 2, 1937 under the sponsorship of The American Tobacco Company's Lucky Strike Cigarettes. For a brief time it originated from the studios of WOR in New York and was heard over several eastern affiliate stations of the Mutual network. Before year's end it moved to the NBC Blue network with Lucky Strike remaining as sponsor.

Song titles contained in skits that were correctly identified by contestants from the studio audience earned them a ten dollar bill and a rendition of the song.

The vocalists were Stuart Allen, Buddy Clark, and Fredda Gibson (Georgia Gibbs). Fred Uttal was the emcee, Richard Himber and Harry Salter led the orchestra, and Ed Herlihy Basil Ruysdael, and Tom Slater announced.

Melody Puzzles faded from the air in 1938.

MELODY RANCH
See: Gene Autry's Melody Ranch

MELODY ROUNDUP
A Saturday morning of western music hosted by Andy Devine was the format for the Melody Roundup show. The series replaced Hook 'n' Ladder Follies on May 6, 1944, sponsored by The Goodyear Rubber Company.

The eight to ten songs crammed into the thirty minutes were performed by The Range Singers, The Song Spinners, and The Sons of the Pioneers. Accompaniment was provided by Perry Botkin's orchestra. Jim Doyle was the announcer.

The end of the trail came for Melody Roundup after the broadcast of November 11, 1944.

MELODY THEATRE
A Sunday afternoon half hour beamed at a juvenile audience, Melody Theatre combined a moralistic message with recorded classical music.

Bill Griffis and Jay Meredith narrated the stories designed to instill respect and responsibility in its youthful listeners.

The series was a sustaining feature of the Mutual network and aired only briefly during the fall of 1947.

MEL-O-ROL JAMBOREE
The zany duo of Tom Howard and George Shelton teamed to bring hilarity to radio on Mel-O-Rol Jamboree. The obscure show aired over the NBC network during the 1936-37 season. Vocalist Peg LaCentra provided a break in the slapstick comedy routines with a song or two.

JAMES MELTON
Tenor James Melton was born on January 2, 1904 in Moultrie, Georgia. He studied law at The University of Florida, but after his sophomore year he transferred to The University of Georgia and changed his curriculum to music. Later he also studied opera at Vanderbilt University.

Melton's rise up the ladder of the music world was slow, but deliberate. He broke into radio in 1927 with Sam Rothafel's Roxy Gang. He went on to become a member of The Revelers Quartet and as a solo performer appeared on radio, concert tours, and in several motion pictures. In December of 1942 he made his debut with The Metropolitan Opera Company. Traversing the spectrum from opera to popular music, Melton was one of the most sought after singers on radio. This fact is evident by his impressive list of airwave credits that included: The Atwater Kent Hour, The Jack Benny Show, The Bromo Seltzer Revue, Circus Night in Silvertown, The Chicago Theatre of the Air, The Ford Summer Hour, Gulf Headliners, Harvest of Stars, The Intimate Program, Music for America, Palmolive Beauty Box Theatre, The Raleigh Revue, The Salada Salon Orchestra, Saturday Night Party, The Sealtest Sunday Night Party, The Seiberling Singers. The Song Shop, The Rise Stevens Show, The Telephone Hour, The Texaco Star Theatre, The Voice of Firestone, Ward's Family Theatre. The White Flash Program, The Wrigley Revue, and Ziegfeld Follies of the Air.

On televison he was a regular on The Ford Festival. He semi-retired from performing in the early 1950s to spend more time with his family and to collect antique automobiles. James Melton died of pneumonia on April 21, 1961. He was fifty-seven years old.

THE MEN ABOUT TOWN TRIO

The vocal group known as The Men About Town Trio sang on several radio series during the 1930s and the early 1940s. Members of the trio were Phil Duey, Frank Luther, and Jack Parker. Later Harold "Scrappy" Lambert replaced Luther. The trio's credits on radio included Believe It or Not, The Kodak Hour, Manhattan Merry-Go-Round, The Mobiloil Concert, Rendezvous Musical, The Saturday Night Terraplane Party, and Three Bakers.

MEN AGAINST DEATH

See: The Federal Theatre Project

MEN AT SEA

Men at Sea was a wartime drama depicting the heroics of the U.S. Merchant Marine Service. The weekly half hour of action was presented under the auspices of The Office of War Information (OWI) and The War Shipping Administration (WSA). It was used a tool in the recruitment drive for The Merchant Marine.

From 1943 to 1945 Men at Sea was the perennial summer replacement for the vacationing Great Gildersleeve show. A varied cast of familiar radio voices dramatized the stories and Merle Kendrich directed the orchestra.

MEN BEHIND THE STARS

During the summer of 1939 a series called Men Behind the Stars occupied fifteen minutes of the CBS network's weekly air time. Professor H.C. Adamson and W.H. Barton delivered lectures on the science of astronomy.

MEN, MACHINES, AND VICTORY

On June 5, 1942 the NBC Blue network inaugurated an eight week series titled Men, Machines, and Victory. The weekly fifteen minute low budget program was dedicated to the prevention of industrial and home accidents.

The aim was to lessen lost productivity in the war effort by means of a mini-drama and a guest speaker. It was presented under the auspices of The National Safety Council.

MEN OF VISION

Life stories of aviation pioneers were chronicled on the Men of Vision series. It premiered on June 17, 1945 over the CBS network sponsored by The Bendix Aviation Corporation.

The weekly thirty minute dramatizations featured a varied cast drawn from the pool of radio actors. News commentator Edwin C. Hill served as narrator, William Stoess directed the music, and Tony Marvin announced. Variety (June 20, 1945) was severely critical of the series and found nothing good to say about the production. Men of Vision filled out the summer and then flew off into the sunset on September 9, 1945.

ADOLPHE MENJOU

Actor Adolphe Menjou was born in Pittsburgh, Pennsylvania on February 18, 1890. After completing his studies at Culver Military Academy and Cornell University he began an acting career. His performing was interrupted by military service during World War I.

The dapper dresser was well known for his debonair roles on the motion picture screen as early as 1916. Later Menjou expanded the scope of his career to include both the vaudeville and legitimate stage, radio, and television. On radio he was one of several to serve in the capacity of emcee on The Texaco Star Theatre, co-starred with his (third) wife Verree (Teasdale) on Meet the Menjous, introduced new talent on Hollywood Star Preview, and frequently appeared as a guest star on shows such as Academy Award Theatre and Lux Radio Theatre.

On television he often guested on late night talk shows and served as host on Favorite Story and Target.

Adolphe Menjou died of hepatitis on October 29, 1963. He was seventy-three years old.

HELEN MENKEN (Helen Meinken)

Actress Helen Menken was born on December 12, 1901 in New York City. She first appeared on stage at the age of five, and at twelve made her debut on Broadway and the vaudevile stage.

Although her principal fame came from the Broadway stage, Helen Menken was also heard on radio. She first turned to the medium of radio in 1937 due to facial paralysis. Her most memorable role on the airwaves was as Brenda Cummings on the serial drama Second Husband. Among her other radio credits were The Kate Smith Show, Stagedoor Canteen. Theatre Guild on the Air, and Women's Exchange.

In addition to performing, she served as both chairman and president of The American Theatre Wing. She also helped to organize The Stagedoor Canteen during World War II. Helen Menken suffered a fatal heart attack while attending a party at The Lamb's Club on March 27, 1966. She was sixty- four years old.

MENNEN SHAVE TIME

Mennen Shave Time was a transcribed five minute morning "filler" show. It was syndicated for distribution during the 1947-48 season.

The format consisted of a comic dialog on a variety of subjects between Lew Parker and a switchboard operator named Annie played by Ann Thomas.

Mennen Shaving Cream and Skin Bracer sponsored the humorous interlude.

JOHNNY MERCER

Songwriter and performer Johnny Mercer was born in Savannah. Georgia on November 18, 1909. Mercer aspired to be an actor, but achieved legendary status as a prolific lyricist.

As a tunesmith he penned words and some music for over a thousand songs, among them were Autumn Leaves; Blues in the Night; How Little We Know; Laura; Moon River; On the Atchison. Topeka, and the Santa Fe; and That Old Black Magic. In 1942 he joined Buddy DeSylva and Glenn Wallichs to found Capitol Records.

Eventually he worked his way into the performing spotlight as an actor and singer on stage, screen, radio, and television. On radio Mercer sang with Paul Whiteman's orchestra and with Benny Goodman's and Bob Crosby's bands during the time they were associated with The Camel Caravan. He was also the star of his own shows and appeared on Call For Music, The Kraft Music Hall, and Your Hit Parade.

Johnny Mercer died on June 25, 1976 at the age of sixty-six. He had undergone brain surgery for the removal of a benign brain tumor three months prior to his death.

JOHNNY MERCER SHOW(S)

During the summer of 1943 Johnny Mercer's Music Shop replaced the vacationing Bob Hope. The weekly thirty minutes of warm weather entertainment was broadcast over the NBC network sponsored by Pepsodent Tooth Paste. Joining Johnny on the musical frolic was Ella Mae Morse, The Pied Pipers. Jo Stafford, and Paul Weston's orchestra.

Mercer's Music Shop again returned to the NBC network's airwaves on June 12, 1944 with a Monday through Friday early evening fifteen minute show. It took over the time period formerly occupied by Fred Waring. Johnny reassembled the gang from his 1943 summer show and signed Wendell Niles on as the announcer. The Music Shop was closed on December 8, 1944 and was replaced by The Chesterfield Supper Club.

Starting on October 10, 1953 a new Johnny Mercer Show took over a full hour in the CBS Saturday evening schedule. The musical variety series also featured The Notables, The Paul Smith Trio, The Roger Wayne Chorale, and weekly guests. Johnny Jacobs was the announcer. The final broadcast aired in the spring of 1954.

MARY ANN MERCER
See: Aunt Jemima

THE MERCURY THEATRE (ON THE AIR)

Young producers Orson Welles and John Houseman organized The Mercury Players in 1937. They first performed on radio that year over the Mutual network with an adaptation of Les Miserables. However, since the company was formed as a theatre group, they appeared in several stage productions before returning to the airwaves as The Mercury Summer Theatre. Welles and Houseman premiered their warm weather series on July 11, 1938 over the CBS network. Come fall, it continued on the air as a sustaining program under the title of The Mercury Theatre on the Air. However it remained relatively obscure and earned poor ratings until the infamous Halloween eve broadcast in October of 1938. That fateful night Orson Welles became a household name when his radio adaptation of H.G. Wells War of the Worlds caused panic from coast-to-coast. Using the premise of interrupting a program of music for a bulletin reporting the landing of hostile Martians, millions of radio listeners believed the attack to be real. The aftermath of the broadcast created a climate for restricting radio drama from duping its audience. On December 9, 1938 Campbell Soups began sponsorship and promptly changed the title to The Campbell Playhouse, which is described further under that heading.

In addition to playing many roles himself, Welles amassed a cast of actors for his dramas who would later go on to become well-known names on stage, screen, radio, and television. Among the more familiar were Ray Collins, Joseph Cotton, George Couloris, Kenny Delmar, Alice Frost, Martin Gabel, Helen Hayes, John McIntire, Burgess Meredith, Agnes Moorehead, Edmund O'Brien, Vincent Price, Frank Readick, Elliott Reid, Everett Sloane, Karl Swenson, and Richard widmark. Music was under the direction of Lud Gluskin and Bernard Herrmann. The announcers were Ernest Chappell and Dan Seymour.

Campbell Soups and Welles came to a parting of the ways on March 31, 1940 and the series left the air.

Welles returned to the CBS airwaves in 1941 with a half hour Mercury Theatre format titled The Orson Welles Theatre which is described under that heading.

The Mercury Theatre ended as it began, as a summer series. It was on the air from June 7th to September 13th of 1946 as a replacement for Danny Kaye's show. The thirty minute program was sponsored by Pabst Blue Ribbon Beer and presented a less "heavy" form of drama for which the earlier series was well-known. Welles again headed the cast of players. The announcer was Ken Roberts.

A revival of The Mercury Theatre's War of the Worlds was aired over National Public Radio on October 30, 1988 with Jason Robards, Jr. filling the late Orson Welles' role.

BURGESS MEREDITH

Versatile actor Burgess Meredith played diverse roles on stage, screen, radio, and television.

He was born in Cleveland, Ohio on November 16, 1908. He attended Amherst College, was employed in the world of business, and went to sea before making his acting debut on stage in 1929.

On radio Meredith was the host of pursuit of Happiness; Roll Call; and We, the People. He was the narrator of The Free Company and briefly The Spirit of '42 and played the title role on Red Davis (the predecessor to Pepper Young's Family). He was also heard on American Music Hall, The Campbell Playhouse (Mercury Theatre), High Adventure, Lincoln Highway, Arch Oboler's Plays (Plays for Americans), Tales of Tomorrow, Theatre Guild on the Air, and We Care.

On television Meredith is probably most remembered for his role as the arch criminal Penguin on the Batman series. His other video credits included frequent guest star roles and regular roles on such shows as Gloria, Mr. Novak, and Search. He also hosted Those Amazing Animals and narrated the video version of The Big Story.

Burgess Meredith died from Alzheimer's disease and melanoma on September 9, 1997. He was eighty-eight years old.

JAY MEREDITH

Youthful radio and stage actress Jay Meredith was heard on a lengthy list of radio shows beginning in the late 1930s and continuing through the mid 1940s.

She played Marion Leighton on Amanda of Honeymoon Hill, Althea Dennis on The Brighter Day, Barbara Crayley on Mary Marlin, Jean Carter on The Mighty Show, Anna on Our Gal Sunday, and Rena Fletcher on Ellen Randolph. Other credits included By Kathleen Norris, Chaplain Jim. Just Plain Bill, The Life and Love of Dr. Susan, The Parker Family, Salute to Youth, Terry and the Pirates, This Life is Mine, and Don Winslow of the Navy. In addition, she co-narrated Melody Theatre with Bill Griffis and was cast in the lead role of Angela on the obscure series called Angel in the House.

JUNE MEREDITH

Actress June Meredith was born on June 8, 1908 in Chicago, Illinois. She attended dramatic school in Chicago and then migrated to New York. There she launched her acting career on the stage. In 1930, when the depression caused a severe decline in theatre attendance, she turned to radio.

On the airwaves she played Dorothy Wallace Webb on Attorney-at-Law, Eve Underwood on Mary Marlin, and Edith Wood on Stepmother. Other credits included: First Nighter, Kitty Keene, and Talkie Picture Time.

UNA MERKEL

Actress Una Merkel was born in Covington, Kentucky on December 10, 1903.

Although she had been applauded by motion picture and theatre audiences dating back to 1920, she would later perform on a limited number of radio and television broadcasts.

On radio Una Merkel played Leila Fairchild's cousin Adeline on The Great Gildersleeve and was a regular on The Texaco Star Theatre. She was also cast in the title role on Nancy Baker Reporting, a newspaper oriented mini-drama included in the Johnny Presents series.

On television she was a frequent guest star on such dramatic productions as Climax, The Kraft Television Theatre, Play-house 90, and Studio One. Una Merkel died at the age of eighty-two on January 2, 1986.

ETHEL MERMAN (Ethel Zimmerman)

Singer and actress Ethel Merman was born on January 16, 1909 in Astoria, New York.

She began singing in amateur shows and worked as a secretary while trying to establish herself as a professional singer in nightclubs. She made her Broadway debut in 1930 and went on to become a legend on the musical theatre stage. A singing "machine," her trademark was a singing voice that could be heard in the back row without the benefit of a microphone! Some of her memorable stage triumphs included Annie Get Your Gun, Anything Goes, Call Me Madam, Girl Crazy, and Gypsy. she also performed on the motion picture screen, radio, and television.

On radio Ethel Merman was the star of her own shows and was a guest or semi-regular on such shows as The Andrews Sisters, The Big Show, Keep 'em Rolling, The Kraft Music Hall, and Stairway to the Stars. She appeared as a guest on numerous musical and variety television programs.

Ethel Merman underwent surgery to remove a brain tumor in April of 1983. She died in her sleep on February 15, 1984 at the age of seventy-five.

ETHEL MERMAN SHOW (S)

Unlike her legendary successes on the musical stage, Ethel Merman's two attempts at a radio show of her own were dismal failures.

The first series, titled Rhythm at Eight, was a 1935 summer replacement for Eddie Cantor. The Show premiered over the CBS network on May 5, 1935 sponsored by Lehn and Fink's Lysol Disinfectant. Merman's featured song of the evening was woven into a weak vignette performed by a small unnamed dramatic cast. Also joining Ethel on her show was emcee Ted Husing, The orchestras of Al Goodman and Kenn Sisson, The Ritz Quartet, and announcer Art Millet. After thirteen weeks Merman and Husing departed the show leaving Goodman's orchestra and the quartet to fill out the balance of Cantor's hiatus.

It was not until 1949 that Merman made her return to the air-waves. The new Ethel Merman show made its debut over the NBC network on July 31, 1949. The half hour situation comedy was built around a feeble story line about show business people.

Ethel Merman was heard as herself, Leon Janney was a piano player named Eddie McCoy, and Allen Drake played Homer Tubbs. The latter character, known as a "floor mop tycoon," was a prospective candidate to bankroll her stage play. Others in the cast were Ethel Browning, Arthur Q. Bryan, Pert Kelton, Joe Marks, Santos Ortega, and Charles Webster. The orchestra was led by Johnny Green and Milton Katims. The announcer was Ed Herlihy.

Like its predecessor, the critics branded this show a flop. Ethel Merman abandoned her place in NBC's schedule when The American Album of Familiar Music returned in the fall. However, the network still owed Merman five more broadcasts on her contract. She was shuttled from Sunday, to Saturday, and finally to Monday before the show folded after the net- work fulfilled the terms of her contract.

GARY MERRILL

Actor Gary Merrill was born on August 2, 1915 in Hartford, Connecticut. He was educated at Loomis Prep School) Bowdoin College, and Trinity College.

Although best remembered as a character actor on the motion picture screen, he began his acting career on the stage in 1937 and not until 1944 (while still on active duty with the Army) did he appear in the first of his many films. Merrill spent less time performing in other mediums, but was not a stranger to radio and television audiences.

On radio he played the title role on Dr. Standish, Medical Examiner; Miles Nelson on The Right to Happiness: Stanley on The Second Mrs. Burton; and Batman on Superman. He was also heard on The March of Time and My True Story.

On television he narrated Winston Churchill-The Valiant Years and was in the cast of Justice, The Mask, The Reporter, and the video version of Young Dr. Malone. Merrill married actress Barbara Leeds in 1941, which ended in divorce. He married superstar Bette Davis in 1950, a union that was dissolved in 1960.

Gary Merrill died of cancer on March 5, 1990 at the age of seventy-four.

HOWARD MERRILL

Youthful actor Howard Merrill was born in New York City c. 1918. The busy lad appeared in several motion pictures and on the Broadway stage before making his radio debut in 1929. His airwave credits included roles on Death Valley Days, The Goldbergs, Hello Peggy, The Lady Next Door, The March of Time, Mountainville True Life Sketches, Mrs. Wiggs of the Cabbage Patch, Penrod, Second Husband, Soconyland Sketches, Way Down East, and Your Unseen Friend.

Also. while still young, Merrill wrote for The New York Times and published the magazine Cross-Town.

Reaching adulthood, he abandoned radio acting in favor of writing. He penned scripts for such radio shows as Archie Andrews, Leave it to Mike, and Sherlock Holmes. In the medium of television Merrill wrote for F. Troop, The Love Boat, and Mrs. G. Goes to College.

JOAN MERRILL

Singer Joan Merrill toured the nighclub circuit, recorded on the Bluebird label, performed on the Broadway stage, appeared in several motion pictures, was heard on radio, and seen on television.

On radio she was a regular for one season on The Edgar Bergen and Charlie McCarthy Show, was heard on The Jack Pearl Show, and was a frequent guest on other programs. On television she was often seen on The Ed Sullivan Show.

Joan Merrill died from Alzheimer's disease on May 10, 1992. She was seventy-four years old.

LOUIS MERRILL

Actor Louis Merrill was born on April 1, 1912 in Montreal, Canada. The rotund, deep voiced Merrill specialized in playing "heavy" roles on both the motion picture screen and the radio airwaves.

On radio he was heard as Santa Claus on the Cinnamon Bear mini-series, narrator Thomas Nyland on Crime Classics, Captain Craig McKenzie on Latitude Zero, Jug Genie on Ed McConnell's Buster Brown Gang, Aaron Saul on Point Sublime, and Ed Neely on Those We Love. Additional credits included Big Town, Dan Carson, Good News of 1938, Hollywood, Hotel, Hollywood Playhouse, Al Jolson's Lifebuoy Show, Lights Out, The Lux Radio Theatre, On Stage, Parties at Pickfair, Joe Penner, Retribution, Irene Rich Dramas, Rogue's Gallery, That's Finnegan, Theatre of Famous Radio Players, and The Rudy Vallee Show.

Louis Merrill died on April 7, 1963 at the age of fifty-one.

ROBERT MERRILL

Baritone vocalist Robert Merrill was born on June 4, 1919 in Brooklyn, New York. His youthful ambition to become an opera singer led him away from his father's shoe business. However, he was unable to afford an expensive formal education in music. As a result, he honed his singing skills playing the summer resort hotels. From there he graduated to radio and eventually reached his goal when he made his debut with the Metropolitan Opera on December 15, 1945.

On radio he was a winning contestant on Major Bowes Original Amateur Hour and Metropolitan Auditions of the Air. With this encouragement under his belt he continued on the airwaves with his own show, as the host of Rest of All, and was both the singing star and emcee on Encore. He was also heard on The Chicago Theatre of the Air, An Evening With Romberg, Metropolitan

Opera on the Air, Music America Loves Best, The Music of Andre Kostelanetz, The RCA Victor Show, Serenade to America, and The Woolworth Hour.

In addition to opera and radio he was frequently seen as a guest star on television, toured the concert circuit, recorded on the RCA Victor label, appeared in one motion picture, often sang the National Anthem at sporting events, and authored two autobiographies under the titles Once More From The Beginning and Between Acts.

THE ROBERT MERRILL SHOW

On December 2, 1945 The Robert Merrill Show premiered with a sustaining program of music broadcast over the NBC network, occupying thirty minutes in the Sunday noontime schedule. Despite being billed as The Robert Merrill Show, he was limited to performing only his vocal renditions. Ed Herlihy actually hosted the show and NBC staffer Robert Denton was the announcer. Music was conducted by Frank Black and H. Leopold Spitalny.

The final broadcast of The Robert Merrill Show was heard in March of 1946.

(THE ADVENTURES OF) FRANK MERRIWELL

Frank Merriwell was a character created in 1890 by author Gilbert Patton under the nom de plume Burt L. Standish. The radio adaption of Standish's story of a turn of the century schoolboy was first broadcast over the NBC network in 1933. It was sponsored by Dr. West's Toothpaste.

Merriwell, a student athlete at Fardale Military Academy, was the forerunner of the Jack Armstrong and the lesser known Dick Cole juvenile serial formats. This initial series, which featured an unnamed cast and announcer Harlow Wilcox was on the air for less than a complete season.

The "new" Adventures of Frank Merriwell returned to NBC's network on October 5, 1946 as a weekly half hour series. The story line was essentially the same, but more characters were added, and the setting was advanced in time to where we find Frank now a student at Yale University.

The title role was played by Lawson Zerbe, Inza Burrage by Elaine Rost, Bart Hodge by Hal Studer, and Elsie Bellwood by Patricia Hosley. Others in the cast were Brad Barker, Jean Gillespie, Al Hodge, Lamont Johnson, and Grace Keddy. Mel Brandt announced, Paul Traubman directed the music, and John Winters was at the organ console.

In the fall of 1948 penners of the script caved-in to those who opposed criminals and violence associated with college life. Such a toned down version spelled doom for Frank and the series. It left the air in March of 1949.

THE MERRY LIFE OF MARY CHRISTMAS

A summer series titled The Merry Life of Mary Christmas occupied a weekly half hour in the CBS network's 1945 warm weather schedule.

The unlikely Christmas in July situation comedy revolved around a Hollywood gossip columnist named Mary Christmas.

Her husband, who hated actors, provided a comedic roadblock to Mary's career. Film star Mary Astor played the title role with support from Wally Maher and Paul Marion. Music was under the direction of Ivan Ditmars and the announcer was Frank Martin.

The show was on the air from July 2nd until September 3rd.

THE MERRY MACS

The McMichael brothers Joe, Judd (George E.), and Ted vocalized as The Merry Macs. They began singing together as youngsters and in 1929 made their radio debut over station WCCO in Minneapolis, Minnesota as The Mystery Trio. Shortly thereafter they went on tour with bandleader Joe Haymes as The Personality Trio. Settling down to perform as The Merry Macs, they were featured on their own radio show during the 1933-34 season. The fifteen minute Monday through Saturday songfest was a sustaining series aired over the NBC Blue network. In 1937 the boys decided they needed a female voice added to the group. Among those who filled that need was Helen Carroll (Helen Marie Faulk), Mary Lou Cook, Marjorie Garland, Imogene Lynn, Cherry Mackay, and Virginia Rees. The Merry Macs continued their radio performances on such shows as Fred Allen's Town Hall Tonight, The Breakfast Club, Climalene Carnival, For Men Only (George Jessel's Celebrity Program), Benny Goodman's Swing School, Al Jolson's Lifebuoy Program, The Old Gold Show, Al Pearce and His Gang (Watch the Fun Go By), The Philco Summer Hour, (Maxwell House) Show Boat, Town Hall Varieties, Tuesday Night Party, and Your Hit Parade.

Joe McMichael was killed in 1944 while serving in the military. His place was taken by Lynn Allen. Jimmy Garland also sang with the post-war group. The Merry Macs continued to perform on radio and in motion pictures into the 1950s.

MESSAGE OF ISRAEL

Produced under the auspices of The United Jewish Laymen's Committee, Message of Israel was first broadcast in 1934 over the NBC Blue network.

The series was founded by Rabbi Dr. Jonah B. Wise, a pioneer in Jewish religious broadcasting. Rabbi Wise and guest rabbi speakers brought a weekly message to radio audiences for more than a quarter century.

Rabbi Wise made his last appearance on the program in 1959, just three weeks before he died.

METROPOLITAN HEALTH TOWER

See: Tower Health Exercises

METROPOLITAN OPERA AUDITIONS OF THE AIR

An operatic talent search was the format for Metropolitan Opera Auditions of the Air. Young singers on the threshold of stardom competed before a coast-to-coast radio audience for their big chance. Winners were awarded contracts with the opera company.

The series premiered on December 22, 1935 over the NBC Red network sponsored by Sherman-Williams (Kem-Tone) Paint. In the fall of 1937 the program was moved from NBC's Red to their Blue network.

Edward Johnson, general manager of The Metropolitan Opera Company, served as emcee. Wilfrid Pelletier conducted the orchestra and Milton Cross announced. Some of the future stars that appeared on the show included Walter Cassel, Robert Merrill, Patrice Munsel, and Rise Stevens. On November 27, 1944 the program's title was changed to The Metropolitan Opera Presents. With the new name came a new format. It limited only one newcomer on each show, sharing the spotlight with an established soloist. The altered format failed to catch on with listeners and the series left the air on April 1, 1945.

It returned on January 4, 1948 with its original title and format over the ABC network. The Farnsworth Company, makers of radio and televison sets, sponsored the revival.

Farnsworth cancelled sponsorship the following year, but again Metropolitan Opera Auditions of the Air bounced back in the fall of 1950 as a sustainer.

The series finally left the air in 1956.

METROPOLITAN OPERA ON THE AIR

If there is a record for tenure of a radio series, it must belong to the Metropolitan Opera of the Air broadcasts. Saturday afternoon performances, originating directly from the Metropolitan stage, began on Christmas day of 1931.

They were initially heard over the NBC Red network, but after one season the program was moved to NBC's Blue network. The Radio Corporation of America was the sponsor until 1940 when Texaco began their long association in that capacity.

The opera company itself was the star of the show; however, Milton J. Cross' name became synonymous with the broadcasts as its knowledgable host. During intermissions Olin Downes conducted The Opera Quiz, Boris Goldovsky presided over Opera News and Roundtable, and Lisa Sergio added her commentary. In 1940 a late-night Metropolitan Opera sampler was aired weekly under the title Remember the Met. Its aim was to enlist funds to pay-off the Opera House mortgage. Although those who were associated with the broadcasts during the "golden age of radio" are gone, the Metropolitan Opera still occupies a place on radio dials into the 1990s.

METROPOLITAN OPERA PRESENTS

See: Metropolitan Opera Auditions of the Air

STUART METZ

Announcer Stuart Metz was born on March 20, 1908 in Buffalo, New York. Metz entered the field of broadcasting in 1929 as an engineer, but switched to announcing in 1931. Among the programs with which he was associated were

The 1937 Jello Summer Show; Light of the World; The Betty Moore Triangle Club; Mr. Keen, Tracer of Lost Persons; Orphans of Divorce; Road of Life; Waltz Time; you Are There; and Pepper Young's Family. He was also one of several to serve as the narrator for Grand Central Station.

MEYER THE BUYER

Ethnic Jewish humor was the format for Meyer the Buyer. The comedy series, adapted from Harry Hershfield's comic strip, aired over the CBS network in 1932. The title role was played by Harry Hersfield himself, with support from Teddy Bergman as Mayor Mizznick, Paul Douglas as Lawyer Feldman, and Adele Ronson as Irma Mizznick. Others in the cast were Geoffrey Bryant, Dot Harrington, Ethel Holt, and Ruth Yorke.

MGM SCREEN TEST

See: Screen Test

MGM THEATRE OF THE AIR

The MGM Theatre of the Air was a program of transcribed hour long radio adaptations of MGM motion pictures. It premiered over New York's station WMGM on October 14, 1949. The series was also syndicated for distribution to other stations by Metro-Goldwyn-Mayer Radio Attractions and was aired over the Mutual network during the 1951-52 season.

MGM's vice president and publicity director Howard Dietz served as emcee, music was provided by WMGM staffer Joel Herron, and a varied dramatic cast was drawn from a pool of radio actors.

MICHAEL AND KITTY

The all too familiar scenario of a husband and wife amateur sleuth team was the basis for the Michael and Kitty series. The weekly half hour mystery drama first took to the airwaves over the NBC Blue network on October 10, 1941. Its sponsor was Canada Dry's soft drink called Spur.

The story line was supposed to be on the light and humorous side; however, there was more than an ample amount of stark terror and heinous murders included.

John Gibson was heard as Michael Piper, and Elizabeth Reller as his wife Kitty.

By year's end the series dumped the spouse and scripted Michael carrying on his amateur detecting alone. The show was renamed simply Michael Piper, but endured only a few weeks.

JAY MICHAEL

Radio actor Jay Michael was born on September 30, 1908 in New York City.
Michael's radio career was spent at Detroit's station WXYZ, but because of several network originations from that facility his voice became recognized na-

tionwide.

He was the first to play Sergeant Preston on Challenge of the Yukon when the series was still heard only locally in the Detroit area. In 1955, when the Yukon adventures began packaging old episodes for rebroadcast, Jay Michael was the narrator. He was also heard in the cast of The Green Hornet and The Lone Ranger. His voice is probably best remembered as that of the evil Butch Cavendish on the latter series.

MARY MICHAEL

Colorado born actress Mary Michael played supporting roles on stage, radio, and television.

On radio she played Ma Fogarty on Big Sister and Mrs. Kelly on Stepmother. She was also in the cast of Aunt Jenny, Bright Horizon, By Kathleen Norris, The CBS Radio Workshop, Stella Dallas, The Goldbergs, Great Plays, Hilltop House, The Lux Radio Theatre, My True story, The New Penny, Pretty Kitty Kelly, and When a Girl Marries.

On television she played Birdie Bodkin on the 1953 summer series titled Wonderful John Action. She was also in the cast of the 1955 comedy special The Women.

Mary Michael died on November 6, 1980. Her age was purported to be seventy-seven.

ELDER SOLOMON LIGHTFOOT MICHAUX

Evangelist and political activist Elder Solomon Light foot Michaux was born on November 7, 1883 in Newport News, Virginia. Labeled "The happy am I" preacher, his charismatic style rallied thousands to his tent meetings and reached many more thousands over the radio airwaves. The exuberant black preacher, a former shellfish peddler, attracted both blacks and whites to share in his hand clapping, foot stomping meetings during the 1930s and 1940s, There he loudly and proudly proclaimed his unabashed humanistic and prosperity-minded beliefs. He also enjoyed the mutual admiration of Presidents Roosevelt, Truman, and Eisenhower.

On radio a program called Elder Michaux and His Congregation was broadcast over the CBS network beginning in 1933 on a series titled The Radio Church of God. The announcer was Rober Trout.

He switched to the Mutual network on May 17, 1937 and renamed his program The Shepherd of the Air. He was also heard on local radio in Washington D.C. where he pastored The Church of God and founded seven other churches.

On television he continued his ministry over the Dumont network from 1947 to 1949.

Elder Solomon Lightfoot Michaux died on October 20, 1968 from a stroke he suffered on August 26th. He was eighty-four years old.

THE MICHELIN HOUR

A program of music and song occupied the NBC Blue network on The Michelin Hour (more accurately half hour). The weekly thirty minute show was broadcast during the 1928-29 season sponsored by the manufacturers and distributors of Michelin Tires.

The vocalists were soprano Louise Bave, baritones Taylor Buckley and Irving Kaufman, and tenor Howard Phillips. The orchestra was directed by Louis Katzman.

THE MICKEY MOUSE THEATRE OF THE AIR

Walt Disney's famous cartoon rodent took to the radio air-waves on January 2, 1938 on The Mickey Mouse Theatre of the Air. The short-lived series was sponsored by Pepsodent Tooth Paste and was heard as a weekly half hour show over the NBC Red network.

Disney himself played the Mickey Mouse role. Others in the cast were Thelma Broadman as Minnie Mouse, Stuart Buchanan as Goofy, Florence Gill as Clarabelle Cow, and Clarence Nash as Donald Duck. Felix Mills directed the music which included Donald Duck's Swing Band and The Minnie Mouse Woodland Choir. Bud Hiestand was the announcer.

The final curtain call for Mickey and his friends took place on May 15, 1938.

MICKEY OF THE CIRCUS

The circus was a popular setting for radio shows during the 1930s. One such adventure drama was Mickey or the Circus. The half hour transcribed program was distributed c. 1935.

Mickey was played by Chester Stratton, Clara Gaines by Gretchen Davidson, Mamie by Betty Garde, and Zephyr by Ray Collins.

MIDSTREAM

The daytime serial drama Midstream was first on the air in 1938 as a local series which aired from the studios of WLW in Cincinnati. It made its network debut on May 1, 1939 in the NBC Red network's morning schedule and was rebroadcast in the afternoon over NBC's Blue network. Later both morning and afternoon episodes were aired over the Red network. Procter and Gamble's Teel Liquid Dentifrice and Drene Shampoo sponsored the serial.

The story chronicled the mid-life crisis of Charles and Julia Meredith, described as "reaching the half way mark between the distant shores of birth and death."

Sidney Ellstrom, Hugh Studebaker, and Russell Thorson all were heard as Charles Meredith. Betty Lou Gerson and Fern Persons played Julia Meredith. The supporting cast included: Helen Behmiller, Bill Bouchey, Elia Braca, Willard Farnum, Laurette Fillbrandt, Josephine Gilbert, Glen Goodwin, Sharon Grainger, Jane Green, Annette Harper, Henry Hunter, Sylvia Jacobs, Bob Jellison, Lenore

Kingston, Nina Klowden, Elliott Lewis, Mercedes McCambridge, Marvin Miller, Pat Murphy, Connie Osgood, Olan Soule, and Leslie Woods. Henry Larson was the organist and the announcers were Gene Baker and Dick Wells. The final episode of Midstream aired on November 27, 1941.

MIDWEEK HYMN SING

Midweek Hymn Sing was a long running program of early evening gospel music. From 1926 to 1936 the fifteen minute series bounced between Tuesday and Thursday in the NBC Red network's schedule. The host of the program was Dr. Arthur Billings Hunt who led a group of singers that included: Joyce Allmand, Clyde Dengler, Helen Jenke, Richard Maxwell, Kathryn Palmer, Sidney Smith, and Muriel Wilson. The organists were Lowell Patton and George Vause. The announcer was Marley R. Sherris. Dr. Hunt was the director of The National Hymn Sing Association and pioneered the airing of religious music as far back as 1923. He also conducted The Shut-in Hour in the New York City area over station WNEW.

Dr. Arthur Billings Hunt died on August 10, 1971 at the age of eighty-one.

THE MIGHTY SHOW

Life under the circus big top was the story line of the Monday through Friday serial drama called The Mighty Show. The show was designed to appeal to both adult and juvenile audiences.

The first of the fifteen minute episodes aired over the CBS network on September 12, 1938. The show (aka The My-T-Fine Circus) was sponsored by Penick and Ford, makers of My-T-Fine Desserts.

Ma Hutchinson was played by Agnes Moorehead; Jean Carter by Jay Meredith; Sally, the trapeze performer, by Helen Lewis; Tex by Artells Dixon; Ruth, the knife thrower, by Anne Boley; and the circus sounds by animal imitator Brad Barker. The large supporting cast included: Jim Boles, Kingsley Colton, Don Costello, Ken Daigheau, Harold DeBecker, Maurice Franklin, Sarah Fussell, Peter Kappel, Ed Latimer. Fred Irving Lewis, Robert Lynn, Jerry Macy, Craig McDonnell, John Milton, James Monks, Arnold Moss, Jack Orrison, William Pringle, Frank Readick, Elliott Reid, Stefan Schnabel, Paul Stewart, and Karl Swenson. Ted Jewett announced and Fred Feibel played the circus organ.

The Mighty Show's mythical circus train chugged off the air on April 28, 1939.

THE MILKMAN'S MATINEE

In 1935 New York's station WNEW was a pioneer in all night broadcasting. To fill the wee hours between two and seven in the morning a program of recorded music and chatter known as The Milkman's Matinee was born. When it made its debut on August 6, 1935 it became an instant companion to night owls, the insomniac, and those working the "graveyard shift." Although it was a local show, it was well known and copied nationwide.

Stan Show presided over the rattling milk bottles with assistance from switchboard operator Millie Enright, John Flora, and Jack Lescoulie. In 1942 Show turned the reigns of the show over to Lescoulie. Shortly thereafter Art Ford took over when Lescoulie entered military service. Ford held sway with the Matinee until 1954.

RAY MILLAND (Reginald Truscott- Jones)

Film star Ray Milland was born on January 3, 1905 in Neath, Wales. He attended The University of Wales, served as a Royal Guardsman, and then decided to pursue an acting career. He made his motion picture debut in 1929 and the following year migrated from his native Wales to Hollywood's film capitol. His subsequent fame was achieved in scores of motion pictures. He is especially remembered for his Academy Award winning role in The Lost Weekend. Milland also performed on stage, radio, and television, produced and directed shows on television, and authored his autobiography Wide-Eyed in Babylon.

On radio he played the title role on the Meet Mr. McNulty series. He was also heard as a guest star on such shows as The Family Theatre, Hollywood Star Preview, The Lux Radio Theatre, Prudential's Family Hour, and Suspense. On television he recreated his radio role of Mr. McNulty on The Ray Milland Show. He was also seen on The DuPont Show of the Month, The General Electric Theatre, The Love Boat, the video version of Suspense, Suspicion, and many more.

Ray Milland died of cancer on March 10, 1986 at the age of eighty-one.

LEE MILLAR

Actor and animal impersonator Lee Millar was born in Oakland, California on February 20, 1888.

His diverse career encompassed both human and animal sounds on stage, screen, and radio. For example, he was heard as the voice of Walt Disney's cartoon character Pluto on the motion picture screen. On radio he played the austere judge on Big Town and provided the bark of Rags, the dog on Those We Love. Lee Millar died of a heart attack at the age of fifty-three on December 24, 1941. He was survived by his widow, actress Verna Felton.

BEATRICE MILLER

Actress Beatrice Miller was heard in supporting roles on radio during a period extending from the late 1930s through the early 1940s. She also appeared in several Broadway plays. Her airwaves credits included: By Kathleen Norris, Stella Dallas, Lincoln Highway, The Lux Radio Theatre, Myrt end Marge, Orphans of Divorce, The Parker Family, Radio Guild, Society Girl, and Valiant Lady.

GLENN MILLER (Alton Glenn Miller)

Bandleader and trombonist Glenn Miller was born in Clarinda, Iowa on March 1, 1904. He made an attempt to gain a college education at The University of Colorado, but the lure of music led him away from the halls of learning and into the dance halls. He played with such bands as Jimmy and Tommy Dorsey, Benny Goodman, Vincent Lopez, Red Nichols, Ray Noble, Ben Pollack, Freddie Rich, and Boyd Senter. However, Miller was not content to play for other bandleaders. His ambition was to create a unique style and lead his own dance band. The first Glenn Miller band formed in 1937 ended in failure, but the determined Miller tried again in 1938. This time he met with success and the Glenn Miller sound was destined to make his band one of the most popular of all time. Miller played the nation's ballrooms and hotels, recorded mostly on the Bluebird and RCA Victor labels, appeared in two motion pictures, and his music permeated the radio airwaves. On radio the Miller sound was frequently heard on the big band remote broadcasts and on several shows aired under the title The Glenn Miller Orchestra. Glenn Miller also provided music for such other shows as The Chesterfield Supper Club, The Fitch Bandwagon, I Sustain the Wings, The Magic Key of RCA, The Million Dollar Band, The Kate Smith Show, and Sunset Serenade.

In 1942 Miller traded his tuxedo for the uniform of an Army Air Force Captain. His assignment was to lead the Army Air Force Band, which he later turned into a morale building dance band. Many of his civilian band members followed him into the service to play with the band. Miller was later rewarded for his innovative approach to popularize military music with a promotion to the rank of major.

On December 15, 1944 Major Miller embarked on a flight from England to France and was never seen again; he was declared dead on December 18, 1944. No trace of Miller's body or the plane was ever found. Despite what seemed to be a lengthy musical career, Glenn Miller was only forty years old at the time of his death. As a testimony to his musical talent, his unmistakable arrangements endure today. Miller's widow Helen, who he married in 1928, died in 1966 at the age of sixty-four.

IRVING MILLER

Musician Irving Miller was born on September 2, 1907 in New York City. After studying music both privately and at Columbia University he launched his career as a composer, conductor, arranger, and pianist.

Miller played piano with symphony orchestras, composed several songs and scores for motion pictures, conducted orchestras on radio, and arranged music for television. Irving Miller was first associated with radio in 1928 when he joined the staff of the NBC network. He subsequently waved his baton to provide music for such radio programs as The Mel Blanc Show, Everything Goes, Finders Keepers, Fun With the Revuers, The Bob Hawk Show, The Jack Kirkwood Show, Meet Millie, Mirth and Madness, The Garry Moore Show, Pleasure Parade, Allen Prescott, Saturday Showwdown, Streamlined Journal, and Sweeney and March.

JACK MILLER (John J. Miller)

Orchestra leader Jack Miller was born on September 4, 1899 in Dorchester, Massachusetts. During Miller's career as an orchestra leader, much of his time was spent on the radio airwaves. He is probably best recalled for his long association with Kate Smith. While others provided music for Miss Smith, Jack Miller was her principal conductor on radio and other mediums. Other radio shows on which Miller conducted included: The Aldrich Family, (Molle) Mystery Theatre, Radio Reader's Digest, Tales of Fatima, and Who-Dun-It?.

On television he followed Kate Smith into the video era on her 1951-52 Evening Hour show.

Jack Miller died on March 18, 1985 at the age of eighty-five.

MARVIN MILLER (Marvin Mueller)

One of the moat familiar voices on radio belonged to actor and announcer Marvin Miller. He was born on July 18, 1913 in St. Louis, Missouri. He received his education at Washington University and then began his busy career in 1931 as an announcer at his hometown station KWK. The following year he moved across town to KMOX. In 1939, after marrying writer Elizabeth Dawson, the newlyweds left for Chicago. There Miller (still known as Mueller until the stigma of a German name during World War II led him to change it to Miller) took to the airwaves as an announcer and soon afterward appeared as an actor in the first of scores of radio shows. In 1944 Hollywood beckoned the Millers and upon arriving on the West Coast, he continued his prolific work on radio. In his "spare time" Miller was active in civic, fraternal, and professional organizations.

As a radio actor he played Anthony Marleybone, Sr. on The Affairs of Anthony; Hands Bannister and Arturo Valdi on Scattergood Baines; Colonel Fitts and Banker Gutherie (and also announced) on The Billie Burke Show; Captain Einman Rogart on Captain Midnight; Sergeant Mike Monihan on Dear Mom; one of several Mr. First Nighters on The first Nighter Program; Gloomy, Moe Hoffman, and Lorson Snells on Great Gunns; Ellis Smith on The Guiding Light; Dr. Bishop on Judy and Jane; Howard Andrews on Midstream; Captain Amhurst, Rodney Brooks, Edward de Manfield, and Fritz Sterner on Mary Noble, Backstage Wife; Consider Martin, Reverend McArthur, and Roderick Stone on One Man's Family; Jack, the crackpot on Play Broadcast; Mark Brandon on Press Club; the title role on Peter Quill; Inspector Ben Lyon (and also announced) on Jeff Regan; voice of the past on The Right to Happiness: Ted Fenton on Road of Life; Gil Whitney on The Romance of Helen Trent; Reginald Brooks on Stepmother; Breezy Jenks and Pop Jenks on Harold Teen, voice of the past on Today's Children; one of several in the title role of The Whistler (and also announced); and Dr. Lee Markham on Woman in White. Miller's other radio credits as an actor included Jack Armstrong; Burns and Allen; Chicago Theatre of the Air (also announced); Cousin Willie; Escape; Family Skeleton; Family Theatre; Phil Harris/Alice Faye Show; I Was a Communist for the FBI; Knickerbocker Playhouse; Lassie; Life With Luigi; The Abe Lincoln Story; Lonely Women (also announced); The Lux Radio Theatre; Maisie; Fibber McGee and Molly; Me and Janie; Mr. District Attorney; My Friend Irma; My Little Margie; The National Barn Dance; Ozzie and Harriet; Ellen Randolph; Roy Rogers' Show; Smilin' Ed McConnell's Busier Brown Gang; Theatre of Famous Radio Players; The Danny Thomas Show; Uncle Walter's Dog House; and Yours Truly, Johnny Dollar. As an announcer Miller was associated with The Don Ameche Show; (The Bickerson's Old Gold Show); The Andrews Sisters; Aunt Mary; Beat the Band; Beulah; The Borden Program; The Billie Burke Show (also in the cast); Chicago Theatre of the Air (also in the cast); The Cisco Kid; A Date With Judy; Dreft Star Playhouse; Duffy's Tavern; Father Knows Best; The Gay Mrs. Featherstone; Lonely Women (also in the cast); Ma Perkins (using the name Charlie Warren); Martin and Lewis; Louella Parsons; Poly Follies; The Quiz Kids; The Railroad Hour; Jeff Regan, Investigator (also in the cast); Irene Rich Dramas; Red Skelton; Songs by Sinatra; The Jo Stafford Show; Stars Over Hollywood; Strange Wills (also in the cast); That Brewster Boy; This is Life; The Rudy Vallee Show The whistler (also was one of several to play title role); Wings of Destiny; Woman From Nowhere; and delivered countless commercials. Miller was also the narrator on Armchair Adventures; Behind the Story; The Coronet Storyteller; Home Edition; Marvin Miller, Storyteller; Moon Dreams; Tell It Again; and Treet Time. He was the emcee of Name the Movie and Stop That Villain.

Despite his unmatched volume of work on radio, Miller is best remembered for his television portrayal of Michael Anthony, the deliverer of million dollar checks from philanthropist John Beresford Tipton on The Millionaire. His other video credits included: Batman, Jack Benny, Burns and Allen, Fantastic Voyage, The Lone Ranger, The Lone Wolf, Mr. Magoo, and Mysteries of Chinatown.

Marvin Miller died of a heart attack on February 8, 1985 at the age of seventy-one.

MARVIN MILLER, STORYTELLER

Actor, announcer, and narrator Marvin Miller presided over two radio storytelling series.

The first Marvin Miller, Storyteller (aka Prelude to Great- ness) was a syndicated five minute "filler" program. It was distributed on transcriptions during the 1948-49 season. Miller not only told the story, but assumed all the voices in a mini-dramatization of men's lives in crisis. In 1958 the series was revived, airing over the CBS network. The scripts from Miller's earlier fifteen minute Behind the Story programs were rewritten and used again. Marvin Miller and his wife, Elizabeth Dawson, penned the scripts.

ART MILLET

Announcer Art Millet was born in Chicago, Illinois in 1909. After completing his education at Tulane University, he made his announcing debut in 1932 at station WRR in Dallas. Shortly thereafter he returned to his hometown of Chicago where he was associated with station WGN and the CBS network. In 1937 Millet became a free lance announcer. Numbered among his numerous network announcing assignments were such programs as The American Album of Familiar Music, Bobby Benson, Eddie Dooley's Sports Broadcast, Famous Jury Trials, The Flying Red Horse Tavern, The Goldbergs, Hammerstein's Music Hall, The Lux Radio Theatre, Maudie's Diary, Ethel Merman's Rhythm at Eight, Mary and Bob's True Story Hour, The Nash Speed Show, Our Gal Sunday, The Packard Show, Popeye the Sailor, Quality Twins, Rich Man's Darling, Second Husband, Valiant Lady, end Waltz Time.

Art Millet died on April 9, 1943 at the age of thirty-four.

MILLIGAN AND MULLIGAN

Although broadcast locally in the Chicago area, the detective spoof titled Milligan and Mulligan is remembered by many. Perhaps it is because the program reached a considerable number of households in the regional area of the mid-west.

It was on the air five nights weekly with Don Ameche playing detective Milligan. Bob White co-starred as his side-kick Mulligan, and also wrote the scripts. According to Ameche, the Milligan and Mulligan series was on the air for only a brief time c.1932.

THE MILLION DOLLAR BAND

A composite band comprised of side men from the well known dance bands and a weekly guest bandleader occupied the NBC network's radio airwaves as The Million Dollar Band. Palmolive Soap began sponsorship of the musical half hour on May 29, 1943. Singer Barry Wood served as the permanent emcee/vocalist with assistance from The Double-Daters singing group.

The show's "gimmick" was to give away diamonds to five women who wrote the best misty-eyed letters requesting "their" song be played.

Although the critics gave the program a poor report, it remained on the air until March 25, 1944. It was replaced by a revamped format under the title The Palmolive Party which is described under that heading.

MILLIONS FOR DEFENSE

Even before the United States formally entered World War II, The U.S. Treasury Department was building a "war chest" through the sale of Defense Bonds.

On July 2, 1941 an "all-star" program that featured top names in the entertainment business, who appeared gratis, along with high level government officials took to the air over the CBS network. The announcers were Larry Elliott and Graham McNamee.

Titled Millions For Defense, the hour-long series replaced Fred Allen's show during the summer months to pitch the sale of the newly created bonds.when Allen returned to the air in October the series was renamed The Treasury Hour and moved to the NBC Blue network.

The new program remained on the air only few weeks and was cancelled after the Japanese attack on Pearl Harbor on December 7, 1941.

BILLY MILLS (William R. Mills)

Orchestra leader and pianist Billy Mills was born in Flint, Michigan on September 6,1894. He attended both Syracuse University and The University of Michigan. He then played piano accompaniment for silent films, served as a U.S, Army Bandmaster during World War I, and arranged music for several bands before organizing his own orchestra in 1922.

He began his association with the medium at radio in 1925 over his hometown station WFDF. In 1932 he joined the CBS network as an arranger and conductor. Later he became the network's musical supervisor in Chicago, and still later its general music director for the western division. Severing his exclusive ties to CBS, Mills proceeded to provide music for many radio shows. He is probably best remembered for his long tenure as the orchestra leader on The Fibber McGee and Molly Show. His other baton waving assignments on the airwaves included Attorney-at-Law, The Victor Borge Show, The Flying Red Horse Tavern, The Gold Medal Hour, Mortimer Gooch, Hap Hazard, Hires' Ice Box Follies, Myrt and Marge. Poetic Melodies, and Alec Templeton Time. He also conducted the orchestra for many local shows broadcast over WBBM in Chicago.

Billy Hills died of a heart ailment on October 20, 1971. He was seventy-seven years old.

THE MILLS BROTHERS

The smooth vocal harmony of The Mills Brothers entertained audiences for nearly six decades. They began singing together in 1925 as Four Boys and a Guitar. They would subsequently perform as The Mills Brothers on stage, record, radio, tele- vision, and in several motion pictures. The unique group not only excelled in their singing of close harmony, but often provided their own accompaniment by imitating the sounds of various musical instruments. On radio The Mills Brothers were heard on their own twice weekly fifteen minute show. It was broadcast over the CBS net- work from 1931 to 1933 sponsored by Vapex Cold Remedy. Later they performed on such other radio programs as The Elgin Campus Revue, Goodrich Silvertown Time, The Kraft Music Hall, and Philco Radio Time, They also made guest appearances on many radio and television shows.

The brothers were born in Piqua, Ohio; John in 1911, Herbert in 1912, Harry in 1913, and Donald in 1915. When John died in 1935 his place was taken by their father John, Sr. He retired in 1956 and died the following year.

The remaining brothers carried on as a trio until 1982 when Harry became ill with an abdominal tumor. He died on June 28, 1982 at the age of sixty-eight, Herbert died on April 12, 1989 at the age of seventy-seven, and Donald on November 13, 1999 at the age of eighty-four.

FELIX MILLS

Musical director and composer Felix Mills was born on July 28, 1901 in Fort Collins, Colorado.

Mills made his radio debut over Hollywood's station KHJ in 1928. He would later go on to conduct and/or compose music for such radio shows as The Aldrich Family, Burns and Allen, Charlie Chan, Chandu the Magician, Cinnamon Bear, A Date With Judy, The Gilmore Circus, Hap Hazard, Hollywood Playhouse, Hollywood Premiere, The Man Called X, Meet Corliss Archer, The Mickey Mouse Theatre of the Air, Results, Inc., Tommy Riggs and Betty Lou, Silver Theatre, Strange as it Seems, and Tarzan.

MARJORIE MILLS (Marjorie Meader Burns)

Columnist and radio personality Marjorie Mills was born in Waterville, Maine in 1892. She attended The Eric Pope Art School, Colby College, and The University of Kansas. Her ambition to become a journalist began at The Waterville Sentinel, but her goal was to write for The Boston Herald. She persevered and was finally hired as the first woman on the Herald's writing staff. She was the women's page editor there for many years.

On radio her pleasant, though croaking, voice endeared her to New England audiences over the regional Yankee network and Boston stations WBZ, WEEI, and WNAC. She brought her "down home" warmth and homemaking expertise to network radio during the 1930s over the Mutual network. One such series was titled The Girl From Maine sponsored by The Maine Development Commission. It was on the air from October 11, 1938 to January 5, 1939.

She remained active on local radio and television into the 1970s.

Marjorie Mills died on April 5, 1979 at the age of eighty-six.

VERLYE MILLS

Harpist Verlye Mills was born in St. John, Kansas on December 16, 1913. She studied her instrument at Curtis Institute and The Paris Conservatory. She was the featured harpist with The Chicago and Cleveland Symphony Orchestras and played at New York's Roxy Theatre and Radio City Music Hall for many years. She also performed on radio, television, records, and in motion pictures. On radio she plucked her harp strings on The Hour of Charm, Your Hit Parade, and as a guest on numerous music and variety shows.

Verlye Mills Brilhart died on October 2, 1983 at the age of seventy-one.

CHARLES MILTON

San Jose, California organist Charles Milton provided music for many obscure local radio series; however, his talents were utilized for a few network shows. They included: California Caravan, Dr. Christian, Meet Miss Sherlock, and Meet the Missus.

MILWAUKEE MUSICALE

See: Down By Herman's

MIND YOUR MANNERS

A juvenile panel program that discussed questions submitted concerning moppet manners was the format for Mind Your Manners. The series was first heard locally in the Hartford, Connecticut area in 1947 over station WTIC. Shortly there- after the program's listening audience was expanded when it became a NBC network sustaining series.

Allen Ludden was the moderator of the weekly thirty minutes of manners mania. The announcer was Ed Anderson. Mind Your Manners remained on the air until 1953.

JAN MINER (Janice Miner)

Character actress Jan Miner was born in Boston, Massachusetts on October 15, 1917.

Her acting career encompassed the mediums of stage, screen, radio, and television.

On radio she shared the role of Mary Wesley on Boston Blackie with actress Lesley Woods; was one of five to play Ann Williams on Casey, Crime Photographer, portrayed the title role on Linda Dale; was heard as Julie Erickson on the latter day series of Hilltop House episodes; took over the title role on Lora Lawton from Joan Tompkins; was one of three to play Della Street on Perry Mason; was one of several cast in the role of Margo on The Shadow; and was heard as Vera on That Hammer Guy. Her other radio credits included: The Big show (latter day version), Big Sister, Cavalcade of America, Cloak and Dagger, Dimension X, Doctor's Wife, Nora Drake, Great Plays, Ma Perkins, MGM Theatre, Philco Radio Playhouse. Radio City Playhouse, Road of Life, and Under Arrest.

On television she continued her role of Ann Williams on the video version of Crime Photographer. She was also seen on Cameo Theatre, The Edge of Night, Friends and Lovers, House on High Street, Lights Out, Love of Life, and the summer version of Robert Montgomery Presents.

Despite substantial exposure on both radio and television as an actress, Jan Miner is most often associated with her portrayal of Madge, the manicurist on the Palmolive Liquid Commercials with the phrase: "You're soaking in it !!"

BORRAH MINEVITCH

Musician and actor Borrah Minevitch was born in Kiev, Russia in 1903. Young Borrah came to the United States with his family in 1913. His Mother ran a boarding house and he hawked newspapers in their adopted city of Boston, Massachusetts.

In 1925 his harmonica playing talent led him to organize a harmonica band comprised of boys plucked from the streets of New York. The group was known as Borrah Minevitch and His Harmonica Rascals and played the nightclubs, the vaudeville circuit, toured Europe, appeared in motion pictures, and were heard on radio.

On radio the Harmonica Rascals starred on their own show aired over the NBC Blue network during the 1933-34 season. They also frequently performed as guests on musical variety shows broadcast during the 1930s.

Menevitch, "The King of the Harmonica," moved to Paris in 1947 and became a motion picture producer.

Borrah Minevitch died of a cerebral hemorrhage at the age of fifty-two on June 25, 1955.

MINSTREL MAN

Singer Benny Fields, The Minstrel Man, performed on his own twice weekly radio show in 1936. The fifteen minutes of song was sustained over the CBS network beginning on July 1, 1936. Fields was accompanied by the orchestra of Lud Gluskin.

THE MINUTE MEN

Stoopnagle and Budd performed their famous comic routines as the stars of the musical variety show titled The Minute Men. The weekly thirty minute series premiered over the NBC Blue network on October 4, 1936. It was sponsored by General foods' Minute Tapioca.

Joining the comic duo on the program were Joan Banks, GoGo deLys, Alice Frost, the orchestra of Donald Voorhees, and announcer Harry Von Zell.

The Minute Men retreated from the airwaves on May 16, 1937.

MIRACLES OF MAGNOLIA

Miracles of Magnolia was a brief serial drama broadcast over the NBC Blue network in 1936.

Actress Fanny May Baldridge was heard in the lead role on the obscure series. The fifteen minute episodes aired on Monday through Saturday for only three or four months beginning in late February.

MIRTH AND MADNESS

A weekday half hour of comedy and musical variety was the format for the Mirth and Madness series.

It initially originated from the studios of station KPO in San Francisco where it first took to the air as a local show in June of 1943. The sustaining shenanigans moved their base of operations to New York City and premiered over the NBC network on December 13, 1943. It was an effort by NBC to compete with ABC's popular Breakfast Club. The antics of wacky comedian Jack Kirkwood replaced Gary Moore's Everything Goes and the brief Music From Manhattan interim program.

Joining Kirkwood was Lee Brody, Bill Grey, Tom Harris, Virginia King, Barbara Lee, Lillian Leigh (Kirkwood's wife), Jean McKean, Mike McTooch, Archie Presby, Don Reid, and Herb Sheldon. The orchestras of Tony Freman, Jerry Jerome, and Irving Miller all took their turn at providing the music.

During its final season on the air Ransom Sherman took over the show from Kirkwood. Mirth and Madness came to an end on February 16, 1945.

MISCHA THE MAGNIFICENT

Mischa the Magnificent was first heard on the airwaves in 1940 as a one time only pilot on the CBS network's Forecast series. On July 5, 1942 CBS brought the show out of mothballs as a summer replacement for Fred Allen.

Comedian Mischa Auer played himself on the weekly half hour of humor. Also on the show were actress Mary Jane Croft, vocalist Buddy Clark, and the orchestra of Wilbur Hatch.

Magnificent or not, Mischa left the air in September.

MISS HATTIE

Miss Hattie was a revived version of the serial drama Lighted Windows. It was broadcast over the ABC network beginning on September 17, 1944, sponsored by The Aluminum Company of America (ALCOA).

The weekly thirty minutes was the continuing story of Hattie Palmer, played by veteran actress Ethel Barrymore. Hattie was a widow who returned to town after forty years to live with her nephew Robert Thompson and his family.

The cast included: Eric Dressler, John Gibson, Warren Parker. Dick Van Patten, Andree Wallace, and Lois Wilson. Betty Garde took over for the ailing Ethel Barrymore for several weeks late in 1944. Doc Whipple led the orchestra and Roland Winters announced.

Miss Hattie left the air in June of J945.

MISS MEADE'S CHILDREN
See: Pilot/Audition

MISS PINKERTON, INC.
See; Pilot/Audition

MISSING HEIRS
See: Court of Missing Heirs

MISSUS GOES A-SHOPPING

The "King of Emcees," John Reed King, presided over the "hilarious" quiz series Missus Goes A-Shopping. The transcribed fifteen minute show aired over the CBS net- work on Monday, Wednesday, and Friday beginning in 1941. It was recorded in local grocery stores in the New York and New Jersey areas. Shoppers won prizes for correct answers to questions posed by King. Mostly the prizes were food products of the program's various sponsors.

Missus Goes A-Shopping moved to television as one of the pioneer quiz shows on that medium during the late 1940s.

MISTER

See: Listings under Mr.

ALBERT MITCHELL

Albert Mitchell, radio's Answer Man, was born in Elsberry, Missouri on May 31, 1893.

Early in his career Mitchell was a scientific writer and musician. He was associated with Paul Whiteman's orchestra from 1920 to 1927 as a conductor and arranger. Mitchell assumed the role of the Answer Man in 1937. He remained on the airwaves answering "off-beat" questions sent in by listeners until 1950. At that time he left his radio post to work for the Marshall Plan in Paris, France. He died there on October 4, 1954 at the age of sixty-one.

EVERETT MITCHELL

Announcer and farm program host Everett Mitchell was born in Austin, Illinois on March 15, 1898.

Mitchell was an insurance adjuster when he made his radio debut as a member of his church choir. He was immediately bitten by the radio "bug" and in 1926 joined the staff of station WENR in Chicago. He eventually became chief announcer and farm director of that station. This position led to his long tenure as host of The National Farm and Home Hour. He also presided over Voice of the Farm and special broadcasts dealing with farming and live stock. In addition, Mitchell announced for a few network programs such as The Carnation Contented Hour and Swift Studio Party.

SHIRLEY MITCHELL

Actress Shirley Mitchell played many roles on radio, several on television, and a few on the motion picture screen. On radio she was heard as Leila Ransom on The Great Gilder- sleeve, Olive "Honeybee" Gillis on The Life of Riley, Kitty "Mouse" Archer on McGarry and His Mouse, Alice Darling on Fibber McGee and Molly, Shirley Ann on The Village Store, and Molly Belle on Young Love. Other airwave credits included: The Morey Amsterdam Show, Author's Playhouse, Blue Ribbon Town, The Joan Davis Show, Eyes Aloft, First Nighter, Girl Alone, The Bill Goodwin Show, Arnold Grimm's Daughter, Kay Kyser's

Kollege of Musical Knowledge, Ma Perkins, Mary Marlin, Romance, The Red Skelton Show, Stepmother, That's Life With Fred Brady, The Rudy Vallee Show, and The Alan Young Show.

On television she recreated her radio role of Leila Ransom on the video version of The Great Gildersleeve. She was also in the cast of Bachelor Father, Pete and Gladys, and Please Don't Eat the Daisies.

TOM MIX (AND HIS RALSTON STRAIGHT SHOOTERS)

One of the most popular and enduring of radio's juvenile adventure serials was Tom Mix and His Ralston Straight Shooters. Initially the story line was loosely based on the life of the real Tom Mix, but with the passage of time, it became a contemporary western mystery drama. Except for some globe trotting adventures during World War II, the stories took place in the vicinity of Dobie Township and The T-M Bar Ranch. For the faithful listeners and regular consumers of' Ralston Cereal there was a windfall of Tom Mix paraphernalia available. For a dime and a Ralston box top the mailman could deliver dozens of different badges, rings, decoders, cowboy clothing, and toys.

The series premiered on September 25, 1933 over the NBC Red network as a fifteen minute serial aired three times weekly. On September 28, 1936 Tom and His Straight Shooters expanded their air time to a Monday through Friday schedule. On September 27, 1937 they moved to NBC's Blue network where they remained (with frequent hiatus periods) until March of 1942.

Tom Mix returned to the air over the Mutual network in June of 1944. The next major change came on September 26, 1949 when the fifteen minute serial was abandoned in favor of a complete thirty minute adventure broadcast three times each week.

Tom Mix himself was never heard on the series. He was "impersonated" by Curley Bradley (Bradley also played Pecos Williams before taking over the title role), Artells Dickson, Jack Holden and Russell Thorson. The Old Wrangler was played by Percy Hemus; Sheriff Mike Shaw by Leo Curley, Hal Peary, and Willard Waterman; Amos Q. Snood by Sidney Ellstrom; Jimmy by Andy Donnelly, George Gobel, and Hugh Rowlands; Jane by Winifred Toomey and Jane Webb; and Wash by Forrest Lewis and Vance McCune. Also heard in the cast were Phil Cord, Patricia Dunlap, Florence Freeman, Betty Lou Gerson, Bob Jellison, Carl Kroenke, Wilfred Lytell, Charles MacDougal, DeWitt McBride, Cornelius Peeples, Arthur Peterson, and Bruno Wick.

Western songs were sung by The Ranch Boys (Curley Bradley, Shorty Carson, and Jack Ross). The announcers were Lynn Brandt, Don Dowd, Franklyn Ferguson, Don Gordon, Les Griffith, and Durward Kirby.

For all its seventeen seasons on the air it was sponsored by The Ralston Purina Company's cereal products. The final Tom Mix radio mystery was heard on June 23, 1950.

MOBILIZATION FOR HUMAN NEEDS

An annual half hour broadcast, Mobilization for Human Needs was heard over all four major networks each October. The program presented radio personalities performing skits and VIPs delivering short talks appealing for contributions. The drive for funds aided The Community Chest, later called The Red Feather, and more recently The United Way.

THE MOBILOIL CONCERT (HOUR)

In the fall of 1929 The Socony-Vacuum Company, makers of Mobil automobile products, began sponsorship of The Mobiloil Concert. The weekly half hour of music and song was heard over the NBC Red network.

Erno Rapee, and later Nathaniel shilkret, conducted the Mobiloil Orchestra. Douglas Stanbury served double duty as the emcee and featured baritone. Others on the program were tenors Lewis James and Robert Simmons, soprano Gladys Rice, The Men About Town Trio (Phil Duey, Scrappy Lambert, and Jack Parker), and announcer John Holbrook.

The series of Mobiloil Concerts concluded in the fall of 1932.

THE MOB1LOIL QUALITY HOUR

The Mobiloil Quality Hour premiered over nineteen affiliate stations of the NBC Blue network on February 6, 1929. It was sponsored by The Socony-Vacuum Company's Mobil automobile products.

The weekly thirty minute series presented a fifteen piece orchestra under the direction of Erno Rapee. Soprano Lois Bennet was the featured vocalist and Alois Havrilla was the announcer.

Despite claims of being "One of the leading radio features of the listeners' week," The Mobiloil Quality Hour faded from the airwaves in the spring of 1929. It was replaced in the fall by The Mobiloil Concert over NBC's other (Red) network.

MODEL MINSTRELS

Three series with a common trace of a minstrel format, and sponsored by U.S. Tobacco Company's Pipe Tobacco (Model and Dill's Best) occupied the radio airwaves.

They were Model Minstrels, Pick and Pat's One Night Stand, and Pipe Smoking Time. The latter two are described under those headings.

Making this history more confusing, at various times these titles were interchanged.

The Model Minstrels part of the trilogy took to the air over the CBS network in December of 1938 starring the comedy team of Pick (Malone) and Pat (Padgett). Also heard on the show was Ray Bloch's orchestra, The Eton Boys vocal group, singer Edward Roecker, and announcers Mel Allen and Harry Clark.

Model Minstrels gave way to the Pipe Smoking Time series on February 27, 1939.

THE MODERN ADVENTURES OF CASANOVA

Swashbuckling motion picture star Errol Flynn was heard on the airwaves in the title role on The Modern Adventures of Casanova. The amorous exploits of Christopher Casanova was a contemporary version of the infamous womanizing rogue of the 1700s (Giovanni Giacomo Casanova de Seingalt).

The weekly half hour sustaining series was broadcast over the Mutual network during the 1951-52 season.

MODERN CINDERELLA

Modern Cinderella was a relatively obscure daytime serial drama that had its beginnings over Chicago's station WGN. On June 1, 1936 it premiered over the CBS network as a fifteen minute segment of an hour-long program of homemaking and drama shows. The sixty minutes of Monday through Friday programming was sponsored by General Mills' Gold Medal Flour.

The lead role of Hope Carter was played by Lucille Barklie and Rosemary Dillon. Others in the cast were Larry Burton, Eddie Dean, Ben Gage, Jimmy Gale, and Ethel Owen. The announcer was Roger Krupp.

Modern Cinderella was dropped from the General Mills' hour on July 2, 1937.

MODERN ROMANCES

Spanning two decades, more than one radio series used the title Modern Romances. Modern Magazines, publishers of Modern Romances, sponsored a weekly thirty minute radio show. It premiered over the NBC Blue network on October 7, 1936. The radio adaptations of the "True-life" stories from the pages of the magazine were selected by a committee comprised of a judge, a psychologist, and a social worker. Heard on the dramas was a varied cast that included: Alan Bunce, Charles Cantor, Adelaide Klien. Hanley Stafford, and Karl Swenson. The announcer was Don Lowe. This series of Modern Romances was last heard on March 31, 1937.

In 1945 NBC's Radio-Recording Division syndicated one hundred and fifty-six transcribed fifteen minute episodes of romantic stories called Modern Romances.

On April 11, 1949 the original Modern Romances returned to the air over the ABC network. Modern Romances Magazine, then published by Dell Publishing, returned as sponsor. Vinton Hayworth, Claire Niesen, and Lyle Sudrow were among the actors in the cast of these romantic dramas. George Henninger was at the organ and Bob Sabin announced.

On November 14, 1949 General Mills' Gold Medal Flour took over as sponsor. The format was changed from a weekly half hour show to a Monday through Saturday fifteen minute series. Included in this batch of dramatic actors was Edwin Bruce, Ralph Camargo, Ethel Remey, Gertrude Warner, and Lawson Zerbe. Andre Baruch was the announcer.

On August 8, 1950 Modern Romances returned to a half hour show aired on Monday through Friday. Sponsorship for this series was taken over by The Norwich Pharmacal Company. This cast included Patsy Campbell, George Petrie, and Scott Thompson. Don Gardiner was the announcer.

A final radio version of Modern Romances was heard over the ABC network from 1953 to 1955 as a Monday through Friday series of fifteen minute episodes. Among the sponsors was Ex-Lax, Junket Brand Food, and The Vick Chemical Company. A television version of Modern Romances was seen over the NBC network from 1954 to 1958.

THE MODERNAIRES
See: Paula Kelly

MOHAWK TREASURE CHEST

Several eastern affiliates of the NBC Red network aired the musical Mohawk Treasure Chest series. The weekly half hour program was on the air for several months during 1934 sponsored by Mohawk Carpet Mills. James Meighan was the emcee, baritones Ralph Kirbery (The Dream Singer) and Howard Phillips vocalized, and the orchestras of Don Allen and Harold Levey provided the music. Interior decorator Lee Cole dispensed home hints, with emphasis on carpeting.

MONTGOMERY MOHN
See: Monty Masters

GERALD MOHR

Actor Gerald Mohr was born on June 11, 1914 in New York City. Mohr was studying medicine at Columbia University when a previous chance acquaintanceship with announcer Andre Baruch led to a part-time announcing job at the CBS network.

This experience resulted in his abandoning medicine in favor of an acting career. This career would subsequently encompass performances on stage, screen, radio, and television. On radio he played Rocky Palmer on Crime is My Pastime; Jules Carlshorn on Dear John; the title roles on Bill Lance, The Lone Wolf (also in the motion picture version), and Philip Marlowe; and was one of several heard as Archie Goodwin on Nero Wolfe. Mohr's other radio credits included The Joan Davis Show, Errand of Mercy, Escape, Hallmark Playhouse, The Lux Radio Theatre, The Mercury Theatre, The Private Practice of Dr. Dana, Rogue's Gallery, and The Damon Runyon Theatre, Sara's Private Capers, and Woman from Nowhere.

On television he played Christopher Storm on Foreign Intrigue and was seen in the cast of The June Allyson Show, Fantastic Four, The Magnavox Theatre, Star Playhouse, and Stars Over Hollywood.

Gerald Mohr died on November 10, 1968 while filming a television series on location in Sweden. He was fifty-four years old.

MOLASSES 'N' JANUARY

Molasses 'n' January were the characters portrayed in a blackface comedy act by Pick and Pat. Among the radio shows on which they appeared were The Dr. Pepper Parade and (Maxwell House) Show Boat.

In 1942 they introduced a Monday through Friday five minute "filler" program broadcast over the NBC Blue network. It was designed to be a wartime morale booster, but the critics labeled it "dismal." As a result it remained on the air for only a short time.

BERNARDINO MOLINARI

Noted Italian conductor Bernardino Molinari was born in Rome on April 11, 1880. The maestro waved his baton at some of the most prestigious symphony orchestras of the world, including The New York Philharmonic and The NBC Symphony.

During the years from 1938 to 1940 Molinari conducted a series of radio concerts by The NBC Symphony from the stage of Radio City.

Bernardino Molinari died of pneumonia on December 25, 1952. He was seventy-two years old.

MOLLE SHOWS

The Centaur Company, makers of Molle Brushless Shaving Cream, sponsored a trio of radio programs under their Molle banner. The Molle Show of musical variety premiered over the NBC Red network in January of 1934. The thrice weekly fifteen minute series featured blues singer Shirley Howard accompanied by guitarist Tony Callucchi and pianist Milt Rettenberg. Also heard on the show were William Edmonson, The Jesters Trio, The Southernaires Quartet, and Roxanne Wallace.

In the fall of 1934 the Molle Show took on a minstrel format and the new title of The Molle Merry Minstrels. This series remained on the NBC Red network, but was broadcast as a weekly half hour program. Wally Butterworth served as the interlocutor, Al Bernard and Emil Casper were the end men, baritone Mario Cozzi and The Melodeers vocalized, and The Molle Orchestra, conducted by Leith Stevens and Milt Rettenberg (a holder from The Molle Show), provided the music. The curtain fell for the last time on The Molle Merry Minstrels in the summer of 1935.

The last of the three Molle series was The Molle Mystery Theatre (see Mystery Theatre).

MOLLY OF THE MOVIES

The initial episode of the serial drama Molly of the Movies aired over the Mutual network on October 10, 1935.

After the first week the fifteen minute Monday through Friday series was sponsored by The Wander Company's Ovaltine. Molly was played by male actor Gene Byron! The supporting cast included: Kay Campbell, Kirby

Hawks, Ray Jones, and Henrietta Tedroe. The announcer was Pierre Andrew.

Molly of the Movies left the air on April 23, 1937

MOMMIE AND THE MEN

The early evening serialized situation comedy titled Mommie and the Men premiered on August 20, 1945. The fifteen minute episodes of domestic humor were broadcast on Monday through Friday over East coast affiliate stations of the CBS network. The show was sponsored by Proctor and Gamble's Ivory Soap. Mommie, a small town writer, was played by Elspeth Eric and her husband by Lon Clark. Others in the cast were Delores Gillen, Jackie Grimes, Richard Keith, Charles Mullen, and Sid Ward. Dick Leibert was the organist and Ron Rawson the announcer.

Mommie and the Men concluded on April 1, 1946.

MONDAY EVENING WITH BUDDY WEED

See: Buddy Weed

MONDAY MERRY-GO-ROUND

An extension of Sunday's Manhattan Merry-Go-Round was broadcast the following evening as a Monday Merry-Go-Round. It retained some of the Sunday talent and Dr. Lyon's Tooth Powder as sponsor. However, while the Manhattan version concentrated on the tunes being played in New York night spots, Monday's ethereal carousel featured songs from nightclubs across the country. For example, a telegram of "what's tops on the floor" might be received from The College Inn in Chicago or The Coconut Grove in Los Angeles.

Monday Merry-Go-Round premiered over the NBC Blue network in the fall of 1941 with Ford Bond as both announcer and host of the show. Victor Arden led the orchestra and vocals were sung by Bea Wain, Phil Duey, Alan Holt, Evelyn MacGregor, Marion McManus, and The Myer Rappaport Chorus.

The Monday Merry-Go-Round came to a stop on April 13, 1942.

MONDAY MORNING HEADLINES

Broadcast on Sunday evenings, Monday Morning Headlines was a prophetic newscast of what was perceived to be the headlines for the next morning.

The long running fifteen minute broadcast aired over the ABC network with newscaster Don Gardiner predicting the important events of Monday.

Monday Morning Headlines made its debut in 1944 with Serutan Laxative (Nature's spelled backwards) as sponsor. Over the years Airwick, Kent Cigarettes, Old Gold Cigarettes, and Seaman took their turn underwriting the newscast.

Monday Morning Headlines remained on the air into the later 1950s.

THE MONDAY NIGHT SHOW

The Monday Night Show was so titled for lack of a more imaginative name to describe a beginning of the week musical variety program. It was first aired on March 7, 1938 over the CBS network. The weekly half hour of varied entertainment was sponsored by The Brewer's Radio Show Association whose aim was to encourage beer drinking (any brand is fine!).

Among those appearing on the show was emcee Ted Husing and comedian Lou Holtz (not the football coach). Holtz was replaced by Henny Youngman in the fall of 1938. Others on the show included: Stuart Allen, Connie Boswell, Richard Himber's orchestra, Agnes Moorehead, Kay Thompson, and Nan Wynn. The announcers were John Reed King, Ken Roberts, and Dan Seymour.

The Monday Night Show departed the airwaves following the broadcast of November 28, 1938.

MONEY-GO-ROUND

The musical quiz show Money-Go-Round began its brief run over the ABC network on March 11, 1944.

The series was co-hosted by announcer Fred Uttal and singer Benay Venuta. They were assisted by the vocal duo of Lanny and Ginger Gray. Benay interviewed the male contestants and joined in the vocalizing while Fred interviewed the female contestants.

Money-Go-Round endured only a few weeks and then joined the endless parade of unsuccessful quiz shows.

MONICA'S MUSIC BOX

See: Monica Lewis

MONITOR

See: NBC Monitor

JAMES MONKS

Actor James Monks was born on February 10, 1913 in New York City. During his acting career Monks appeared on stage, in motion pictures, on radio, and on television. Much of his time was spent before the radio microphones as evidenced by his impressive list of credits in that medium. He played the title roles on The Avenger and Mr. Moto; Torben Reimer on Against the Storm; Luther Warren on Front Page Farrell; Edgar Jarvis on Joyce Jordan, M.D.; Victor Maidstone on Our Gal Sunday; and Wade Douglas on Woman of America. He was also in the cast of Armstrong Theatre of Today, The Ave Maria Hour, Bobby Benson, Big Sister, The Campbell Playhouse, Captain Tim's Spy Stories, Great Plays, Kate Hopkins, Junior G-Men, Light of the World, Little Orphan Annie, Manhattan at Midnight, The Mighty Show, My True Story, Ellery Queen, Radio Reader's Digest, The Shadow, Short Short Story, Superman, Theatre Guild on the Air, Martha Webster, Who Knows, and Pepper Young's Family.

On television he hosted a 1950 syndicated series title Tales of the Black Cat. During the 1950s Monks changed careers, becoming a male fashion model.

James Monks died of cancer on October 9, 1994 at the age of eighty-one.

LUCY MONROE

Singer Lucy Monroe was born on October 23, 1906 in New York City. She was known as "The Star Spangled Soprano" because of her dedication to patriotic music and activities in both her public and private life.

On radio Lucy Monroe was a regular vocalist on The American Album of Familiar Music, Concert Revue, Echoes of New York, The Goodrich Program, Hammerstein Music Hall, The Kraft Music Hall, Lavender and Old Lace, Manhattan Merry-Go-Round, Palmolive Beauty Box Theatre, Swing Shift Frolics, and Waltz Time.

She also sang the National Anthem at a variety of occasions, toured military bases, volunteered her services to Civil Defense organizations, she was a member of the Army/Navy Committee on Welfare and Recreation, and was RCA Victor's director of patriotic music.

Lucy Monroe died of cancer on October 13, 1987. She was eighty years old.

VAUGHN MONROE

Singing bandleader Vaughn Monroe was born in Akron, Ohio on October 11, 1911. He began singing and playing musical instruments while a teenager. Later he studied at Carnegie Tech School of Music and The New England Conservatory of Music. Monroe played and sang with the bands of Larry Funk and Jack Marshard before organizing his own band in 1940. The combination of Monroe's distinctive baritone voice and his listenable dance band afforded him a very successful career in popular music. He played the hotels and ballrooms (particularly at Robin Hood's (Seiler's) Ten Acres located in Wayland, Massachusetts and later as owner of The Meadows in nearby Framingham), turned out many hit recordings on the Bluebird and RCA Victor labels, performed on the motion picture screen, on radio, and on television.

On radio Vaughn Monroe was heard on his own show and was frequently featured on the dance band remote broadcasts. He was also associated with such other radio series as The Camel Caravan, How'm I Doin'?, Penthouse Party, and Spotlight Bands.

On television he presided over his own Vaughn Monroe Show during 1950-51 and 1954-55. He also hosted Air Time '57 and was an occasional guest on other shows.

Following the break up of his band he remained active as a pitchman for products manufactured by RCA.

Vaughn Monroe died on May 21, 1973 at the age of sixty-one.

THE VAUGHN MONROE SHOW

Popular singer and bandleader Vaughn Monroe took his songs and music to the radio airwaves on his own show. The show premiered on June 29, 1942 over the CBS network as a summer replacement for Blondie. This marked the beginning of his association with sponsor R.J. Reynold's Camel Cigarettes. Again in 1946 Reynolds Tobacco enlisted Monroe and his orchestra to "pinch hit" for the summer. This time it was for the vacationing Abbott and Costello Show. The announcer was Mike Roy.

Finally, in the fall of 1946, Vaughn Monroe was emancipated from vacation relief duties and took over The Camel Caravan. That series was aka The Camel Show and The Vaughn Monroe Show. Regulars on the program included: Colonel Stoopnagle, The Moon Maids (Mary Lee, twins Ruby and Ruth Simmons, and Ruth Winston) and The Moon Men (Nace Burnert and Olie Olson) vocal groups, the Sauter-Finnegan band (after Monroe's band broke up in 1953), The Stroud Twins comic duo, and announcers Hugh Conover and Bert Parks.

Vaughn Monroe and The Camel Caravan reached the end of the trail in the spring of 1954.

PATSY MONTANA (Rubye Blevins Rose)

Country singer Patsy Montana was born on October 30, 1914 in Hot Springs, Arkansas. During her career she entertained with her western warblings on tour, records, television, and in motion pictures.

Most of her work on radio was on the local or regional level; however, she was heard on the coast-to-coast broadcasts of The National Barn Dance from WLS in Chicago. She performed on that show both as Patsy Montana and as a member of the Prairie Ramblers vocal group. She also sang on the Wake Up and Smile show.

Patsy Montana died on May 3, 1996 at the age of eighty-one.

MONTANA SLIM (Wilf Carter)

Western singer Montana Slim was born on December 18, 1904 in Guysborough, Nova Scotia. A cowboy and rodeo performer, he abandoned that line of work in the 1930s to become a radio singer in Canada. Shortly thereafter he migrated south of the border where he continued his new-found singing career.

During the latter half of the 1930s Montana Slim was the star of his own fifteen minute daytime show aired over the CBS network. He also recorded as both Wilf Carter and Montana Slim on the Bluebird and RCA Victor labels.

RAY MONTGOMERY

Young actor Ray Montgomery began performing on radio in juvenile roles during the 1930s. Montgomery grew to maturity in front of radio microphones and motion picture cameras. On radio he played Noel Chandler on the serial drama

Dear John. He was also heard in the cast of Dealer in Dreams, Dr. Christian, I Want a Divorce, The Lux Radio Theatre, and (Maxwell House) Show Boat.

In later years Ray Montgomery owned a successful real estate business in the Hollywood area.

ROBERT MONTGOMERY (Henry Montgomery, Jr.)

Actor and producer Robert Montgomery was born on May 21, 1904 in Beacon, New York. He spent his early years as the son of a wealthy rubber company executive, but his father's death left his family without funds. Robert then worked on the railroad and went to sea before trying to establish himself as a writer. Failing as an author, he turned to acting, making his stage debut in 1924. He subsequently expanded his acting and producing horizons to include motion pictures, radio, and television. During the 1930s he served as president of The Screen Actors' Guild (SAG) and during World War I I he distinguished himself as a decorated combat Naval officer.

On radio he both hosted and frequently appeared in the cast on Suspense and joined other notable performers who were guest stars on Nobody's Children. From 1949 to 1951 he delivered political news and commentary on a weekly fifteen minute series called Robert Montgomery Speaking. It was aired over the ABC network sponsored by Lee Hats. He was also heard in guest roles on such dramatic shows as The Doctor Fights and The Lux Radio Theatre.

On television he produced and hosted the live dramatic series Robert Montgomery Presents, which endured for seven seasons during the 1950s. He also produced and appeared on several other video series before becoming disenchanted with the medium.

His dislike of the television industry was chronicled in his book titled An Open Letter From A Television Viewer. He was married twice and was the father of actress Elizabeth Montgomery who starred on the Bewitched television series. Robert Montgomery died of cancer on September 27, 1981. He was seventy-seven years old.

MOODS FOR MODERNS

Moods for Moderns was a half hour of sustaining music and song aired over the CBS network. Lyn Murray's orchestra and chorus were joined by The Four Clubmen, tenor Earl Rogers, and soprano Genevieve Rowe. The announcer was Charles Stark.

Moods for Moderns was on the air from December of 1938 through April of 1939.

TITUS MOODY SPEAKING

From 1952 to 1954 rural humorist Parker Fennelly recreated his Allen's Alley (see Fred Allen's show) character of Titus Moody. The on-again, off-again fifteen minute show was aired on Monday through Friday over the Mutual network. It was sponsored by Bromo-seltzer, Dodge Automobiles, and Wildroot grooming products. Country singer Elton Britt joined Fennelly on the program.

MOON DREAMS

Teleways Radio Productions of Hollywood syndicated a transcribed fifteen minute series of poetry and music called Moon Dreams. The one hundred and fifty-six programs began making the rounds of local radio stations in 1946 and continued to be heard into the early 1950s.

Marvin Miller recited the poetry, Ivan Eppinoff (Scott) was the violin soloist, Warren White sang the songs, and Del Castillo directed the orchestra.

MOON OVER AFRICA

Twenty-six serialized episodes of Professor Anton Edward's adventures in Africa were produced under the title Moon Over Africa. Winston Radio Transcriptions syndicated the fifteen minute series during the mid-1940s.

MOON RIVER

The oldest and longest running of the poetry and music series was Moon River. It began in 1930 and originated from the studios of WLW, The Crosley Radio Corporation "Nation's Station" in Cincinnati. The combination of the late night hour and the five hundred thousand watts of power delivered into the ether made Moon River receivable by listeners from almost anywhere in the country. However, when The Federal Communications Commission decreed a power limit of fifty thousand watts for radio stations, the coverage declined until the program was forced to network into far flung stations. A transcribed fifteen minute version was also distributed during the mid-1940s.

Among the many to narrate Moon River were Lon Clark, Don Dowd, Peter Grant, Harry Holcomb, Jay Jostyn, Palmer Ward, and Charles Woods. The opening and closing Moon River poems were written by the show's creator and WLW program director Edward Byron. Vocalists included: Betty and Rosemary Clooney, The Devore Sisters, Anita Ellis, and Ann Ryan. The announcer was Bill McCord (married to Ann Ryan).

MOONBEAMS

Moonbeams was a late night program of music and song aired over the Mutual network. It was first broadcast in 1929 from the studios of New York's station WOR. That station's music director George Shackley produced the show and conducted the orchestra. Several combinations of female vocal trios were heard as The Moonbeams (Rhoda Arnold, May Merker, Verna Osborne, Annette Simpson, and Veronica Wiggins). Also on the program were baritone soloist Douglas Stanbury, The Choir Invisible, and announcer Jerry Lawrence.

During the early 1930s the series was sponsored by Lentheric Perfume, later in the decade Gambarelli and Davitto's Italian Swiss Colony Wine assumed sponsorship.

Moonbeams left the air on December 23, 1938.

ART MOONEY

Bandleader Art Mooney formed his first band in the late 1930s in Detroit, Michigan. He played locally around the Motor City area until entering military service during World War II. After being discharged in 1945 he returned to baton waving on the ballroom circuit and recording on the MGM label. The Lowell, Massachusetts native's exposure on radio was mostly limited to dance band remote broadcasts and occasional guest appearances. However, in 1949 he was briefly on the air with his own Art Mooney's Talent Train series. The weekly thirty minute sustaining program toured various cities ferreting out new talent. It premiered over the ABC network on March 22, 1949, but endured only until the network's summer schedule took over.

On television Mooney presided over the 1954 Let's Dance program. During the 1970s he toured with The Big Band Cavalcade.

MOONSHINE AND HONEYSUCKLE

A drama of mountain life and family feuding was portrayed on Moonshine and Honeysuckle. The weekly half hour sustaining series was heard over the NBC Red network beginning with the broadcast of July 28, 1930.

The idealistic young man from "Ole Lonesome Mountain" named Clem Betts was played by Louis Mason. The remainder of the cast included: Brad Barker as the dog Mr. Bones, Jeannie Begg as Annie Bevens, Claude Cooper as "Peg Leg" Gaddis, Anne Elstner as "Cracker" Gaddis, John Milton as Pa Betts, Anne Sutherland as Ma Betts, and Queenie Walker as Piney Hyatt. Moonshine and Honeysuckle vanished from the airwaves in February of 1933.

BETTY MOORE (HOME DECORATING) (TRIANGLE CLUB)

The Benjamin Moore Paint Company first sponsored their home decorating series on radio in 1931 over the NBC Red network. Betty Moore, a trademark name tied to the sponsor, delivered household hints on beautifying homes using a plethora of pigments from Moore's color charts. The fifteen minute weekly program underwent numerous changes and extended periods of absence from the air over two decades. In 1943, following such an absence, Miss Moore hopped to the ABC network.

Among those who portrayed Betty Moore were Margaret MacDonald and Vicki Vola. Also on the program were organists Arthur Chandler, George Crook, Dolph Gobel, and Lew White, vocalist Johnny Thompson, and announcers George Gunn, Stuart Metz, and Hjerluf Provensen.

In 1950 Moore's Paints moved their show to the Mutual network and renamed it Your Home Beautiful.

COLLEEN MOORE (Kathleen Morrison)

Actress Colleen Moore was born in Port Huron, Michigan on August 19, 1900. She was educated in a convent and later studied the piano, but her claim to fame would be as a silent film star. Radio did not figure prominently in her career; however, she did appear as The Story Lady on the Safety Leigon Time series during the mid 1940s. Her intense interest in safety grew out of a movie set accident in which she broke her neck.

In later years the thrice married Miss Moore rekindled her fame by exhibiting a half million dollar doll house to raise money for crippled children. She also authored her autobiography titled Silent Star.

Colleen Moore died in January 25, 1988 at the age of eighty-seven.

GARRY MOORE (Thomas Garrison Morfit)

Popular radio and television personality Garry Moore was born on January 31, 1915 in Baltimore, Maryland. After attending Baltimore City College, he began his broadcasting career in 1935 as a writer and comic. His early days on radio were spent at his hometown station WBAL. However, in an effort to extricate himself from comedy, he left Baltimore in 1938 to broadcast news and sports at St. Louis' station KWK. It was not long before his style of delivery on radio dictated he also host a daily local variety show. Up to this point in time he was using his real name of Morfit, but in 1940 his new name of Garry Moore was selected by a listener contest. Armed with his nom de radio, Garry set out to amass a long list of credits on radio and television. With his crewcut hair style as a trademark, Moore combined comedy with a pleasing personality to become one of radio's outstanding emcees.

He would eventually preside over his own Garry Moore Show, but he would also host and appear on many other series. He was heard on The Fred Allen Show, Beat the Band, Breakfast in Hollywood, Club Matinee, The Durante-Moore Show (aka The Camel Caravan during the time it was sponsored by Camel Cigarettes), Everything Goes, The Fitch Bandwagon, The Mighty Memorymobile, The Radio Hall of Fame, Service With a Smile, The Dinah Shore Show, and Take It or Leave It.

On television he hosted his own Garry Moore Show. He also served as emcee of I've Got a Secret, and on the syndicated version of To Tell The Truth.

Garry Moore retired in 1977 due his battle with throat cancer. He died of emphysema and other complications on November 28, 1993. He was seventy-eight years old.

THE GARRY MOORE SHOW

After years of hosting other radio shows and co-starring with Jimmy Durante on the Durante-Moore series, Garry Moore took to the airwaves with his own Garry Moore Show. The variety format occupied a full hour in the CBS network's afternoon schedule on Mondays through Fridays. The sustaining Moore show made its debut on September 12, 1949 with some of Garry's old radio friends on board. Those joining Garry included: Howard Petrie, vocalists Ken Carson, Alice Cornett, and Eileen Woods, and the piano duo of Irving Miller and Bill Wardell. The announcer was Jimmy Matthews.

The Garry Moore radio show left the air on March 31, 1950. The series was an ambitious effort for a daytime variety show and although short-lived, it provided a springboard for Moore's next twenty-seven seasons on television. Garry and old friend Durward Kirby returned to the CBS radio airwaves with a new Monday through Friday show beginning on September 1, 1959. Despite being a waning era for network radio, the series endured for five seasons. It left the air on September 4, 1964.

GRACE MOORE (Mary Willie Grace Moore)

Actress and operatic soprano Grace Moore was born near Jellico, Tennessee on December 5, 1901. During her singing career she sang with The Metropolitan Opera, performed on the Broadway stage, was seen on the motion picture screen , and heard on radio.

Radio did not occupy a prominent place in Miss Moore's list of performing credits; however, she did make her presence known on several series. Among them was The Chesterfield Program, General Motors Concerts, The Nash Program, The Tele- phone Hour, and Vick's Open House.

Grace Moore was expected back from a trip to Sweden to rejoin The Metropolitan Opera when she was killed in a plane crash in Denmark. She died on January 26, 1947 at the age of forty-five.

HAL MOORE

Announcer Hal Moore arrived on the network radio scene in 1934. That year he left station WQAM in Miami, Florida to join the announcing staff of the CBS network in New York. The Mount Vernon, Indiana native was also associated with New York's station WNEW as an announcer and newscaster. After serving as an Army officer during World War II, he returned to his New York based announcing duties.

Among the network programs on which he served as announcer were Mrs. Wiggs of the Cabbage Patch and Pick and Pat.

JOHN MOORE

Actor John Moore was born on May 8, 1906 in Bangor, Ireland. He attended Queen's University in Belfast and made his radio debut over the BBC performing in Shakespearean plays. Upon his arrival in the United States Moore embarked on a busy radio acting schedule, especially on daytime serial dramas. He played the dual role of Jeffery Barton and Davis Jeffers on Hilltop House, Hank O'Hoolihan on Life Can Be Beautiful, the title role's spouse on Mrs. Miniver, Tracey Endicott on The Strange Romance of Evelyn Winters, and Captain Goodhue on Terry and the Pirates. He was also in the cast of Just Plain Bill, Pretty Kitty Kelly, The O'Neills, Our Gal Sunday, and Young Widder Brown.

TOM MOORE

Announcer and emcee Tom Moore, not to be confused with the silent film star, was heard plying his trade over the radio airwaves on several shows during the 1940s.

Moore worked his way to the network plateau by way of WIBG in Glenside, Pennsylvania, and WAIT in Chicago. He announced for Captain Midnight and Dear Mom, hosted Design for Happiness and Let's Be Lazy, was the quizmaster on Meet Your Match, presided over Smoke Dreams as "The Dreamer," and took over the emcee duties on Ladies Be Seated for that series' final season on radio.

On television he continued as the emcee on the video version of Ladies Be Seated. Much later he was the voice of a dog named Boomer on the short-lived series Here's Boomer.

VICTOR MOORE

Actor and comedian Victor Moore was born on February 24, 1876 in Hammonton, New Jersey. Starting at the age of seventeen, Moore's long career began on the vaudeville stage. He would later perform in motion pictures, Broadway stage productions, and on radio.

On radio he teamed with comedienne Helen Broderick on the Twin Stars series in 1937. In the fall of 1943 Moore and his stage partner William Gaxton signed on as regulars to appear on The Edgar Bergen and Charlie McCarthy Show, and on the last day of 1947 he joined the cast of Jimmy Durante's show. Moore was also a semi-regular on The Kraft Music Hall. He was married to vaudevillian Emma Littlefield who died in 1934. He was later wed to ballerina Shirley Paige.

By 1957 Moore had bowed out of the performing limelight to work on writing his memoirs.

Victor Moore's bumbling and confused style of comedy was silenced by a fatal heart attack on July 23, 1962. He was eighty-six years old.

AGNES MOOREHEAD

Actress Agnes Moorehead was born in Clinton, Massachusetts on December 6, 1906. She received her education at The American Academy of Dramatic Art, Bradley University, Muskingum College, and The University of Wisconsin.

Her critically acclaimed acting career encompassed stage, screen, vaudeville, radio, and television. Miss Moorehead's versatile acting ability ran the gamut from heavy dramatic roles to comedy.

Agnes Moorehead made her radio debut in 1925 over St. Louis' station KMOX as a singer! Her subsequent list of radio acting credits was prolific. She was cast in the title role on The Amazing Mrs. Danbury and Calamity Jane, played Mrs. Brown on The Aldrich Family, Sarah Heartburn on Phil Baker's Show, Maggie on Bringing Up Father, Brenda's mother on Brenda Curtis, Rosie on Dot and will, Min Gump on The Gumps, Mrs. Thompson on Bess Johnson, Nellie Conrad on Life Can Be Beautiful, Eleanor Roosevelt (one of several) on The March of Time, Marilly on Mayor of the Town, Ma Hutchinson on The Mighty Show, Mrs. Van Alastair Crowder on The New Penny, Margot Lane (one of many) on The Shadow, The Dragon Lady (one of three) on Terry and the Pirates, Catherine Allison on This Day is Ours, Anna Bartlett on Way Down East, and Mrs. Mollet on Leonidas Witherall. She was also heard on such other radio shows as Fred Allen's Town Hall Tonight; America's Hour; Aunt Jenny; Believe It or Not; Ben Bernie and all the Lads; Betty and Bob; Big Sister; The Jack Carson Show; Cavalcade of America; The CBS Radio Mystery Theatre; Columbia Workshop; Death Valley Days; Doc Rockwell's Brain Trust; Dreft Star Playhouse; Bulldog Drummond; Evening in Paris; Grand Central Station; Hillbilly Heart-Throbs; Sherlock Holmes ; Joyce Jordan, Girl Interne; Les Miserables; Life Begins (Martha Webster); Meet Mr. Meek; Mercury Theatre of the Air; The Monday Night Show; Mysteries in Paris; Mystery in the Air; The Orange Lantern; Radio Hall of Fame; Short Short Story; Spy Secrets; Strange As It Seems; Suspense (Miss Moorehead's performance on the series' radio adaptation of Sorry Wrong Number proved so popular that it was repeated no less than eight times between 1943 and 1960); There Was a Woman; This is My Best; and Orson Welles' Almanac.

On television she appeared in over a dozen series, but is probably best remembered for her role as the witch Endora on Bewitched. She was troubled by this fact and was quoted as saying "I don't particularly want to be identified as a witch."

Agnes Moorehead died of lung cancer at the age of sixty-seven on April 30, 1974.

MOORISH TALES

During the summer of 1936 the NBC Blue network aired a weekly fifteen minute series titled Moorish Tales.

Actor George Gaul narrated these stories of the North African Moors. The tales were based on writings of well known author Washington Irving.

MORAN AND MACK

See: Two Black Crows

BETTY MORAN

Radio actress Betty Moran successfully achieved almost total anonymity concerning her life and acting career; however, there does exist a record of some of her airwave credits. She played Bingle's wife on The Busy Mr. Bingle, shared the title role on The Career of Alice Blair, was the police commissioner's secretary on Dangerous Assignment, was heard as Carol Chandler on Dear John, portrayed Therese on Today's Children, and played Ellen Norris on The Whisperer. She was also in the cast of Night Beat.

GEORGE MORAN (George Searcy)

Comedian George Moran was born on October 3, 1881 in Elwood, Kansas.

Moran was touring the vaudeville circuit when he met fellow vaudevillian Charles Mack. Together they formed the blackface comedy team of Mack and

Moran (aka Two Black Crows). The duo continued to perform on the vaudeville stage and later branched out to include motion pictures, radio, and recordings.

Moran and his partner made their radio debut in 1928 They were heard on The Eveready Hour, The Majestic Theatre Hour, and appeared frequently as guests on shows of that era. Moran was injured in the same automobile accident that killed his partner Mack on January 11, 1934. For several years thereafter Moran continued the act with other partners.

George Moran died on August 1, 1949 at the age of sixty- seven. He had suffered a stroke five days before.

PATSY MORAN

Comedienne Patsy Moran was born in the state of Pennsylvania on October 13, 1903. She was featured in many films during the 1930s and 40s and was also heard on several radio series.

On the latter medium she played a maid named Hilda on the first version of Junior Miss, was cast in the role of Martha on Major Hoople, and was heard as Mrs. Flanagan on the Sad Sack series.

Patsy Moran died on December 10, 1968 at the age of sixty-five.

MARCOS MORENO

See: Lloyd M. Shaffer

CLAUDIA MORGAN (Claudeigh Louise Wuppermann)

Actress Claudia Morgan was born in Brooklyn, New York on June 12, 1912. The oft married and divorced star of stage, screen, radio and television was the daughter of actor Ralph Morgan and the niece of actor Frank Morgan.

On the radio airwaves Claudia Morgan was cast in key roles on several series. She played Christy Allen Cameron on Against the Storm, Clarissa Oakley on David Harum, Nita Bennett on Lone Journey, Carolyn Kramer Nelson on The Right to Happiness, Nora Charles on The Thin Man, and Andrea Reynolds on We Love and Learn. She was also in the cast of Dimension X and Light of the World.

On television she appeared in numerous dramatic productions such as Armstrong Circle Theatre, Celanese Theatre, The Kraft Television Theatre, and Robert Montgomery Presents. She was also in the cast of the daytime serial dramas The Doctors, The Edge of Night, Our Five Daughters, and Way of the World.

Claudia Morgan died on September 17, 1974 at the age of sixty-two.

ELIZABETH MORGAN

Actress Elizabeth Morgan began performing at the age of five. She went on to pursue a long career in films, nightclubs, on the stage, radio, and television.

Her radio credits included roles on Stella Dallas, Murder Clinic, My True Story, Our Gal Sunday, When a Girl Marries, and Young Dr. Malone. She was also heard on Believe It or Not, The Campbell Playhouse, Suspense, and Leonidas

Witherall. In 1961 she hosted a daily talk show over station WJRZ in Newark, New Jersey.

On television she appeared on Armstrong Circle Theatre, Crime Photographer (the video version of Casey, Crime Photographer), Hallmark Playhouse, The Kraft Television Theatre, and Man Behind the Badge.

She Morgan served as a board member and treasurer of AFTRA (The American Federation of Television and Radio Artists).

Elizabeth Morgan died following a stroke on May 31, 1987. She was eighty-four years old.

FRANK MORGAN (Francis Philip Wupperman)

Actor Frank Morgan was born on June 1, 1890 in New York City. Young Morgan rejected the idea of entering the family business that produced the famous Angostura Bitters. Rather he chose to pursue a career as an actor. To that end, in 1913 he enrolled in The American Academy of Dramatic Arts. He subsequently performed on stage, screen (best remembered as the Wizard in The Wizard of Oz), and radio.

He was the star of his own radio show, was cast in the title role on The Fabulous Dr. Tweedy, and was a frequent guest and summer host of The Kraft Music Hall. Morgan was also heard on Good News of 1938-39, Maxwell House Coffee Time, The Old Gold Show, and The Radio Hall of Fame.

Frank Morgan was apparently in good health when he died in his sleep on September 18, 1949. He was fifty-nine years old.

THE FRANK MORGAN SHOW

The principal segments of the hour-long Maxwell House Coffee Time series was split into two separate thirty minute shows in the fall of 1944.

One of these programs was The Frank Morgan Show. The weekly comedy series was broadcast over the NBC network with Maxwell House Coffee remaining as his sponsor.

The boisterous Frank and his tall tales was augmented by British actor Eric Blore, comical vocalist Cass Daley, Latin song stylist Carlos Ramirez, the orchestra of Albert Sack, and emcee Robert Young. The announcer was Harlow Wilcox. Morgan's ratings did not measure up to expectations and the show endured for only a single season. The final broadcast of The Frank Morgan Show aired on May 31, 1945.

GENE MORGAN (Eugene Schwartzkopf)

Actor and orchestra leader Gene Morgan was born in Racine, Wisconsin on March 12, 1893. This Gene Morgan should not be confused with the announcer of the same name who announced on local radio stations in New York and Philadelphia. Many sources have intermixed biographical data of these two Gene Morgans.

Morgan's airwave acting credits included the role of Gary Crandall on Carol Kennedy's Romance, Bill Taylor on Mary Marlin, Rex Marvin on Myrt and

Marge, and another character named Bill Taylor on Today's Children. He was also a member of the cast on The Columbia Workshop, Gangbusters, Heinz Magazine of the Air, and Romance.

Gene Morgan died of a heart ailment at the age of forty-seven on August 15, 1940.

HARRY MORGAN
See: Henry Morgan

HELEN MORGAN (Helen Riggins)
Actress and "torch singer" Helen Morgan was born in Danville, Illinois on August 2, 1900. The popular vocalist gained fame during the 1920s and 1930s on stage, screen, records, radio, and in nightclubs.

On the radio airwaves she sang in guest appearance on many of the musical shows of that era and was a regular on Broadway Melodies and Laugh With Ken Murray. As an actress she was heard on Death Valley Days.

Helen Morgan died penniless of cirrhosis of the liver on October 8, 1941. She was forty-one years old.

Her life was portayed on the motion picture screen in the 1957 film The Helen Morgan Story. Actress Polly Bergen played the title role.

HENRY MORGAN (Harry Van Ost, Jr.)
Humorist and announcer Henry Morgan was born in New York City on March 31, 1915. Early in his life he expressed an interest in broadcasting. To that end he became a page at New York's station WMCA at the age of seventeen. He was soon to graduate to the announcing staff at WMCA and later in the employ of WCAU in Philadelphia, WEBC in Deluth, WNAC in Boston, and WOR in New York. During his fledgling years as an announcer he retained his real first name of Harry (not to be confused with the film and televison actor Harry Morgan).

Morgan initially departed from announcing duties in 1937 to host his own fifteen minute show aired over WOR under the title Meet Mr. Morgan, later renamed Here's Morgan. In 1943 he took over as host of WHN's Gloom chasers Show, but soon afterwards left for military service in the Army Air Corps. Following his discharge, he returned to the radio microphone of WJZ in New York. Morgan's cynical style and caustic treatment of commercials endeared him to his fans, but often led to trouble with the sponsors. This earned him the reputation as "the bad boy of radio" which would follow him throughout his career.

The Henry Morgan Show premiered as a prime time comedy show in 1946 over the ABC network. His other exploits on network radio included narrating psychic dramatizations on Mysteries of the Mind and guest appearances on a variety of series from the comedy of Fred Allen's show to the terror of Suspense.

The Henry Morgan Show was cancelled in 1950, but Morgan returned to radio's airwaves with a late night talk show. It was broadcast every night Monday through Sunday over station WMGM in New York. Morgan's other exploits on New York radio included hosting a talk show over WOR and airing comedy routines over WNEW.

On television he presided over Draw to Win, Henry Morgan's Great Talent Hunt, and On the Corner. He was a panelist on I've Got a Secret and What's My Line, played Philip Jensen on My World and Welcome to It, and regularly appeared on That Was the Week That Was. Henry Morgan died of lung cancer on May 19, 1994 at the age of seventy-nine.

THE HENRY MORGAN SHOW

The Henry Morgan Show (aka Here's Morgan) premiered over the ABC network on September 3, 1946. The weekly comedy series first took to the air without benefit of a sponsor, but Eversharp shaving and writing materials soon signed on to underwrite the show.

The program opened with a calliope rendition of For He's a Jolly Good Fellow and the greeting "Good evening anybody, here's Morgan." There followed thirty minutes of cynical humor, Morgan's irreverent treatment of the sponsor's products, and a few musical interludes thrown in.

Over the years Morgan was joined by many of radio's familiar voices on both his local and network shows. They included his principal side-kick Arnold Stang, together with Ralph Bell, Art Carney, Kenny Delmar, Betty Garde, Maurice Gosfield, Florence Halop, Pert Kelton, Madeleine Lee, Louis Neistat, Alice Pearce, Minerva Pious, and Mae Questal. The vocalists were Elton Britt, Jeff Clark, The Golden Gate Quartet, Betty Harris, Lisa Kirk, and The Billy Williams Quartet. The orchestra was conducted by Bernie Green and Milton Katims. The announcers were Art Ballinger, Doug Browning, Ben Grauer, Ed Herlihy, Charles Irving, Kelvin Keech, Glen Riggs, David Ross, and Doug Sheppard.

"The Bad Boy of Radio" continued his trouble with sponsors for his less than enthusiastic approach to their products.

This resulted in Eversharp cancelling sponsorship of the show on December 24, 1947. After a five week layoff Morgan was back on the air with Rayve Shampoo enduring his treatment of their products until they too cancelled in June of 1948.

Morgan next returned to the airwaves on March 13, 1949 over the NBC network on a sustaining basis and on July 6th he was moved to replace Duffy's Tavern for the summer. In the fall the network found Morgan a place in their schedule and kept him on the air until June 18, 1950.

NOTE: Another radio series titled Afloat With Henry Morgan had no connection with this show and is described under that heading.

JANE MORGAN

Actress Jane Morgan (not to be confused with singer Jane Morgan) was born in England in 1880. As a child she came to the United States with her family.

Jane Morgan became well known for her work on the vaudeville stage and on radio. She also performed to a lesser degree in motion pictures and on television. She specialized in the roles of mothers, maids, and elderly women.

On radio she played the title role on Aunt Mary, Martha on The Jack Benny Show, Nora Mawson on Brenthouse, Mrs. Foster on The Jack Carson Show, Lillian on Glorious One, Alice's mother on The Phil Harris-Alice Faye Show, Mrs. Hemp on Honest Harold, Mrs. Morgan on The Jack Paar Show, Evelyn Hanover on Point Sublime, and Mrs. Margaret Davis on Our Miss Brooks. She was also heard on Dr. Christian, Hollywood Playhouse, I Want a Divorce, The Lux Radio Theatre, Mystery in the Air, One Man's Family, and The Silver Theatre.

She recreated her role of landlady Mrs, Davis on both the film and video versions of Our Miss Brooks.

Jane Morgan died of a heart attack on January 1, 1972. She was ninety-one years old.

THE JOHNNY MORGAN SHOW

Obscure "second banana" Johnny Morgan from radio's Broadway Showtime briefly rose to "top banana" status on two radio series aired under his name.

In June of 1944 Morgan took over Broadway Showtime's weekly half hour on the CBS network sponsored by Ballantine Beer and Ale. The new Johnny Morgan Show remained on the air only until March of 1945 when Morgan and P. Ballantine & Son came to a parting of the ways.

During the summer of 1946 Johnny Morgan returned with a warm weather sustaining thirty minutes of benign comedy broadcast over the NBC network. Morgan was joined by Jack Arthur, Norman Brokenshire, Bill Keene, Walter Kinsella, Gloria Mann, The Smoothies vocal group, and announcer Jack Costello.

RAY MORGAN   (Raymond Storrs Morgan)

Announcer and broadcast personality Ray Morgan, who closely guarded his birth date, began his career on radio during World war II with The Office of War Information (OWI). His broadcasts were aired over the facilities of The Voice of America.

Morgan attended Dartmouth College and was a Congregational minister before devoting full time to radio. On network radio he was more than just an announcer. He was often included in the cast, narrated, or served as host. Morgan's radio credits included: Americans at Work; Counterspy; Dr. Susan; Gangbusters; Murder at Midnight; Valiant Lady; and We, the People.

On television he hosted or announced such shows as The Kraft Music Hall, Ted Mack's Amateur Hour, The Magic Clown, Robert Montgomery Presents, and Toast of the Town.

In later years he was involved with The American Cancer Society, The Heart Association, and Recordings for the Blind.

Ray Morgan died of cancer on January 5, 1975.

ROBIN MORGAN

Juvenile performer Robin Morgan was born in Lake Worth, Florida on January 29, 1942.

At the age of six she was billed as "Radio's youngest disc jockey." Her weekly Sunday morning fifteen minute show aired over New York's station WOR in 1948. Robin also appeared as a panelist on Juvenile Jury.

On television she played Dagmar on I Remember Mama. Her other video credits included: The Alcoa Hour, Meet Corliss Archer, Star Stage, and Tales of Tomorrow.

RUSS MORGAN

Bandleader and trombonist Russ Morgan was born in Scranton, Pennsylvania on April 29, 1904. Young Morgan began working with his father in the coal mines, but soon abandoned mining for music. While still in his teens he was arranging music for Victor Herbert and John Philip Sousa. He played trombone with The Scranton Sirens and the bands of Ted Fio Rito, Jean Goldkette, Freddy Martin, and Phil Spitalny before organizing his own band in 1935.

"Music in the Morgan Manner" was played in the ballrooms and hotels, on records, radio, the motion picture screen, and television.

On radio Martin and his aggregation was heard on the dance band remote broadcasts and on his own show Johnny Presents Russ Morgan. Other airwave appearances included Flying High, Here's to Veterans, The Ken Murray show, One Night Stand, The Philip Morris Playhouse, spotlight Bands, and The Rudy Vallee Show.

On television he hosted In The Morgan Manner, The Russ Morgan Show, and shared the orchestral spotlight with the Vincent Lopez orchestra on Welcome Aboard.

Russ Morgan died of a cerebral hemorrhage on August 7, 1969. He was sixty-five years old.

THE MORIN SISTERS

The singing Morin Sisters warbled their way into loudspeakers during the 1930s. Sisters Evelyn and Pauline ("Birdie") were born in Dunn, Indiana on March 27, 1911 and February 24, 1909 respectively. The third sister Marge was born in Continental, Ohio on April 26, 1913.

The girls sang on such radio shows as The Breakfast Club, Club Matinee, Jamboree, The Princess Pat Program, The Sealed Power Side Show, and Sunset Dreams (an early version of The Fitch Bandwagon). They also starred on their own fifteen minute program of songs aired over the NBC Blue network from 1932 to 1935.

The trio of siblings faded from the airwaves at the beginning of the 1940s.

THE MORMON TABERNACLE CHOIR

The three-hundred voice Mormon Tabernacle Choir, during its long history, transcended its Mormon faith roots to attain popularity with ecumenical and secular audiences.

Their radio broadcasts (aka Music and the Spoken Word and Music from Utah) were first aired On July 15, 1929 over the NBC network from the studios of Salt Lake City's station KSL. Three years later the choir moved to the CBS network, when KSL switched its affiliation to that network.

Various sources differ as to the personnel on the program, but correspondence with The Mormon Temple's Historical Department in Salt Lake City provided the following: The first choir director was Anthony C. Lund, the organist was Edward P. Kimball, and the announcer was Ted Kimball (the organist's nineteen year old son). Many of the others that followed included: director J. Spencer Cornwall, organists Frank Asper and Alexander Schreiner, and announcers Richard Evans and Earl Glade. Later the duties of the announcer were expanded to include delivery of a "Spoken Word" message. The Mormon Tabernacle Choir was still being heard over the CBS network in the 1990s.

MORNING ALMANAC

See: The Phil Cook Show

MORNING DEVOTIONS

The NBC Blue network sustained a fifteen minute program of Morning Devotions during the 1930s.

Those heard on the inspirational interlude of music were contralto Joyce Allmand, tenor Richard Dennis, soprano Kathryn Palmer, and baritone John Wainman. The organist was Lowell Patton.

The series was on the air from September of 1933 to October of 1937.

MORNING MARKET BASKET

See: Isabel Manning Hewson

MC KAY MORRIS

Actor McKay Morris was born in Fort Sam Houston, Texas on December 22, 1891.

He made his debut as an actor on the stage on May 1, 1912 and subsequently appeared in dozens of theatrical productions. Although best known for his work on the stage, Morris saw limited duty in acting roles on the radio airwaves. He was cast in the title role on The Abe Lincoln Story and played Gregory Ivanoff on the Ma Perkins serial drama. He was also a guest star on various other series such as Grand Central Station.

McKay Morris died on October 3, 1955 at the age of sixty-four.

RUSTY MORRIS (Rolland Morris)

Actor Rusty Morris began his radio career in 1938 at the age of fifteen on the Dramas for Youth series. The Colorado native later went on to perform on stage, screen, and television.

Following service in the Navy during World War II, Morris returned to acting. His radio credits included such shows as Dr. Christian, Halls of Ivy, The Lux Radio Theatre, Mayor of the Town, The Railroad Hour, Screen Guild Theatre, and This Is Your FBI.

On television he appeared on several series. They included The Ray Bulger Show, Death Valley Days, Omnibus, and The Ann Sothern Show.

Rusty Morris died of cancer on May 14, 1986 at the age of sixty-three.

WILLIE MORRIS

Female vocalist Willie Morris was featured on several radio shows during the 1930s. Although her life and career is not well documented, Willie's soprano talent won her a place on the musical programming of that era.

Willie Morris vocalized on such series as Fireside Recitals, The Flying Red Horse Tavern, Home on the Range, Musical Camera, Palmolive Beauty Box Theatre, (Maxwell House) Show Boat, and Your Hit Parade.

BERT MORRISON

Actor and announcer Bret Morrison was born on May 5, 1912 in Evanston, Illinois. Young Bret was first heard on radio in 1930 while still an eighteen year old high school student.

He later attended Northwestern University while continuing his work on the airwaves from Chicago.

Morrison's subsequent long list of radio credits is headed by a twelve year stint as Lamont Cranston, The Shadow. As an actor, announcer, or narrator he was also heard on a long list of programs. He was one of more than a half dozen to portray Mr. First Nighter on the First Nighter program, he played Chris Gunn on Great Gunns, Stanley Westland on Arnold Grimm's Daughter, Clifford Foster on The Guiding Light, Jonathan on Mary Marlin, Linden Wake on Road of Life, Jonathan Hayward on The Romance of Helen Trent, Paul on Son of Man (annual Easter drama), The Stranger (Pierre Varnay) on Song of the Stranger, and Dave Talbot on Woman in White. He was also heard on Jack Armstrong; Attorney at Law; Author's Playhouse; Best Sellers; CBS Radio Mystery Theatre; Chicago Theatre of the Air; Clara, Lu, and Em; The Contented Hour; The Falcon; Heartbeat Theatre; Hollywood Hotel; Kitty Keene; Listening Post; Light of the World; Love Song; The Lux Radio Theatre; Ma Perkins; Manhattan Mother; My True Story; Parties at Pick-Fair; Irene Rich Dramas; Superman; The Thin Man; Vanity Fair; Vick's Open House; Win Your Lady; Wings For America, and Woman in White.

Bret Morrison died of a heart attack on September 25, 1978 at the age of sixty-six. Ironically, he was on his way home from a taping session of Heartbeat Theatre when he succumbed.

HERB MORRISON

Newscaster Herb Morrison was born in 1905 in Scottdale, Pennsylvania. Morrison began his quest for the news after graduating from high school in 1923. Several years later he took his news reporting to the radio airwaves.

He was associated with KQV and WJAS in Pittsburgh; WLBD in Waukegan, Illinois; WLS in Chicago; WOR in New York; WTMJ in Milwaukee, Wisconsin and XER in Villa Acuna, Mexico. It was during the time he was with Chicago's WLS that the well traveled and relatively obscure newscaster was catapulted into radio broadcasting history. On May 6, 1937 he was sent to record the landing of the dirigible Hindenburg in Lakehurst, New Jersey. His emotional eyewitness account of the tragic explosion of the airship was broadcast the following day by transcription.

Morrison served with the Army during World War II and then returned to his broadcast journalism career. He served as news director of stations KQV and WJAS in Pittsburgh and televised newscasts over WTAE-TV.

He retired from broadcasting in 1967, but was occasionally seen on television talk shows with regard to his historic coverage of the Hindenburg disaster.

Herb Morrison died on January 10, 1989 at the age of eighty-three .

JEFF MORROW

Actor Jeff Morrow was born on January 13, 1907 in New York City. Morrow's acting career was confined mostly to the stage; however, he also appeared on the motion picture screen, radio, and television.

On radio he was included in various supporting casts on many shows following military duty during World War II. He also played the title role on the Dick Tracy series for a brief time.

On television he played Dr. Lloyd Axton on Temperatures Rising (1973-74), Bart McClelland on Union Pacific, and in supporting roles on several other series.

Jeff Morrow died on December 26, 1993 after a long illness. He was eighty-six years old.

CARLTON E. MORSE

Writer and producer Carlton E. Morse was born in Jennings, Louisiana on June 4, 1901. He studied at The University of California and worked as a newspaperman before turning his attention to radio script writing in 1929.

Although not known as a performer, the scripts Morse penned for radio set a standard of excellence in two categories. As creator and writer of I Love a Mystery and One Man's Family he became the dean of the spine tingling adventure arid the folksy family drama formats. Morse was also responsible for such other radio scripts as Adventures By Morse; Family Skeleton; His Honor, the Barber; The Upper Room; and Woman in My House.

He introduced his One Man's Family saga to television in 1949 and scripted the daytime video drama Mixed Doubles the same year.

In later years the prolific writer continued to grind out new mystery novels.

Carlton E. Morse died on May 24, 1993. He was ninety-one years old.

SIDNEY MOSELEY
See: Headlines of Tomorrow

ANOLD MOSS

Actor Arnold Moss was born on January 28, 1910 in Brooklyn, New York. He was educated at City College of New York, Columbia University, and New York University, He directed and apprenticed at Eva LeGallienne's Repertory Theatre and served on the staff of the speech and theatre department of Brooklyn College.

During his acting career Moss specialized in the classical and Shakespearean theatre, but was equally at home on the motion picture screen, radio, and television.

On radio he played Philip Cameron on Against the Storm, Dr. Reed Bannister on Big Sister, Dr. Fabian on Cabin B-13, Colonel Maurice Lesko on Cafe Istanbul, Ted White on The Guiding Light, Frank Flippin on The Man I Married, and Giles Henning on Mary Marlin. In addition he was heard on such other shows as Jane Arden; By Kathleen Norris; Columbia Presents Corwin; Stella Dallas; Grand Central Station; Joyce Jordan, Girl Interne; Manhattan Mother; The Mighty Show; Road of Life; This is Our Enemy; Valiant Lady; and Warriors of Peace. Moss also hosted broadcasts of various symphony orchestras, was the narrator on the Mrs. Miniver series, and served double duty as announcer and narrator for The Open Door and Radio Reader's Digest.

On television he was in the cast of such dramatic series as The Campbell Television Soundstage, The Clock, Lights Out, The Motorola Television Hour, Suspense, Tales of Tomorrow, and in transient roles on daytime serial dramas.

Arnold Moss died of lung cancer on December 15, 1989 at the age of eighty. He had been married for many years to radio script writer Stella Reynolds.

REV. DR. LESLIE BATES MOSS

Rev. Dr. Leslie Bates Moss was born in Minneapolis, Minnesota in 1888. Rev. Moss graduated from Harvard University and was ordained a Baptist minister in 1915.

He served as a missionary in China, authored several books, was an executive of Church World Service, and broadcast religious commentary on radio.

His ministry over the airwaves began in 1936 and continued through 1945. Rev. Moss presided over At Home in the World, This World of Ours, and other similar types of programming. Rev. Dr. Leslie Bates Moss died in his sleep of a heart attack on April 2. 1949. He was sixty years old.

MOTHER AND DAD

Weekday afternoon meetings of "downeast" neighbors and friends in the "sitting room" was the atmosphere created in the mind of the radio listner on Mother and Dad. The folks spent their daily fifteen minutes together in conversation, song, and reading letters from their radio audience. Mother and Dad made its debut over the CBS network on August 9, 1942. Rural humorist Parker Fennelly played Dad, with Charme Allen and Effie Palmer in the role of mother.

The weekday visits with Mother and Dad came to an end in the fall of 1943. However, they shortly returned as a weekly half hour show sponsored by Allegheny-Ludlum Steel Corporation. The final broadcast aired in the fall of 1944.

MOTHER KNOWS BEST

Mother Knows Best, an audience participation series aimed at a female audience, was first heard over the Pacific Coast net- work of CBS in the fall of 1948. It was actually transcribed in New York for airing on the West Coast. On October 8, 1949 Mother Knows Best was brodcast live in the New York City area over station WCBS during the recording sessions.

Games, interviews, and songs comprised the all too familiar format of the weekly half hour program. It was sponsored by Kelloggs Cereals.

Warren Hull served as emcee, assisted by New York Journal American's food editor Isabella Beech. The announcer was Ralph Paul.

The live New York broadcasts were short-lived and left the air before the close of 1949.

MOTHER O' MINE

The daytime serial drama Mother O' Mine made its debut on October 7, 1940. The fifeen minute episodes were heard over the NBC Blue network, sponsored by Clapp's Baby Food.

The well-worn story line chronicled the plight of Mother Morrison, a widow who sold her debt ridden farm and moved in with her son and his family.

Agnes Young was heard in the title role. Her son and daughter-in-law, John and Helen Morrison, were played by Donald Cook and Ruth Yorke. Others in the cast were Arthur Allen, Patte Chapman, Jackie Kelk, Paul Nugent, and Betty Jane Tyler. The announcer was Charles Stark.

Mother O' Mine had a relatively short radio life. The final chapter in the woeful widow's quest for happiness aired on July 4, 1941.

MOUNTAINVILLE TRUE LIFE SKETCHES

Mountainville True Life Sketches (aka Tiny Tots Theatre) was the brainchild of businessman Morris Littman, owner of a chain of New York stores. He conceived the idea of a rural drama series for radio while vacationing in a quiet little hamlet named Mountainville.

The saga revolved around a kindly schoolteacher and his wife as they attempted to educate their adopted children. The weekly half hour program was broadcast over the CBS network in 1930.

Frank Knight played the role of schoolteacher David Peters and Yolande Langworthy served double duty co-starring as David's wife Marilyn and also penning the scripts. Others in the cast were Howard Merrill and Pat Ryan.

MOVIE QUIZ

During the 1952-53 season General Mills' Kix Cereal sponsored a show with a Hollywood flavor titled Movie Quiz.

The program was heard over the Mutual network as a weekly half hour question and answer bee about doings in filmdom. Johnn Olsen served as host and quizmaster.

THE MOYLAN SISTERS

The youthful singing sisters Marianne and Peggy Joan Moylan from Long Island, New York started their vocalizing at about the same time they began to walk. The eldest sister Marianne was born on August 16, 1932 and kid sister Peggy Joan came along on October 2, 1934.

The Moylan Sisters are best remembered for their exposure on radio, but they also appeared in several film shorts and made a few records.

They made their network radio debut in 1938 over the NBC Blue network on The Children's Hour. The following year they were awarded their own Moylan Sisters Program. They were also heard as guests with Fred Allen, Ilka Chase, and Alec Templeton. During World War II they joined the multitude of talent appearing on The Stage Door Canteen series and later wrote to many of the GIs they met at the Canteen.

By the mid 1940s the singing careers of the Moylans faded. Marianne became a laboratory technician and Peggy Joan a medical secretary.

THE MOYLAN SISTERS PROGRAM

Seven year old Marianne Moylan and five year old Peggy Joan Moylan became the stars of their own radio show aired over the NBC Blue network. The fifteen minute Sunday afternoon series premiered on October 15, 1939. It was sponsored by The Modern Process Company, makers of Thrivo Dog Food.

Labelled "Angels of the Airwaves" or "Cherubs of Radio," the girls were closely tied to the sponsor's product. They sang the Thrivo jingle, presented a weekly National Dog Hero Award, and the title of their theme song was Sittin' on a Log Pettin' My Dog. Piano accompaniment was provided by Morty Howard and the announcer was Don Lowe.

Due to wartime restrictions, Thrivo Dog Food cancelled as the sponsor in 1942. Hecker Products quickly stepped in to bankroll the show, but they too cancelled in the spring of 1943.

By popular demand The Moylan Sisters Program continued on the air as a sustainer until June of 1944.

JACK MOYLES

West Coast based actor and announcer Jack Moyles first stood before a radio microphone in the early 1930s.

He was associated with California stations KGO-KPO and KSFO in San Francisco and KROW on Oakland. Moyles was heard on local, network, and syndicated radio shows. He was cast in the title role on A Man Named Jordan (Rocky Jordan), played Major Daggett on Fort Laramie, and Mel Sherwood on Hawthorne House. His other radio credits included: Alias John Freedom, Scattergood Baines, Frontier Gentleman, Lady of Millions, Philip Marlowe, My Children, Night Editor, Romance, Twelve Players, and The Whistler.

Jack Moyles was the announcer for My Secret Ambition and Watch the Fun Go By (Al Pearce and His Gang).

MR. ACE AND JANE

The official, but unorthodox, way of writing the title of this radio show was mr. ace and JANE. The sustaining domestic comedy was a revival of the Easy Aces series. It premiered on February 14, 1948 as a sustaining feature of the CBS network.

The weekly thirty minutes of humor shed the low key image of its predecessor by employing a full orchestra and performing before a live studio audience.

Goodman Ace created, wrote, and starred on both series. His wife Jane co-starred as the whiney master of malapropism. The supporting cast included: Frank Butler, Eric Dressler, John Griggs, Leon Jauney, Pert Kelton, Florence Robinson, and Everett Sloane. The orchestra was under the direction of Morris Surdin and the announcer was Ken Roberts.

On July 4, 1948 the show was moved into the summer lineup to replace the vacationing Baby Snooks. General Foods' Jello was the sponsor. Come fall, mr. ace and JANE remained in the CBS schedule, but lost their sponsor on the last day of 1948 due to low ratings.

The final chapter of domestic mayhem at the Ace home was broadcast on May 24, 1949.

MR. ADAM AND MRS. EVE

See: Crumit and Sanderson

MR. AND MRS.

Mr. and Mrs. (aka Joe and Vi) was a domestic comedy based on the comic strip by Clare Briggs. The radio adaptation aired over the CBS network beginning in 1929. It was sponsored by Graybar Electric.

Initially Mr. and Mrs. was a weekly half hour program, but in the fall of 1930 it was reduced to a quarter hour. Jack (J. Scott) Smart was heard as Mr. (Joe) and Jane Houston as Mrs. (Vi). The announcer was Harry Von Zell. Mr. and Mrs. left the air in 1931.

Other radio series using the same title were produced locally at such stations as KNX in Los Angeles and WGN in Chicago.

MR. AND MRS. BLANDINGS

A radio adaptation of the novel and film Mr. Blandings Builds His Dream House was aired as Mr. and Mrs. Blandings. The weekly half hour situation comedy made its debut over the NBC network on January 21, 1951. Trans World Airlines (TWA) sponsored the show.

The marital madness starred the husband and wife team of Cary Grant and Betsy Drake as Jim and Murial Blandings (Myrna Loy played Murial in the motion picture). Among those appearing in the supporting cast were Gale Gordon and Sheldon Leonard. The announcer was Don Stanley.

Amid disdain of the critics for a show that lacked a credible story line, Mr. and Mrs. Blandings struggled to stay on the air. However, they lost the battle and the Blandings saga left the air on June 17, 1951.

MR. AND MRS. F.C.H.

Mr. and Mrs. F.C.H. was a little known show with a well known format. The husband and wife chatter occupied fifteen minutes of CBS network airtime three times weekly. The series was broadcast during 1931 with Phil and Ann Brae as the F.C.H.s.

MR. AND MRS. MUSIC

See: Andre Baruch and Bea Wain
Ted Steele

MR. AND MRS. NORTH

Mr. and Mrs. North were characters created by Frances and Richard Lockridge. Their adventures unfolded on the printed pages of New Yorker Magazine, on stage, the motion picture screen, radio, and television.

The radio version of the amateur sleuthing exploits of Pam and Jerry North took to the airwaves over the NBC Red network on December 30, 1942. A not generally remembered earlier Mr. and Mrs. North series premiered on March, 12. 1942. It was a situation comedy, devoid of crime drama, that endured only briefly. The Norths attracted a parade of personal care products as sponsors during their tenure on the air. They included Colgate Toothpaste, Halo Shampoo, Jergen's Lotion, Palmolive Soap, and Woodbury Soap.

Jerry North, a mystery story publisher, and his wife Pam lived in the Greenwich Village section of New York. Their offbeat lifestyle led them into mystery and mayhem as an everyday occurrence.

The initial brief situation comedy series starred Carl Eastman and Peggy Conklin in the title roles. Music was directed by Donald Voorhees and the announcer was Dan Seymour.

The more familiar tongue-in-cheek crime drama format cast was led by Joseph Curtin and Alice Frost as the Norths. The supporting players included: Staats Cottsworth, Francis DeSales, and Frank Lovejoy as detective Bill Weigand; Walter Kinsella as Sergeant Mullins; Mandel Kramer as taxi driver Mahatma McGloin; and Betty Jane Tyler as the North's niece Susan. Others who appeared from time-to-time in the cast were Jean Ellyn, Larry Haines, Allan Hewitt, Santos Ortega, Frank Readick, Anne Teeman, Arthur Vinton, and Linda Watkins. Music was composed and conducted by Charles Paul. Among the announcers were Joseph King, Ron Rawson, and Charles Stark. Mr. and Mrs. North departed the NBC airwaves in December of 1946. After a hiatus of six months they returned to the air on July 1, 1947 over the CBS network.

A major change took place in 1955 when the series became a Monday through Friday serial. At that time Richard Denning and Barbara Britton took over the title roles on radio. They had been playing Jerry and Pam on the video version since it made its debut in July of 1949. Ironically, the radio Norths outlasted their televison counterpart; however, the fifteen minute radio serial format continued only briefy and left the air by the end of 1955.

MR. CHAMELEON

Another of the airwaves' super crime stoppers with a unique gimmick was Mr. Chameleon. The "famous and dreaded" detective (aka The Man of Many Faces) used his mastery of disguise to confound and capture fugitives from justice. The contrived capers of Mr. Chameleon were first brodcast on July 14, 1948 over the CBS network. The thirty minute weekly adventures were sponsored by The Sterling Drug Company's Bayer Aspirin. Karl Swenson was cast in the title role, Frank Butler played his assistant Dave Arnold, and Richard Keith was heard as the police commissioner. Other supporting actors included: Audrey Egan, Mary Jane Higby, Alexander Scourby, Grace Valentine, Charles Webster, and Ethel Wilson. The announcers were Howard Claney and Roger Krupp. The music was under the direction of Victor Arden.

Wrigley Chewing Gum assumed sponsorship in 1952, but the series failed to survive to year's end.

MR. DISTRICT ATTORNEY

"Mr. District Attorney; champion of the people; defender of truth; guardian of our fundamental rights to life, liberty, and the pursuit of happiness."

Although fictitious, the Mr. District Attorney character was patterned after the crusading style of then New York District Attorney Thomas E. Dewey. It realistically presented stories of crime and punishment that both informed and entertained the radio audience.

The series began as a Monday through Friday fifteen minute serial drama on April 3, 1939 over the NBC Red network. On June 27, 1939 the show was moved into the weekly half hour vacated by Bob Hope for the summer. Hope's sponsor, Pepsodent Tooth Paste, bankrolled the warm weather substitute.

On October 1, 1939 Mr. District Attorney underwent a change of venue to the NBC Blue network. Pepsodent continued as sponsor until March 31, 1940. The program was then taken over by Bristol Myers Company (Ipana, Sal Hepatica, and Vitalis) and moved back to the NBC Red network on April 11, 1940. There it remained until switching to the ABC network on September 21, 1951 for a final season during 1951-52.

The title role was played by Dwight Weist during the fifteen minute serial format. Raymond Edward Johnson assumed the role for the 1939 summer series. Jay Jostyn then took over as Mr. District Attorney for the long haul from 1940 to 1952. The regular supporting cast members included Len Doyle and Walter Kinsella as the D.A.'s Inspector Harrington, Arlene Francis and Eleanor Silver as Miss Rand, Vicki Vola as Miss (Edith) Miller, and Maurice Franklin and Jay Jostyn as The Voice of the Law. Others on the series included: Jackson Beck, Jeffrey Bryant, Fran Carlon, Helen Choate, Helene Dumas, Adelaide Klein, Ed Latimer, Frank Lovejoy, Craig McDonnell, Thelma Ritter, Eric Rolf, Stefan Schnabel, Amy Seidell, Paul Stewart, James Van Dyk, and Lawson Zerbe. Harry Salter and Peter Van Steeden conducted the orchestra. The announcers were Ben Grauer, Mark Hawley, Ed Herlihy, Bob Shepard, and Fred Uttal.

The final radio broadcast of Mr. District Attorney was aired on June 20, 1952.

The video version finally gave Mr. District Attorney the name Paul Garrett. Until then he was always referred to as "Boss" or "Chief."

The television series was seen on the ABC network during the 1951-52 season and was later syndicated.

MR. FIXIT

Do-it-yourself home improvements and repairs were described on the Mr. Fixit radio series. The weekly fifteen minute informational program first aired over the Mutual network on June 5, 1949. Greystone Press, publishers of a fixit book, was the sponsor.

Jim Boles appeared as Mr. Fixit offering information and answering questions from a "typical domestic couple." The series was moved to the NBC network in the fall of 1949 and left the air in 1950.

MR. KEEN, TRACER OF LOST PERSONS

The "most celebrated cases of the kindly old investigator" were chronicled on Mr. Keen, Tracer of Lost Persons. Based on the book of the same name, the radio adaptation was first broadcast over the NBC Blue network on October 12, 1937. Initially the series aired three times weekly as a fifteen minute serial drama. Each episode was cleverly introduced by the theme song Someday I'll Find You. American Home Products' (Whitehall Pharmacal Company) Anacin, BiSoDol Mints, Kolynos Toothpaste, and other products sponsored the programs.

In the fall of 1942 Mr. Keen moved to the CBS network and on December 2, 1943 abandoned the serial format in favor of a complete weekly half hour case.

During the 1950s Mr. Keen flip-flopped between the NBC and CBS network on both fifteen and thirty minute episodes. Subsequent sponsors included Chesterfield Cigarettes and Procter and Gamble products.

With the passage of time, the story lines concentrated less on missing persons cases and more on homicides. Despite having no official affiliation with any police department, Keen conducted his investigations with an implied authority.

Mr. Keen was played by Bennett Kilpack, replaced during the series' latter days by Arthur Hughes. "Saints preserve us Mr. Keen" was regularly uttered with astonishment by Keen's assistant Mike Clancy. The role, complete with Irish brogue, was played by Jim Kelly. Others in the cast were Joseph Curtin, Florence Freeman, Walter Greaza, Irene Hubbard, Florence Malone, Erin O'Brien Moore, John Raby, Vivian Smolen, and Bill Zuckert. Music was under the direction of Al Rickey and the organists were Ann Leaf and John Winters. The announcers included: Jim Ameche, Jack Costello, Milton Cross, Larry Elliott, James Fleming, Ben Grauer, and Stuart Metz.

Mr. Keen, Tracer of Lost Persons was last heard in October of 1954.

MR. MERCURY

Mr. Mercury was the improbable scenario of a masked silver clad circus acrobat who doubled as a crime buster.

The twice weekly series premiered over the ABC network on July 3, 1951, sponsored by General Mills' products. Mr. Mercury was played by Bob Haig and John Larkin. His circus pals included Raymond Edward Johnson as Goliath, Gilbert Mack as Impe, and Ann Shepherd as Eve Costello. Music was provided by Bob Briner and John Gart. The announcer was Michael Fitzmaurice.

The brief adventure fantasy left the air at the conclusion of 1951.

MR. MOTO

International detective and philosopher Mr. I.A. Moto was adapted for radio from the writings of J.P. Marquand. It aired as a NBC weekly half hour summer sustainer in 1951.

The adventures of the Japanese investigator were laced with eastern mysticism as he went about the business of thwarting the spread of global communism. The timely story line went hand in hand with the era of bleak times during the Korean conflict.

James Monks appeared in the title role. He was assisted by a supporting cast that included: Gavin Gordon, Peter Kappel, John Larkin, and Scott Tennyson. The announcer was Fred Collins.

MR. PRESIDENT

The human side of many United States chief executives were dramatized on the Mr. President radio series.

The distinguished actor Edward Arnold portrayed a different president each week on the thirty minute informative and entertaining program. The identity of the particular president being featured was withheld until the end of the story. Supporting Mr. Arnold was a weekly cast of familiar radio voices. The music was under the direction of Basil Adlam. The announcers were Owen James, Ed Michael, and Dick Tufeld.

Mr. President was inaugurated over the ABC network's airwaves on June 26, 1947 as a sustaining summer series. In the fall he was moved into the network's regular schedule. Radio's Mr. President failed to complete his second full term in the White House. He resigned from the airwaves after the broadcast of October 8, 1953.

MR. TWISTER, MIND TRICKSTER

Jim Jordan, the Fibber half of The Fibber McGee and Molly Show, soloed as the emcee of a quarter hour series titled Mr. Twister, Mind Trickster. The obscure fifteen minute audience participation show aired three times weekly over the NBC Blue network from Chicago's station WMAQ. Mr. Twister occupied the airwaves from January 24, 1932 to November 10, 1933.

MRS. MINIVER

Mrs. Miniver, a character created by novelist Jan Struther, was made into a motion picture in 1942 and adapted for radio the following year.

The weekly sustaining half hour drama traced the Minivers migration from war weary England to a new beginning in the United States. Mrs. Miniver made her debut over the CBS net- work on December 10, 1943.

The roles of Mrs. (Kay) Miniver and Mr. (Clem) Miniver were first played by Judith Evelyn and Karl Swenson, but they were shortly replaced by Gertrude Warner and John Moore. Their children Toby and Judy were played by Alastair Kyle and Betty Jane Tyler. Carl Eastman and Sara Burton rounded out the cast of regulars as the Minivers friends the Bixbys. Arnold Moss was the narrator and Nathan Van Cleve was musical director.

Mrs. Miniver and her family left the air in June of 1944.

MRS. WIGGS OF THE CABBAGE PATCH

Mrs. Wiggs of the Cabbage Patch, Alice Hegan Rice's pathos filled novel of poverty and suffering, was adapted for radio as a daytime serial drama. There was a time when the poor section of town was referred to as "the cabbage patch," hence a clue to the story line was included in the title.

The tear jerking woes of the Wiggs first came to radio on February 4, 1935 over the CBS network. The fifteen minute Monday through Friday episodes were sponsored by American Home Products. The series moved to the NBC Red network on September 14, 1936.

The title role was played by Eva Condon and Betty Garde. Others in the cast were Jay Jostyn and Robert Strauss as Pa Wiggs, Andy Donnelly as Billy Wiggs, Mary Lou Forster and Estelle Levy as Europina, Amy Sedell and Peggy Zinke as Australia, Patricia Ryan as Asia, Van Heflin as Joe, Edmond O'Brien as Gregory, Joe Latham as Mr. Stebbens, Alice Frost and Agnes Young as Miss Hazy, William Johnstone and Frank Provo as Mr. Bob, Marjorie Anderson as Miss Lucy, John McGovern as Mr. Prentiss, and Pat Calvert as Mrs. Prentiss. The announcers were George Ansboro and Hal Moore.

The listening audience put away their crying towels after the final episode of Mrs. Wiggs of the Cabbage Patch was aired on December 23, 1938.

MUCH ABOUT DOOLITTLE

Much About Doolittle was a summer comedy series starring funnyman Jack Kirkwood premiered on July 2, 1950 over the CBS network. The weekly half hour of Kirkwood's typical raucous humor replaced the vacationing Red Skelton.

Joining Jack on the show was a supporting cast that included: Verna Felton, Bob Jellison, Joe Kearns, Hal March, and Marylee Robb. The orchestra was conducted by Leith Stevens.

NOTE: A recording of an earlier audition program of Much About Doolittle is widely circulated among old time radio collectors. This show starred Hans Conried and a completely different cast.

Kirkwood and his pun filled show of "file" gags relinquished its time to Skelton when he returned to reclaim his place in the network's 1950 fall schedule.

MARVIN MUELLER

See: Marvin Miller

MERRILL MUELLER

Newsman Merrill Mueller covered world events in print and on both radio and television. Mueller launched into broadcast journalism in 1939 with the NBC network. In 1950 he was also seen delivering the news on television.

In 1968 he shifted his allegiance to the ABC network, in 1975 he abandoned the airwaves to teach journalism, and in 1979 he retired.

Merrill Mueller died on November 30, 1980 at the age of sixty- four.

THE MULLEN SISTERS

One of the many, but somewhat obscure, of the singing sisters to appear on radio were The Mullen Sisters. Hilda, Kathleen, and Mary performed on their own show heard locally in the New York City area over station WOR during the 1936-37 season. They were also a mainstay on Singin' Sam's Reminiscin' series and regulars on one of Robert Q. Lewis' series of shows.

MOON MULLINS
See: Pilot/Auditions

FRANK MUNN

Vocalist Frank Munn was born on February 27, 1895 in New York City. Orphaned at an early age, he was reared by his grandmother. Unable to afford any formal musical education, he went to work as an errand boy for three dollars a week. He gained singing experience on amateur shows and in church which led him to make his radio debut in December of 1923. Munn would devote the major portion of his career to the radio, with a few recordings being the only exception. As a result, he was later labelled "The Golden Voice of Radio."

Munn appeared as a regular vocalist on such radio shows as The American Album of Familiar Music (Bayer Musical Revue), The American Melody Hour, Champion Sparkers, Lavender and Old Lace, The Palmolive Hour (using the name Paul Oliver), The Philco Hour of Theatre Memories, Sweetest Love Songs Ever Sung, and Waltz Time.

Never at ease in the performing spotlight, Munn retired in 1945 to enjoy the fruits of his vocalizing labors. Frank Munn died of a heart attack on October 1, 1953. He was fifty-eight years old.

THE MUNROS

Husband and wife dialog was the format for The Munros radio series. The weekday fifteen minute visits had overtones of the more familiar Easy Aces series, with a smattering of Vic and Sade, coupled with The Fitzgeralds chatter.

Gordon Munro, a New York newspaper reporter, was played by Neal Keehn. His scatterbrained wife Margaret was played by Margaret Heckle.

The Munros were on the air over the NBC Blue network from April to September of 1941.

PATRICE MUNSEL

Singer and actress Patrice Munsel was born on May 14, 1925 in Spokane, Washington. Although she gained fame from her career on the operatic stage, she also entertained in other mediums. She toured the nightclub circuit, was heard on radio, and seen on both the motion picture and television screens.

She made her debut with The Metropolitan Opera Company on December 4, 1943 at the age of eighteen. The following year she became a regular on the Prudential Family Hour radio series. Her guest appearances on the airwaves included Metropolitan Opera Auditions of the Air, Metropolitan Opera Broadcasts, The Telephone Hour, and The Voice of Firestone.

On television she was the star of her own Patrice Munsel Show during the 1957-58 season. She was also a guest on many other shows.

ONA MUNSON

Actress and singer Ona Munson was born in Portland, Oregon on June 16, 1906. She began her career at the age of fourteen on the vaudeville circuit and subsequently performed on stage, screen, and radio.

On the airwaves Ona Munson was one of a trio to play the role of Lorelei Kilbourne on Big Town and hosted the CBS Open House series. Her other radio appearances included Cavalcade of America, Hammerstein Music Hall, David Harum, Manhattan Merry-Go-Round, and delivered the commerecials on Rich Man's Darling.

Ona Munson died on February 11, 1955 at the age of forty-eight. She left behind an empty bottle of sleeping pills and a suicide note.

MURDER AND MR. MALONE

The courtroom dramatics of criminal lawyer John J. Malone were chronicled on the series Murder and Mr. Malone. The character was created by Craig Rice, appearing in print and on the motion picture screen before being adapted for radio. The initial broadcast of Murder and Mr. Malone was gaveled to order on January 11, 1947 over the ABC network. The series was sponsored by Wine Growers' Guild Wine.

Frank Lovejoy was cast as the somber and calculating attorney for the defense. He was billed as "Fiction's most famous criminal lawyer," a claim to which Perry Mason might take exception! The weekly supporting cast was drawn from radio's pool of players. The music was provided by Richard Aurandt and John Duffy. The announcer was Art Gilmore. Murder and Mr. Malone adjourned from the air in March of 1948.

On September 21, 1949 the series returned to the ABC airwaves on a sustaining basis renamed The Amazing Mr. Malone. Gene Raymond assumed the title role, later replaced by George Petrie. Larry Haines was heard as the police lieutenant, Rex Koury directed the music, and Dresser Dahlstead and Dick Tufeld were the announcers.

The second series of lawyer Malone cases came to an end in the fall of 1950.

Amazingly enough, The Amazing Mr. Malone received a third chance. This time a video version seen from September of 1951 to March of 1952.

MURDER AT MIDNIGHT

First syndicated in 1946 and produced in the studios of Los Angeles' station KFI, Murder at Midnight was another anthology of trembling terror and horrendous horror. The transcribed programs were produced by Louis G. Cowan and distributed by The World Broadcasting System. The fifty-two episodes made the rounds of local stations during the 1946-47 season.

The tolling of midnight and the foreboding strains of organ music played by Charles Paul set the stage for thirty minutes of bizarre and macabre tales.

Raymond Morgan was the narrator and some of the cast who appeared on a semi-regular basis included: Frank Behrens, Betty Caine, Elspeth Eric, Carl Frank, Barry Hopkins, Berry Kroeger, Robert Lynn, Mercedes McCambridge, Frank Readick, Amzie Strickland, Agnes Young, and Lawson Zerbe. On May 1, 1950 Murder at Midnight returned to the air with repeat broadcasts heard over the Mutual network.

MURDER BY EXPERTS

Tales of foul killings were scripted by well known mystery writers on Murder by Experts. The sustaining series took to the air over the Mutual network on June 18, 1949.

The weekly half hour was narrated by authors John Dickson Carr and Brett Halliday. Music was under the direction of Emerson Buckley and the announcer was Phil Tonken. Among the many radio voices heard in the weekly dramatic casts were Cameron Andrews, Frank Behrens, Ronald Dawson, Robert Donnelly, Ian Martin, Bryna Raeburn, Miriam Wolfe, Lawson Zerbe, and Bill Zuckert.

Murder by Experts remained on the air through the summer of 1951.

MURDER CLINIC

"Stories of the world's greatest detectives of fiction—men against murder" was used to describe the radio series titled Murder Clinic.

The sustaining half hour of murder cases made its debut over the Mutual network on July 21, 1942.

Such guest actors as Juano Hernandez, Elizabeth Morgan, Mark Smith, Maurice Tarplin, and Herbert Yost headed a varied weekly supporting cast. Bob Stanley conducted the music and Frank Knight announced.

Murder Clinic left the air in 1945.

MURDER IS MY HOBBY

The exploits of ficticious detective Barton Drake were dramatized on Murder is My Hobby. The series premiered over the Mutual network on October 14, 1945. The sponsor was The Knox Company's Mendaco.

The weekly half hour whodunit starred film actor Glenn Langan as Barton Drake. The supporting cast included Tom Collins, Joe Duval, Norman Field, and Jean Leighton. Rod O'Connor was the announcer and Len Salvo was at the organ. Accounts of Barton Drake's unusual avocation came to an end on July 7, 1946.

A later syndicated series called Mystery is My Hobby utilized a similar story line and the same cast.

MURDER WILL OUT

A mystery quiz called Murder Will Out was hardly a unique radio format. Such other series as Ellery Queen, Armchair Detective and Who-dun-it? also tested the ability of radio and studio audiences to play detective.

The audience attempted to solve the dramatized murder mystery in exchange for cash prizes before the culprit was revealed and brought to justice.

The series was broadcast over the Pacific Coast network of ABC during the 1945-46 season. The sponsor was The Rainier Brewing Company.

William Gargan and Edmond MacDonald headed the cast in the role of Inspector Burke. His assistant was Detective Nolan, played by Eddie Marr. Larry Keating was the announcer.

KERMIT MURDOCK

Radio and motion picture actor Kermit Murdock appeared in supporting roles over the airwaves during the 1940s. He was heard as Clarence K. Muggins on Lorenzo Jones and Rod Buchanan on The Whisper Men. He was also in the cast on The American School of the Air, Columbia Presents Corwin, Great Plays, My True Story, and Under Arrest.

Kermit Murdock died on February 11, 1981 at the age of seventy-two.

GEORGE MURPHY

Entertainer and politician George Murphy was born in New Haven Connecticut on July 4, 1902. After establishing himself as a song and dance man, he expanded his horizons to include acting and serving as an emcee. Murphy performed on stage, screen, radio, and television in these capacities for many years.

On radio he presided over such shows as Good News From Hollywood, Hollywood Calling, Let's Talk Hollywood, and The Screen Guild Theatre. He was a regular on The Kraft Music Hall and a frequent guest on other shows.

On television he was seen briefly as the host of The MGM Parade.

In later years Murphy became active in actors' organizations and public relations, which eventually led him to quit show business in favor of politics. In 1965 he was elected to the United States Senate from California.

Murphy faded from the political scene in 1971 following throat surgery which affected his speaking voice. In 1970 he authored his autobiography titled Say—Didn't You Used To Be George Murphy?

George Murphy died of leukemia on May 3, 1992; he was eighty-nine years old.

PAT MURPHY (Patrick Howard Murphy)

Actor Pat Murphy was born on September 29, 1911 in Bismark, North Dakota. Murphy made his radio debut as an announcer in 1931 over station KTSP in Minneapolis-St. Paul. At the time he was attending The University of Minnesota. In 1935 he journeyed to Chicago where he began his acting career on the airwaves.

He was one of a trio of actors to play "scoop" Curtis on Girl Alone. He was heard as Timothy Storey on Midstream, as the assistant district attorney on Hot Copy, and Dr. Reginald Travers on The Romance of Helen Trent. Other radio credits included: Attorney-At-Law, The Bartons, First Nighter, Flying Patrol, Grand Hotel, Dan Harding's Wife, It Can Be Done, Lights Out, Mary Marlin, Painted Dreams, Public Hero Number One, Right to Happiness, Silver Eagle, There Was a Woman, Thunder Over Paradise, We Are Four, Welcome Valley, Don Winslow of the Navy, Woman in White; Young Hickory; and Zenith Foundation.

In addition to radio acting, Pat Murphy was an accomplished concert pianist and taught music.

ARTHUR MURRAY (Arthur Murray Teichman)

Legendary dancing instructor Arthur Murray was born in New York City on April 4, 1895.

On the air he is best remembered as the sedate co-host of his 1950s television series The Arthur Murray (Dancing) Party. Actually his effervescent wife Kathryn carried the show while Arthur watched the proceedings with his familiar "dead pan" expression.

On radio Arthur Murray was a pioneer in the broadcasting of dance music, predating network radio by a decade. During the early 1920s he was heard giving dance instruction on radio over station WOR in New York. The NBC Blue network broadcast The Natural Bridge Dancing Class during the 1930-31 season with Arthur Murray in charge of teaching the latest steps.

Beginning on December 1, 1934 Murray presided over a series known as Something New—Something Old. He was joined by baritone Earl Oxford and Leith Steven's orchestra. The program aired over the CBS network during the 1934-35 season.

Arthur and Kathryn Murray's principal business was the ownership of a chain of over four hundred dance studios. In 1964 they sold their business and retired to Hawaii.

Arthur Murray died of pneumonia on March 3, 1991. He was ninety-five years old.

THE FEG MURRAY SHOW

Syndicated Hollywood cartoonist Feg Murray, creator of Seein' Stars, hosted a celebrity gossip series on radio. The weekly half hour show (aka Baker's Broadcast) made its debut over the NBC Blue network on October 3, 1937. It was sponsored by Standard Brands' Fleischmann's Yeast. Between Murray's interviews and inside news from filmdom the orchestra of Ozzie Nelson and vocalist Harriet Hilliard provided musical interludes. The announcer was John Hiestand.

The Feg Murray Show came to an end on June 26, 1938.

JAN MURRAY (Murray Janofsky)

Entertainer and emcee Jan Murray was born in New York City on October 4, 1917. A high school dropout, Murray began his show business career touring the vaudeville circuit. He would subsequently perform on stage, screen, radio, television, and in nightclubs. He even earned his belated high school diploma in 1962!

On radio Murray played Albert's brother on the comedy series It's Always Albert. He served as emcee of Meet Your Match and Songs for Sale and was a regular on Hildegarde's Campbell Room.

On television he hosted the video versions of Sing it Again and Songs for Sale. He also presided over Blind Date, Dollar a Second, Go Lucky, Jan Murray Time, and Treasure Hunt. He appeared in the cast of several comedy and dramatic series and was a frequent guest celebrity on panel shows.

KEL MURRAY

See: Let's Dance

KEN MURRAY (Kenneth Abner Doncourt)

Show business personality Ken Murray was born in New York City on July 14, 1903. Murray made his debut on the vaudeville stage in 1925. He was to become readily identified by his trademarks of a crew cut hair style, a clarinet, and a large cigar.

During his lengthy career Ken Murray performed on stage, screen, radio, and television. He authored several books and was the producer of the famous Ken Murray's Blackouts stage show and the Academy Award winning fantasy film Bill and Coo.

For many years he captured candid film footage of celebrities which he later edited and titled Murray's Shooting Stars. He made his radio debut on The Rudy Vallee Show in 1932 and shortly thereafter became the star of his own radio shows.

His other airwave credits included: Hollywood Hotel, Rexall's Parade of Stars, Stop or Go, The Texaco Star Theatre, and Which is Which.

On television he hosted his own Ken Murray Show. He was also seen on Fun for 51, The Judy Garland Show, Hollywood's Private Home Movies, The Bob Hope Show, and Where Are You?.

Ken Murray died on October 13, 1988 at the age of eighty-five.

THE KEN MURRAY SHOW(S)

Versatile performer and producer Ken Murray was the star of several of his own radio shows.

The first premiered over the NBC Red network in 1932 only a few weeks after Murray's radio debut on The Rudy Vallee Show. It was titled The Royal Vagabond and was sponsored by Royal Gelatin. The series was on the air during the 1932-33 season. Next came Laugh With Ken Murray, a short-lived show sponsored by Lever Brothers' Lifebuoy and Rinso soap. It aired over the CBS network from March 24th to December 15th of 1936.

Lastly, The Ken Murray and Oswald Show occupied a weekly half hour in the CBS network schedule during 1937. The sponsor for this show was Campbell's Tomato Juice. Among those who joined Ken on these shows were Eve Arden, Tony "Oswald" Labriola, Helen Morgan, Phil Regan, Harry Richman, Shirley Ross, and Marilyn Stuart, and Dink Trout. The orchestra was conducted by Lud Gluskin and Russ Morgan.

The announcers were Fred Uttal and Ward Wilson.

LYN MURRAY (Lionel Breese)

Composer and conductor Lyn Murray was born in London, England on December 6, 1909. He came to the United States in 1925 with an ambition to become a seaman, a newspaperman, or an actor. However, after trying all three, he decided to follow in his father's footsteps as a musician. He received his musical training at Juilliard and then applied his acquired talents on the radio airwaves. He began as a pianist and singer at station WGH in Newport News, Virginia. He next moved on to Philadelphia's WCAU where he teamed with Virginia Baker. They co-starred on a program of songs and domestic dialog called Bill and Ginger.

Murray later directed and/or scored music for such radio shows as The Phil Baker Show, The Campbell Playhouse, The Columbia Workshop, Norman Corwin, The Joan Davis Show(s), The Fighting Senator, The Ford Theatre, Hallmark Playhouse, The Danny Kaye Show, Life With Luigi, Christopher London, The March of Time, Philip Marlowe, Meet the Music, Moods for Moderns, Ellery Queen, Radio Reader's Digest, They Live For- ever, and To Your Good Health.

In addition to composing and waving his baton, Murray also directed The Lyn Murray Singers. This vocal chorus was heard over the airwaves on The Flying Red Horse Tavern, Harvest of Stars, Home on the Range, Ninety-Nine Men and a Girl, Penthouse Party, Pursuit of Happiness, The Sealtest Saturday Night Party (leading The New Yorker Chorus), Sound Off, The Texaco Star Theatre, The Westinghouse Program, and Your Hit Parade.

Other aspects of his career encompassed music for films, recordings, and television.

Lyn Murray succumbed to cancer on May 20, 1989 at the age of seventy-nine.

EDWARD R. MURROW (Egbert Roscoe Murrow)

Newscaster and journalist Edward R. Murrow was born in Pole Cat Creek, North Carolina on April 25, 1908. Murrow graduated from Washington State University in 1930 and five years later began his long association with the CBS network. He was catapulted into prominence at the start of World War II.

His eyewitness reports by shortwave radio from London rooftops during German bombings brought the horrors of modern warfare into American living rooms.

In October of 1941 CBS brought him home for a rest from the rigors of overseas reporting. After several months on the lecture trail and "stateside" newscasts, in April of 1942

Murrow was again assigned to cover the war as a foreign correspondent. He returned to broadcasting his first hand descriptions of the allied battle against Nazi tyranny. Returning to the United States in 1946, the post war world offered Murrow the opportunity to continue his influential grip on the CBS network's news operation both on the air and behind the scenes.

On radio, in addition to regular newscasts, he hosted and co-produced with Fred Friendly the documentary series Hear it Now. On television he was seen on the video version called See it Now. However, he is best remembered for his popular in-depth interview series titled Person to Person.

In 1961 Murrow left CBS when President John F. Kennedy appointed him chief of The United States Information Agency.

Late in 1963 he underwent surgery for the removal of a malignant lung tumor. Shortly thereafter he resigned his post at the USIA.

Murrow became one of the most honored and respected men in his profession, especially among contemporary and succeeding generations of broadcast journalists.

Edward R. Murrow died of cancer on April 27, 1965. He was fifty-seven years old.

MUSIC ALONG THE WIRES

The Bell Telephone Company sponsored a radio series titled Music Along the Wires. The Sunday evening half hour of music was broadcast over the CBS network during the fall and winter of 1931.

Fritz Reiner led The Philharmonic of the Air Orchestra. The orchestral presentation was augmented by guest soloists and a sixteen-voice chorus. There were also special features such as a telepone conversation between Grace Moore in New York and Richard Tauber in Berlin or a monologue by Cornelia Otis Skinner.

MUSIC AMERICA LOVES BEST

Music America Loves Best was the title of the RCA sponsored half hour of varied musical entertainment broadcast during the 1944-45 season. The show premiered over the (ABC) Blue network on March 4, 1944. The initial format featured both concert and popular music. The chorus and orchestra were under the direction of Jay Blackton. Also on the program were weekly guest vocalists, emcee Louis Calhern, and announcer Jack Costello.

Bandleader Tommy Dorsey took over the show in April of 1945 when it moved to the NBC network. At this time the classical portion of the program was abandoned. The announcer was Frank Barton.

On December 2, 1945 Music America Loves Best gave way to a revamped version called The RCA Victor Show which is described under that heading.

MUSIC AND THE MUSE

Actress Janet Logan turned her talents to poetry readings on the Music and the Muse radio series. Providing the mood music were harpist Katherine Juleuz, cellist Ray Kramer, violinist Thomas Manchini, and organist William Sobransky.

The weekly thirty minute program was broadcast over the NBC network during the 1949-50 season.

MUSIC AND THE SPOKEN WORD

See: The Mormon Tabernacle Choir

THE MUSIC APPRECIATION HOUR

"Good morning, my dear young people" was the salutation from Dr. Walter Damrosch to his radio audience awaiting their weekly instruction in understanding classical music.

The hour long program was first broadcast over the NBC Blue network on October 26, 1928, Its value as an educational tool was enhanced by beaming the series into schoolrooms from coast-to-coast during normal school hours. A companion workbook was also offered at a nominal cost. Dr. Damrosch, the acknowledged dean of conductors and a renowned composer, imparted his vast knowledge of music to his juvenile audience with the assistance of an orchestra under the direction of Ernest LaPrade. The announcers were Milton Cross and Gene Hamilton, both well known for their association with music on the airwaves.

The final Music Appreciation Hour aired on May 1, 1942.

MUSIC AT THE HAYDNS

A musical sketch titled Music at the Haydns was a 1935 series aired over the NBC Red network. The initial program was broadcast in January, with The Colgate-Palmolive-Peet Company as its sponsor.

Librettist Otto Harbach was joined by weekly guests and the orchestra of Al Goodman on the thirty minute show. Jean Paul King was the announcer.

Music at the Haydns retired from the airwaves in July of 1935 after a seven month run.

MUSIC AT WAR

Conductor Josef Stopak led the NBC Orchestra playing cymbal crashing martial music on Music at War.

The program was designed to bolster home front morale and improve the war effort. However, the critics complained it was too loud and unnerving for late night radio listeners.

Music at War was on the air at 11:30PM for only a six week period beginning on July 8, 1943.

MUSIC BY GERSHWIN

Composer and pianist George Gershwin was the star of his own radio series called Music by Gershwin. The initial broadcast was aired over the NBC Blue network on February 19, 1934. The fifteen minutes of Gershwin tunes were heard twice weekly sponsored by Feenamint Laxative. Don Wilson announced.

After a 1934 summer hiatus, a new Music by Gershwin series returned to the airwaves in the fall. It was moved to the CBS network and expanded to a weekly half hour musical variety show.

Joining the cast of regulars were vocalists Rhoda Arnold, Lucille Peterson, and Dick Robertson, comedian Robert Boran, emcee Harry Von Zell, and the orchestra of Louis Katzman.

Apparently losing the Gershwin personal touch, Music by Gershwin left the air at the close of 1934.

MUSIC BY MALNECK

Bandleader Matty Malneck presided over his Music by Malneck show during the summer of 1939. The weekly fifteen minutes of warm weather dance band music was sponsored by The American Tobacco Company's Pall Mall Cigarettes. The program premiered over the CBS network on June 1st. John Hiestand was the announcer.

Music by Malneck faded from the radio bandstand after the broadcast of August 24th.

THE MUSIC DEPRECIATION PROGRAM

Upbeat arrangements of music written as classical, march, and sophisticated styles were performed on the irreverent Music Depreciation Program.

The show originated from the studios of KHJ in Los Angeles and was first heard over some affiliate stations of the Mutual network in the fall of 1944.

Rubin Gaines served as the comedic emcee, with Frank DeVol's orchestra providing the accompaniment for the weekly guest vocalists. The announcer was Tony LaFrano.

The final program in the series aired on April 22, 1945.

MUSIC FOR AMERICA

During Fred Allen's 1943 and 1944 summer vacation, Music for America filled the half hour void in the CBS network's schedule.

The program starred vocalist James Melton with support from guest performers and an orchestra led by Morton Gould.

MUSIC FOR AN HOUR

The first Music for an Hour series occupied the Mutual net- work's airwaves from May to October of 1943. The Sunday evening sustainer presented a concert orchestra under the baton of Alfred Wallenstein. It also featured such guest soloists as tenor Donald Dame, soprano Frances Geer, pianist Milton Kaye, and violinist Samuel Kissel.

Apparently for the lack of a more inspired title, Music for an Hour reappeared over Mutual's network on May 4, 1947. Initially it was only forty-five minutes of music, but on May 25th the program was expanded to live up to its title. Bill Berns served as the emcee and Sylvan Levin conducted the orchestra. Like its predecessor, there were weekly guest artists, but unlike the earlier version, both classical and popular music were included in the hour.

The second and final Music for an Hour program enjoyed only brief tenure and then vanished.

MUSIC FOR HALF AN HOUR

Thirty minutes of song was the format for the obscure Music for Half an Hour program. It was broadcast over the Mutual network during 1944 and featured vocalists Annette Burford and Earl Palmer.

MUSIC FOR MODERNS

At least two radio series were broadcast under the title of Music for Moderns.

One was heard locally in the New York City area during the late 1930s. It featured dance music performed by Jan Savitt's band.

The network version of Music for Moderns was sustained over NBC's Red web during 1940. The weekly thirty minutes of "concert pops" music originated from the studios of station KYW in Philadelphia.

Clarence Fuhrman and Jan Savitt conducted the orchestra, anonymous male and female singers provided the vocals, and an announcer, who was identified only as Gulliver, hosted the program.

MUSIC FOR TODAY

See: Morton Gould

MUSIC FROM HOLLYWOOD

Hal Kemp's orchestra and vocalist Alice Faye were featured on the Music from Hollywood program. The weekly half hour of music and song aired over the CBS network, sponsored by Liggett and Myers' Chesterfield Cigarettes. This was just one of many Chesterfield Programs. It used the title Music From Hollywood only from July 2nd to December 24th of 1934. The announcer was Carlton KaDell.

MUSIC FROM MANHATTAN

Music from Manhattan was an interim morning series broadcast over the NBC network in 1943. The half hour of "fill music" occupied a place in the schedule from November 15, 1943 until Mirth and Madness made its debut in December.

MUSIC FROM THE HEART OF AMERICA

Music from the Heart of America was broadcast regionally over thirty-five southern and midwestern affiliates of the NBC network. The series premiered on February 5, 1948 and originated from the studios of station WMAQ in Chicago. The Falstaff Brewing Company sponsored the weekly half hour of melodic entertainment.

Joseph Gallicchio led the orchestra, Jack Haskell and Anne Hershey vocalized, and John Holtman announced.

Music from the Heart of America occupied its limited share of NBC's airwaves during the 1948-49 season.

MUSIC FROM THE HOUSE OF SQUIBB

See: To Your Good Health

MUSIC HALL OF THE AIR

See: Radio City Music Hall of the Air

MUSIC HALL VARIETIES

Music Hall Varieties was a 1950s transcribed thirty minute program syndicated by The RCA Thesaurus Library. The series starred Joe E. Howard and Beatrice Kay. Also heard were Irving Kaufman and Aileen Stanley.

Music Hall Varieties was a latter day revival of the two network shows titled The Gay Nineties Revue and Gaslight Gayeties.

MUSIC IN THE MOONLIGHT

A weekly half hour of late night romantic tunes called Music in the Moonlight was broadcast over the NBC Red network during the 1941-42 season.

The program originated in the Nashville studios of station WSM. Lionel Rieger was the host, Beasley Smith led the orchestra, Jane Grant was the featured vocalist, and additional vocals were provided by The Moonlighters.

MUSIC IS MY HOBBY

Amateur musicians, whose fame was in other professional fields, performed on Music is My Hobby. The weekly quarter hour program was first broadcast over the NBC Red network, and was later switched to the Blue web.

Music is My Hobby was aired during the 1935-36 season.

THE MUSIC MAIDS

On radio the Music Maids vocal group was regularly featured on The Kraft Music Hall for several seasons. They were also heard on The Screen Guild Theatre.

The female voices at various times belonged to Bobby Canvin, June Clifford, Virginia Erwin (later performing as a single she was known as Trudy Erwin), Alice Ludes, Dotty Messner, Alice Sizer, and Denny Wilson.

In addition to radio, The Music Maids were seen on the motion picture screen and recorded on the Decca label.

MUSIC OF MANHATTAN

Included in the 1945 NBC Thesaurus recorded library of syndicated programming was Music of Manhattan.

The fifteen and thirty minute formats included vocalists Louise Carlyle and William Young. The "all star" orchestra of twenty-eight network musicians was led by Norman Cloutier.

MUSIC OF YESTERDAY AND TODAY

See: Blue Barron

MUSIC ON THE AIR

Music on the Air presented sentimental stories behind the songs. The fifteen minute series was brodcast over the CBS network three times weekly during the 1933-34 season.

The show (aka Tydol Jubilee) was sponsored by Tide Water Associated Oil Corporation's Tydol products. Music on the Air was narrated by Jimmy Kemper and the orchestra was under the direction of Robert Armbruster and Dolphe Martin. There was also a dramatic cast, a male octet, and The Three Humming Birds.

MUSIC OUT OF THE BLUE

New works by contemporary composers were performed on the Music Out of the Blue program.

The thirteen week series premiered over the ABC network on September 5, 1944. Paul Whiteman led the orchestra on the first four of the half hour sustaining shows. Other radio conductors took turns during the remaining nine weeks.

MUSIC QUIZ

Sigmund Spaeth, The Tune Detective, answered questions posed to him by the studio audience and sent in by listeners. Contrary to the impression given by the Music Quiz title, the series was a musical answer man type of program.

The fifteen minute sustaining Music Quiz was broadcast over the Mutual network during 1947. Keyes Perrin assisted Spaeth as both emcee arid announcer.

THE MUSIC SHOP

See: Johnny Mercer

MUSIC THAT SATISFIES

See: The Chesterfield Program

MUSIC VALLEY
See: Jimmy Wakely

MUSIC WE LOVE
Music We Love was the Armed Forces Radio title for The Voice of Firestone.

MUSIC WITH THE HORMEL GIRLS
The Hormel (Meat) Packing Company began sponsoring Music With the Hormel Girls on March 20, 1948 over Los Angeles' station KHJ. Shortly thereafter, ten affiliate stations of Mutual's Don Lee network carried the show for west coast audiences.

The following year the half hour program was heard coast-to-coast over the ABC network. During the 1950-51 season, Music With the Hormel Girls was moved to the CBS network for its final season on the air. The Hormel Girls thirty-six voice chorus was directed by Louise Mulvany and was accompanied by The Hormel Orchestra.

The show was hosted by Betty Dougherty and Elina Hart. Marilyn Wilson was the announcer.

MUSIC WITHOUT WORDS
Bob Stanley led the orchestra on a 1943 series titled Music Without Words. The program, devoid of vocals, aired over a half dozen east coast affiliate stations of the Mutual network.

THE MUSIC YOU LOVE
The Music You Love was a forty-five minute program of Sunday afternoon concert music.

It premiered over the CBS network on September 13, 1936 under the sponsorship of The Pittsburgh Plate Glass Company. The series originated from the stage of The Pittsburgh Carnegie Music Hall and was broadcast through the facilities of station WJAS.

Antonio Modarelli directed The Pittsburgh Symphony Orchestra, weekly guest soloists performed, and Ernest Neff announced. MusicYou Love endured only three months on the air. The final broadcast was heard on December 13, 1936.

MUSICAL ALBUM (AUTOGRAPHS)
See: Guy Lombardo Shows

MUSICAL AMERICANA
The first of the programs titled Musical Americana was broadcast in 1937. This obscure series featured Freddie Rich's orchestra entertaining over a "handful" of CBS affiliate stations.

The best remembered of the Musical Americana series took to the NBC Blue network's airwaves on January 25, 1940 under the sponsorship of Westinghouse.

The original plan was for the weekly half hour, originating from Pittsburgh was to play music by only American composers, but as time went by this stipulation was relaxed. Ray Perkins, Deems Taylor and Kenneth L. Watt took their turn as emcee. Raymond Paige conducted The Westinghouse Orchestra (actually The Pittsburgh Symphony Orchestra). There was a twenty-four voice mixed chorus and weekly guest performers. Milton Cross was the announcer.

Despite critical acclaim, this version of Musical Americana departed the airwaves in September of 1940.

A final Musical Americana show was revived as the 1947 summer replacement for the vacationing Burns and Allen. It premiered on June 5, 1947 over the NBC network and starred the popular songstress Frances Langford. Carmen Dragon led the orchestra and Tobe Reed and Del Sharbutt were the announcers.

THE MUSICAL CAMERA

Mental portraits in music were painted for the radio listener by The Musical Camera. The program of music and song first aired over the NBC Red network on October 25, 1936. It was sponsored by The International Silver Company.

Conductor Josef Cherniansky was the "musical" photographer as he led the orchestra, while guest songsters developed vocal pictures. The announcers were William Farren, Del King, and Lyle Van.

Left sponsorless in April of 1937, The Musical Camera moved to Emery Auditorium in Cincinnati, Ohio. There they continued to be heard over a few stations through the facilities of station WLW.

MUSICAL CARTOONS

Orchestra leader Victor Irwin's Musical Cartoons program occupied a weekly thirty minutes in the Mutual network's schedule. Adding words to the music was vocalist Benay Venuta.

The relatively brief and obscure series was on the air from the fall of 1937 through the winter of 1938.

THE MUSICAL CLOCK

The prolific use of the title The Musical Clock would indicate that at some time almost every radio station aired such a program. The popular format, most often broadcast during early morning hours, combined recorded music with frequent time checks.

Most notable of these programs was The Musical Clock hosted by John B. Gambling. This long running series was heard over New York City's station WOR.

THE MUSICAL COMEDY HOUR
See: Jessica Dragonette

MUSICAL CRUISE
A mythical ocean voyage was the setting for a Musical Cruise. The fifteen minute weekly series was broadcast over the NBC Red network during the 1934-35 season. It was sponsored by The William Wrigley Company's chewing gum. Orchestra leader Harry Reser and his "Spearmint Crew" was the principal entertainment on the imaginary high seas of melody. The announcer was Ben Grauer.

MUSICAL CRUSIER
See: Plough's Musical Cruiser

MUSICAL DOCTORS
Jokes and songs were the prescription on the Musical Doctors radio show.

Clyde Doerr, George Greer, and Charles Magnanti cavorted on the weekly half hour airwaves laugh clinic. The music was under the direction of Milton Rettenberg.

The Musical Doctors was broadcast over the NBC Blue network during the 1930-31 season, sponsored by Vapex Cold Remedy.

MUSICAL GROCERY STORE
Thirty minutes of songs and comedy were on the shopping list when Best Foods' Musical Grocery Store took to the air. The weekly show was heard over the NBC Red network from March to July of 1933.

Regulars on the program included: Teddy "Blubber" Bergman (Alan Reed), Tom Howard, Jeannie Lang, Herb Polesie, The Singing Clerks, and The Three X Sisters. The orchestra was led by Harry Salter.

MUSICAL MELODRAMAS
The futile search for an arch criminal was the continuing story line on Musical Melodramas.

The series first aired on September 17, 1929 over the NBC Blue network, sponsored by The Johnson & Johnson Company.

The small band of crime fighters included: newspaper reporter Jimmy Otis played by Lorin Raker, nurse Dorothy Brent by Joyce Meredith and Nora Sterling, and Detective Sergeant McCarthy by Jack Smart (J.Scott Smart). The elusive under-world character, known as "The Chief," was played by Joe Granby. The Johnson & Johnson Orchestra was conducted by Victor Arden and Gene Rodemich. The orchestra was called upon for various styles of music that played an important part in the plot, hence the title.

Musical Melodramas left the air at the conclusion of the 1929-30 season.

MUSICAL MEMORIES

Musical Memories was yet another popular title used by several radio series. They were mostly obscure and local shows; however, one was worthy of note.

The Household Finance Corporation sponsored a Musical Memories program heard over the NBC Blue network. It was on the air from late 1932 through the 1934 season.

Featured on Musical Memories were readings by poet Edgar Guest, songs by soprano Alice Mock and tenor Charles Sears, and an orchestra conducted by Josef Koestner.

The program was later known as Welcome Valley, which Is descr ibed under that heading.

THE MUSICAL MEMORY BOOK

The Musical Memory Book was a program of music and song broadcast over several stations of the Mutual network during the 1934-35 season. It originated from the studios of station WOR (then located in Newark, New Jersey). The sponsor was Baum Benguay (Ben-Gay).

Norman Cordon served double duty as the show's emcee and featured vocalist. He was joined by soprano Licille Peterson and the orchestra of Louis Katzman.

MUSICAL MEMORY CONTEST

See: Brunswick Programs

MUSICAL MEMOS

A salon orchestra directed by Rex Maupin was heard on Musical Memos. The Saturday morning half hour musical interlude was sustained over the ABC network during the 1952-53 season.

THE MUSICAL MILLWHEEL

Pillsbury Flour Mills sponsored The Musical Millwheel program over the NBC Blue network. The half hour program was heard on Thursday through Sunday mornings during the 1941-42 season. Tenor Walter Paterson and The Harmony Singers provided the vocals. They were accompanied by a small instrumental group called The Pillsbury Besters. Dan Donaldson announced.

MUSICAL MOCK TRIAL

See: Ben Bernie and All the Lads

MUSICAL MOMENTS

Musical Moments was an obscure program of recorded music that has found its way into the main stream of old time radio collectors' catalogs. It aired over Chicago's stations WBBM and WGN six nights weekly during 1935 and 1936. Chevrolet Automobiles sponsored the transcribed fifteen minutes of music from

The World Broadcasting Library. Pierre Andre, Hugh Conrad, and Tom Shirley all took their turn presiding over the revolving turntables.

MUSICAL MOMENTS REVUE
See: Rubinoff Programs

MUSICAL MOSAICS
See: Cheerio

MUSICAL PLAYHOUSE
See: Gulf Musical Playhouse

MUSICAL ROMANCE

Mabelline Mascara introduced their Musical Romance program to radio listeners on September 16, 1934. It was broadcast over the NBC Red network.

The thirty minute Sunday matinee show featured actor and singer Don Mario (Alvarez), Hollywood gossip reporter Jimmy Fidler, a guest star from movieland, and Harry Jackson's orchestra.

In January of 1935 the program underwent a format change and emerged as Penthouse Serenade, which is described under that heading.

MUSICAL STEELMAKERS

The Wheeling Steel Corporation sponsored a radio show featuring talent culled from the ranks of their workers in the steel mill. Musical Steelmakers began as a local program heard over station WWVA in Wheeling, West Virginia.

The singers and musicians first gathered at Wheeling's Capitol Theatre on Novembr 8, 1936 for the weekly half hour Sunday broadcast.

On January 8, 1938 the Mutual network began carrying the unique series over forty-six of their affiliate stations. John "The Old Timer" Wincholl was the emcee. The orchestra was conducted by Lew Davies, Earl Summers, and Tommy Whitley.

The announcers were Lew Clawson and Walter Patterson.

Included among the performing steelworkers were Mary Bower, Regina Colbert, Claude Colvin, Dorothy Ann Crowe, Alma Custer, Betty Dougherty, The Evans Sisters (Betty Jane and Margaret June), The Singing Millmen (Bill Griffiths, Frank Nalepa, Walter Schane, and Bill Stevenson), The Steele Sisters (Lucille Bell, Kathleen Nelson, and Lois Mae Nolte), and Ardenne White. Steele Sister member Lois Mae Nolte later became co-host of the show with John Wincholl.

In October of 1941 the program moved to the NBC Blue network. The Musical Steelmakers was last broadcast in June of 1944. name of the lead character.

Mystery Without Murder was without air time when Judy Canova returned in September.

MY-T-FINE CIRCUS
See: The Mighty Show

BearManorMedia
P O Box 750 * Boalsburg, PA 16827

The Baby Snooks Scripts
by Philip Rapp   ISBN: 1-9321338-0-1

First time in print! These 10 old time radio scripts by Philip Rapp are taken from OTR's Golden Age shows: *Maxwell House Coffee Time, Good News*, and more. Not transcriptions, but the original scripts! Introduction by John Conte. **$16.95**

Information Please
by Martin Grams, Jr.   ISBN: 0-9714570-7-7

Information Please, the popular radio quiz program that played experts for fall guys, was capital, dependable, adult radio fun for more than a decade (1938 – 1952). OTR historian Martin Grams. Jr. provides the definitive biography and log on this classic panel game. **$29.95**

Private Eyelashes: Radio's Lady Detectives
by Jack French   ISBN: 0-9714570-8-5

Phyl Coe Mysteries, The Affairs of Ann Scotland, Defense Attorney, The Adventures of the Thin Man, Front Page Farrell…radio was just full of babes that knew how to handle themselves. Get the lowdown on every honey who helped grind a heel into crime. **$18.95**

For all these books and more, visit
www.bearmanormedia.com or write info@ritzbros.com
Visa & Mastercard accepted. Add $2.50 postage per book.

BearManorMedia
P O Box 750 * Boalsburg, PA 16827

Welcome, Foolish Mortals...
THE LIFE AND VOICES OF PAUL FREES By Ben Ohmart

The official, heavily illustrated biography of the Master of Voice. Read all about the man behind the voices of Disneyland's *Haunted Mansion*, the pirates in the *Pirates of the Caribbean* ride, Boris Badenov from *Rocky & Bullwinkle*, The Pillsbury Doughboy and thousands of radio shows including *Suspense*, *Escape*, *The Whistler* and more.

ISBN: 1-59393-004-6 $29.95

Every old-time radio and cartoon fan in the world will want this book. Foreword by June Foray. Afterword by Jay Ward biographer, Keith Scott.

"For the first time in print, the real Paul Frees is revealed. Author Ben Ohmart looks beyond the voices to uncover the man within, coming up with an even-handed, but honest portrait of a very complicated individual. This is the definitive biography of an amazing artist." — Laura Wagner, *Classic Images*

BOB AND RAY AND TOM by Dan Gillespie

This booklet is the first publication focusing specifically on Bob & Ray's writer, Tom Koch. Includes complete biography, information on the un-famous collaboration, list of published Bob & Ray works, and reproductions of Mad magazine panels written by Koch featuring Bob & Ray!   ISBN: 1-59393-009-7 $8.95

The story of a guy who wrote a lot of stuff for radio's greatest satirists.

-- by Dan Gillespie --

The Bickersons Scripts Volume 2
by Philip Rapp

Be the first to grab the NEW collection of Bickersons scripts! Includes squabbles from *The Charlie McCarthy Show* and *Drene Time*—plus never-before-seen commercial scripts (for Coffee Rich and other products) and the infamous Christmas episode written for the animated series! Foreword by Marsha Hunt.

ISBN: 1-59393-007-0 $18.95

Add $2.50 postage per book.

For all these books and more, visit
www.bearmanormedia.com

www.ingramcontent.com/pod-product-compliance
Lightning Source LLC
Chambersburg PA
CBHW022103160426
43198CB00008B/329